POCKETS OF
INSIGHT

A Collection of
Provocative Quotations
and Life Affirming Essays

Rasheed Mohammed

The publisher and the author make no warranties of any kind with respect to the ideas, suggestions and recommendations described in this book.

First Edition, 2021

Library of Congress Control Number: 2021905439

ISBN: 978-1-736-7901-2-0 (print)
ISBN: 978-1-736-7901-1-3 (E-book)
ISBN: 978-1-736-7901-3-7 (Apple E-book)

www.pocketsofinsight.com

WHY I WROTE POCKETS OF INSIGHT

I am a first-time writer and if you are like me, at some time in your life you may have heard or read something that you found to be especially clever and intuitive but could not later remember the precise words or order in which it was expressed. Of course, you could have looked it up on the internet, but that may turn out to be a vexing experience especially when you have to maneuver through so many competing options. Software businessman Mitch Kapor noted, *"Getting information off the internet is like taking a drink from a fire hydrant."*

Won't it be wonderful to have at your fingertips a handy guide with down-to-earth, straightforward ideas and suggestions on how to better deal with life's everyday challenges — a book that contained the kind of snippets you wished you could remember and whose compositions were short in length, but 'long' on message?

It happened one day I was scanning the internet looking for one of those elusive kernels of truth, when I accidently came across these two quotations. The first was by German writer and statesman, Johann von Goethe (1749-1832) who observed, *"All intelligent thoughts have already been thought; what is necessary is only to try to think them again."* The other was by English cleric & writer, Charles Caleb Colton (1780-1832) who concluded, *"That writer does the most, who gives his reader the most knowledge, and takes from him the least time."*

Therein, the idea was born to create a piece of literature that would embrace these two remarks. However, since there were hundreds of quote books, plaques, etc., already in circulation and on active websites, I decided it would be better to compile a list of smart, unsung observations outside the reach of appreciative eyes and marry them with straight-forward, engaging narratives. What better way to advise another how to get noticed by management, how to deal with feelings of jealousy or loss than the observations of both ordinary and famous men and women (past and present) whose lives were intimately affected by these very experiences. There was no need to re-invent the wheel.

Furthermore, I chose not to frame my narratives along the old clichéd lines as: "The (5) easy steps to achieve this or that" or "The ten ways to get whatever it is you need to get." Instead, I opted to convey bold and functional messages like, "If you are truly interested in obtaining inner peace, the first thing you should do is — stop lying."

Pockets of Insight is like a 'visible' conscience and a reminder of the hidden dangers associated with old habits and customary ways of thinking. It provides guidance and suggestions on how to better deal with our most troublesome faults and weaknesses.

Here is what I hope this book may do for you!

- Help you to recognize 'fluff' when you see and hear it.

- Demonstrate the need to be more responsible for the things you do and say, because it affects your destiny.

- To remind you, when you care it shows - everything else is just ink.

- To recognize that outside disease and disability much of the unhappiness we generally feel originates from malice, jealousy and transgression.

Everyone respects the person who is in control of his or her life. It is the author's hope you'll find in this book enough words to inspire and motivate you to act and behave in ways that'll make you feel proud of yourself afterwards. To remind you that decency is not an option, but a responsibility— not only does it define you, but it follows you to the grave.

TABLE OF CONTENTS

Anger & Patience

———

hat makes us angry? Often, it's when someone demonstrates a lack of respect to us. The image we have of ourselves is offended. Following a fit of anger, if we were able to read the secret thoughts of those on the receiving end, we'd be shocked and surprised to learn the degree of dislike they harbor toward us—never for once imagining our berating statements were the triggering mechanisms behind their ill feelings. It is far better to let others know how their words or actions affect our feelings than feed their anger with profanities and accusations. When you say, "You hurt my feelings," that remark may not guarantee a fruitful outcome, but by verbalizing your distress that way, you provide a valid and identifiable reason for a possible reconciliation. The trouble with most arguments is that people aren't satisfied or willing to concede until they are able to prove the other side wrong and the comfort or discomfort felt after a fiery exchange is usually determined by the quality and quantity of blows, they're able to get in. In any argument consider being brief instead of harsh and bitter-you will not regret it.

The person who never pardons or forgives, is usually the one who is the biggest offender, but he or she will never admit to that. The trouble is, if given a choice, many of us would rather be the brute. The following is a re-phrased comment made by writer Christopher Morley, "If we suddenly discovered that we had only five minutes left to say what we all wanted to say, every telephone would be occupied by people trying to call up other people to tell them how sorry they were or how much they loved them." A good way to measure your "goodness" is to live your life so that at those times when you lose, you don't feel weighed down by guilt.

ILLUSTRATION:

One Sunday morning, Moshe was talking with his neighbor Ahmed about his 100-mile commute each workday.

Moshe: "How do you do it? I've tried and I can't even go ten miles without getting so angry at those crazy drivers who cut you off, go too slow, or change lanes without warning. Nobody seems to care about rules."

Ahmed: "My friend, I think you feel that way because you are trying to drive every car around you. With me, I only drive one—my own."

We tend to recognize and appreciate patience only when we observe others displaying it. But when it comes to ourselves, we acknowledge that trait only when we are successful in concealing our obvious impatience. Author Eknath Easwaran,(1910-1998) declared, "Patience can't be acquired overnight. It is just like building up a muscle. Every day you need to work on it." And sculptor and architect, Leonardo di Vinci (1492-1519) added, "Patience serves as a protection against wrongs as clothes do against cold. For if you put on more clothes as the cold increases, it will have no power to hurt you. So in like manner, you must grow in patience and when you meet with great wrongs, they will then be powerless to vex your mind."

Here are a few ways you can tell whether you've acquired patience:

- To have patience, you should be able to wait without worrying. Can you find something else to do while you are waiting?

- Are you able to remain calm and not let your impatience be visible to those around you, or is it the other way around with you?

- If you are usually stingy and distrustful of others, know immediately that patience is not one of your virtues.

Within a relationship and following a heated argument, feelings of regret may surface afterwards. As often happens, an apology from one or both sides may not be enough to neutralize all the hurtful words exchanged. So what is a person to do? First, we should recognize this. When we feel angry at another, chances are our anger stems from a need to punish the other person for trying to get away with something and for which he or she should be held responsible. But to suffer in silence is seldom a good response either. Author Perry Buffington wisely pointed out : "Keeping emotional pain inside, is like bandaging an unwashed wound and inviting the probability of infection."

There is no simple or cozy answer of how best to address the upsetting feelings that follow a heated argument. There is remorse but gladness too, as we are able to lay bare that which bothers us the most. At times like these, perhaps these words by Mother Teresa, are worth considering "Peace begins with a smile"

Here is a final thought on this subject. Before you speak, determine whether the words about to leave your tongue are able to pass these three censors: Is it true?; Is it kind?; Is it necessary?

"Anger blows out the light of reason, but like a roaring hurricane, after it expends its fury, the lull of calm sets in." (Dr. Paul J. Parker)

An Essential Guide in Toddler Management

DENIAL & LIES:

The child who is told not to spill milk or slam a door tends to focus on the milk spilling or door slamming. She/he must see your statement first in their mind, right down to its negative end. Within this context, it is much better to say, "Take this milk and hold it with both hands" and "close the door gently".

Additionally, kids may tell lies not because they want to mislead you but because they want to get out of doing something. Don't let them off the hook. You may say, "Who pulled all these toys out?" and you'll likely get the response, "Not me." Don't focus on the lie; instead, say something like, "Well, it doesn't matter how they got here, please help me pick them up." In the end, the child still has to do what he or she didn't want to do. If, however, you feel a need to punish your child, then do it not for what he or she did wrong but for lying about it.

NIGHTMARES:

"Don't take your scared child into your own bed. This sends a subconscious message that their bed is frightening and yours is safe. You'll never get them back into their own bed again".(Alison Maloney, The Mom's Book),Once tucked into his or her own bed, say to your child. "Now tell me what horrible thing you imagine will happen to you." Listen and address their fear head on. If, for instance, your child says the 'bogey-man' will come into the room and take him away. You could say, "Then couldn't you yell for help? You know I will hear you and come into your room immediately."

SELF ESTEEM:

Help your child develop integrity. Parents should practice speaking the truth always. Your children will copy and imitate your behavior and also take that model with them into adulthood. Though you may feel your kids aren't paying attention, they do notice all the kind things you do. So if you are truly concerned about teaching your kids about the "right" path, make sure you are already headed in that direction. We should all have parents we can look up to.

SLEEP:

When a newborn is asleep, new parents go out of their way not to disturb the sleeping infant. They not only tiptoe around the house, they are so quiet that the child becomes used to sleeping in the silence in an 'unreal' world. If you rear kids in an environment where silence is the norm, they will come to expect this silence in every sleep environment. Allow your child to get accustomed to background noise. Vacuum in the adjacent room, talk in a normal tone of voice, let the phone ring without immediately rushing over. Children can sleep through almost anything. Resist the urge to restrict background noise while the infant is asleep and the child will learn to sleep more soundly.

TEMPER TANTRUMS & WHINING.

If your child is aggressive with other children, it is perhaps because your child hasn't spent enough time with other kids his or her own age. Organizing a play group with other moms and dads can do wonders for improving your kid's social skills. Know that your over-reaction to your child's aggressive behavior may scare the living daylights out of him and the other children as well. If you try to lecture him or her, it will sound like "Blah blah" coming from you. Swiftly remove the child and firmly say in a few words (making it quite clear) that you will not tolerate such mean behavior. "Don't ask your two-year-old for his or her opinion. That is only setting up yourself for a tantrum. Don't say, "Can I put Mr. Bunny here on the couch while we go have lunch?" Say instead, "Mr. Bunny is going to sit on the couch while you eat your lunch" and then proceed to take their hand and lead them away. You'd be surprised how much trouble you can avoid when you don't seek your little tyke's permission". (Michelle Kennedy; Tantrums,-Ivy Press ltd.)

Put your hands over your ears and, in a sing-song voice, say, "I can't hear you when you whine." Your child may ask you to stop, but keep your hands cupped over your ears and say, "I am going to listen to you only if you use a nicer voice or tone." Chances are your childish behavior will shock your child so much, he or she may be inclined to stop the whining. Another trick is to whisper in your child's ear gently, unintelligibly. This will stop the whining momentarily because your child will want you to repeat it, so they can understand what you just said.

Small children tend to be very protective of their favorite toys, and it hurts them to watch other children play with their stuff. Do a little role playing before a scheduled meet-up with other kids. Sit on the floor and share the toys. Make your child ask your permission to play with one of your toys, and when you say, "No," teach him or her to ask if there is another toy that can be played with. Practice other scenarios and figure out constructive ways he or she can get around them.

GENERAL ADVICE:

Encourage your kids to express their feelings by teaching them words to express their thoughts.For instance, say something like, "I felt bad and unhappy after I slipped on the floor at work today. Did you feel bad about something that happened today, too?"

Practice letting the parent who discovers the bad behavior be the one who executes the punishment. This way no one enters the equation to "save the day." as that only teaches your child to play one against the other. The child must know the parent who imposed the punishment is still in charge and responsible for carrying it out.

Know that after age 5, children learn how to be smart, than be honest.

ILLUSTRATION

There was once a spoiled little boy named Jeremy whose father wanted to teach him a lesson. Jeremy was always fussy about eating the food given him.

Father: "Jeremy you can have anything you want for supper. Anything! So tell me, what do you want?"

Jeremy : "An earthworm."

The father bit his lip when he heard that but nevertheless he went out, dug up a worm, came back and then placed it on Jeremy's plate.

Father: "Ok Jeremy, here is the worm you asked for ."

Jeremy (in a loud voice) : "I want the worm cooked!"

His father obligingly sautéed the worm in a pan with some butter and presented it again to Jeremy.

Jeremy: "Before I try it you must eat half of it." (The father obliges reluctantly)

Jeremy:(throwing a tantrum) : "Dad, you ate my half."

"If you want your children to turn out well, spend twice as much time with them and half as much money." (Abby,D.)

Arrogance

*A*n arrogant person may be defined as one who acts as if he or she is superior, more valuable, or more important than another. Equally so, the arrogant person longs to be admired and respected for his or her "special qualities" or accomplishments and is subconsciously always measuring himself/herself against others. When their boastful assertions are exposed for what they are, they excuse themselves by saying their exaggerations were only a joke. When they feel not included or left out, they express their dissatisfaction by saying, "Nobody ever tells me anything." If they feel someone will question their decision or authority, you may hear comments like, "No one is going to tell me what to do"; "I will not be responsible for what happens," or "They can do what they want, I couldn't care less."

Arrogance may also serve as a defense mechanism, i.e., to reject someone before they have a chance to reject you. Consider two individuals introduced to each other for the first time. If Party A's expectations falls short of Party B's, then there is a greater probability that Party A's attitude may be more reserved and less friendly, triggering a somewhat arrogant response. Party "B," with no unfavorable thoughts or agenda would be unfavorably disadvantaged by that chance meeting. Transactions like these tend to happen when people become more successful or goal-oriented. Sometimes we forget how hard life is for those who are still struggling. When we master a skill, we have little tolerance for those who are slow in learning the trade. We frown contemptuously at a face covered with pimples but forget that at a younger age, we too struggled to control them.

There are people, though we pay them no mind, seem to have an uncanny ability to always steer the conversation back toward themselves. Seek a hasty exit if you can. You won't miss anything, and you'll be glad you did. Those individuals are so into themselves that they're just like a rooster who continues to believe its crowing at dawn is what causes the sun to rise.

"Do not keep company with people who speak of [their] careers. Not only are such people uninteresting, but also have no interest in anything interesting." (Roger Rosenblatt)

ILLUSTRATION:

Just before takeoff on an overseas flight, a cabin attendant reminded the late heavyweight boxing champion Muhammad Ali, to fasten his seat belt.

Ali arrogantly replied, "Superman don't need no seat belt." Without missing a beat, the irritated attendant responded in likewise fashion, "Superman don't need no aircraft either."

There will always be people who will want to be perceived as important, forward-thinking pillars of society. Think, for instance, of the pomp and extravagance that is sometimes associated with a funeral. Isn't it more a display of the vanity of the living than an honoring of the dead? Why, you say? Well, ask yourself, how come the inside of the coffin is not as ornamented and shiny as the outside? Makes you think about who the casket was really designed for, doesn't it?

To the arrogant and conceited, it would be well to reflect more deeply upon these words by entrepreneur and investor Justin Kan. He asserted, "Impermanence of everything is a universal constant. No matter what kind of legacy, family, foundation, or business you've created, one day it will disappear and no one will remember anything of your life."

"Some people have modesty in their clothes, but arrogance in their hearts." (Cleric Hasan al Basri)

Blame Game

*W*hen we blame another, it is usually precipitated by what the other party did or failed to do. Since we are often intimately involved in the conflict, we seldom consider our role in the sequence of events, as we are more focused on exposing the culprit standing before us. We want to jab that person in the heart with hurtful words and witness the anxiety on their face.

It is worth noting that fault-finding and truth do share a few similarities. Each produces disagreement and denial—and oftentimes little learning. They awaken deep fears, and generally there is a need to seek some restitution or punishment.

In their book titled *Difficult Conversations,* the authors, Douglas Stone, Bruce Patton & Sheila Heen suggested that our invented stories about other people's intentions may not be accurate. People's motivations may be complex, and at times when we attempt to interpret them, we arrive at unfounded assumptions. There is only one way to understand another person's story. The book's authors suggest, "Instead of asking yourself, 'How can they think that?' ask yourself, 'I wonder what information they have that I don't?'Instead of asking, 'How can they be so irrational?'ask, "How might they see the world such that their view makes sense?'"

To avoid these mistakes, we should practice structuring our blame statements so that they do not assume an accusatory tone but instead take the form of, "This is how you have hurt me." avoid words like "you always" or "you never," and replace them with "It seems to me you often" or "It seems to me you hardly," and let the conversation proceed forward from that tonal angle. Remember, those who deserve love and affection the least are usually the ones who need it the most. All people want to belong and feel accepted.

When we accuse and blame, we shut doors and deny others certain privileges. Too often, in situations where there is a need to blame another, it is quite likely that what happened was a result of the things *two or more people did*. Therefore, when competent, sensible people do something stupid, here are two smart approaches to bring about a resolution:

- Try to figure out what 'kept' each party from anticipating the consequences.

- Determine a way or ways to prevent the mess from happening again.

ILLUSTRATION:

From the Sourcebook of Wit & Wisdom- a story by Denis Waitely.

> *"In the Old Testament, the book of Leviticus tells of a sacred custom called the "escaped goat." When the troubles of the people became too much, a healthy male goat was brought to the temple. There, in a solemn ceremony, the high priest of the tribe placed his hands on the head of the goat and recited the list of woes that plagued the people of the village. The problems were then transferred over to the goat, which was then set free, taking with it the troubles of the day." (pg # 6)*

This is the root beginning of the word *scapegoat*. But unlike the old traditions, today we've replaced goats with people.

Some other thoughts to consider on the subject of blame

- The greater a person's sense of guilt, the greater a need to blame others for causing it.
- "When we blame ourselves, we feel that no one else has a right then to blame us." (Oscar Wilde)

♦ "The man who can smile when things go wrong has thought of some-one else, he can blame it on."(Robert Bloch,1917-1994)

♦ "When a man blames others for his failures, it's a good idea to credit others with his successes." (Howard Newton)

ILLUSTRATION:

In their monthly sales meeting the boss admonished his employees for their poor sales performance.

The Boss: "All I hear is, this excuse and that excuse. We have a functional product and if you guys can't get your act together, then I'll have to replace you with others who can."

Silence drenched the room and each salesman had a frightened look on his face. However, one brave sales agent who once played professional football, decided he would reply to the boss. He said, "Sir,during my football days, it was customary when the whole team was doing poorly, we'd get a new coach, perhaps we need a new coach."

Wouldn't it be nice if we could find other things as easily as we find fault?

Busy People

usy people enjoy working independently and are most energized and productive between the hours of 8:00 a.m. and 11:00 a.m. People who are always busy are seldom seeking new knowledge. They are also less likely to be receptive to new ideas. They function on the premise that their efforts are necessary for creating something real or worthwhile. They operate on the illusion that someday, somewhere, they will finally be able to slow down and be free. Essayist Tim Kreider writes, "Notice that people who claim they are always busy *are not* those individuals working back-to-back shifts or who labor at two or more minimum-wage jobs. They who claim they never have the time fail to recognize that their situation is a self-imposed condition that they've created and chosen of their own accord.

If individuals were to take a closer look at their lives and chart all they did in a given week, about 15–20% of all those activities could be eliminated with little or no loss in quality or value. The always-busy person is more consumed with satisfying a deeper psychological need. They are subconsciously validating their self-worth and importance. Since their time is limited, it is often perceived as more valuable. They conclude that those whose time is considered valuable are usually more sought after, needed, and respected. However, remove these feel-good notions and you will notice that the important "me" becomes a much less motivated "me."

Ariana Huffington, editor of the *Huffington Post*, ceded this, "Work is a necessary ingredient for good emotional health, but we should not live to work." And although a good work ethic is commendable, no one is going to thank you for it. People will more likely remember you as a person who participated in their lives and who was there to enjoy it with them. Don't be like those whose attention is always focused on their mobile devices, rushing around looking for dragons to slay or to save the company from a horde of incompetents.

We are all encouraged from an early age to keep busy, be productive, and stay out of trouble, but being busy doesn't necessarily keep you out of trouble. Being busy leaves you with little or no time to keep in touch with your feelings, and unexpressed feelings do have a way of manifesting themselves in undesirable ways. You are more likely to ridicule others, have less patience, and feel frustrated more often. The busy person has no time to spend on creative activities and therefore loses out on the opportunity to nourish and energize their soul.

When we look at a baby, we see evidence of creativity and learning as time passes by. Why as adults do we suspend this creative wonder and joy and settle for day after day of unsatisfying drudgery? We should consider planting, visiting, singing, building, exploring, etc., and experience the gift of life while we can.

HUMOROUS ILLUSTRATION:

> One day, a little girl asked her mother, "Mommy, why does Daddy bring home so much work every night?"
>
> Mother: "Well, dear, it is because he doesn't have time to finish it at work."
>
> Little Girl: "Then why don't they put him in a slower class?"

"At any given time, there are more important people in the world than important jobs to contain them."(Bunk Carter, 1979). Despite how necessary and important you may feel you are, you are not indispensable. When a forever-busy person hears this line, he/she always acknowledges its truth but never thinks it pertains to him or her.Their situation or circumstance is always different. Each falsely imagines that if the ship does begin to sink, *everyone* on board will drown together, and since that is unlikely to happen, there is safety in continuing along. Such faulty thinking is likely to be found among people with too much money or education.

"The graveyards are full of indispensable men".(Former French President, Charles de Gaulle). And Rabbi Harold Kushner added, "Nobody says on their deathbed, 'I wish I had spent more time at the office.'"

"If you begin to think you're changing the culture of the world, just ask your mom what she thinks you do for a living." (Jurgen Stringenz)

Charity

The Jewish Talmud says true charity is practiced in secret. The best type of charity is where the person who gives does not know the person who receives it; and the person who receives does not know who gave it. True friendship is somewhat similar. It consists of forgetting what one gives but remembering what one receives.

The following is an English translation of an Islamic Hadith:

> "On the day of resurrection, God would say, "O child of Adam! I was sick, and you did not visit me. I asked you for food and drink and you did not give it to me." "And he would say, 'Oh God, you are the lord of the universe, how could you be sick and how could I visit you and how could I give you food and drink since you are free of the worldly desires of hunger and thirst?" Then God answered, "Such and such person was sick, and you did not visit him and such and such person asked you for bread and drink and you did not give it to him.'" (Sahih Muslim 2569)

What evidence is there that loving or helping another less-fortunate soul will make you feel better? Have you ever planted a seedling? Do you remember how you felt when you saw the first tiny leaves struggling upward toward the sunlight? Do you remember when you made it your business to water that plant at every opportunity? And of the joy you felt as you monitored its slow, steady growth? How proud and happy you were when the first bud began to bloom, knowing it was just a matter of time before other wondrous developments would occur? It is the same joy you feel when you invest in another and are able to witness first-hand the promise of your efforts. The knowledge that your presence is instrumental in changing the course of events is profoundly satisfying. And best of all, the pleasure you feel can be replayed many times over in your mind, whenever you want.

ILLUSTRATION:

One lady was talking to her next-door neighbor when the conversation shifted to the subject of charity. The first lady said, "Listen, I consider myself a very charitable person. Even this morning, I gave a bum five dollars." The neighbor asked inquisitively, "And, what did your husband have to say about that?" She responded, "Oh! He just said thanks!"

Imagine if a huge amount of wealth was an over-the-counter medicine, there would be a need for the following warning messages on the package:

- Warning: May cause arrogance.

- Extra precaution should be taken not to offend people.

- If taken for prolonged periods, may impair judgement and cause false pride.

This is what Mother Theresa had to say about charity: "It is not how much we give that is so important, but how much love we put into that giving."

Your use of money demonstrates what you think about God, and regardless of your belief, it is a good indicator of your philosophy about life. When you reflect back on your life, the moments that will stand out the most are those moments when you have done things for others. "Every man who goes down to his death, bears in his hands only that which he has given away." (Persian Proverb)

It is, however, wrong for those who are less fortunate to suppose if they were somehow rich, they would behave differently than the rich. It is like assuming that one could drink alcohol all day long and still remain sober.

There is no universal rule to follow when it comes to giving. Often, it is a personal decision that we should all respect. Charity, however, should be conditioned on need and whether the receiver is deserving of it. Genevan poet Jean Petit Senn,(1792-1870) offered this insight:" In giving alms, let us rather look at the needs of the poor than his claim to your charity." Why is it we feel so angered when the "well-off "person chooses not to share his bounty with the less fortunate -but on a hot, humid day not for once do we ever consider making a charitable donation of a bottle of cold water to a street vagrant out in the hot noon sun? It is only when we share the same basic comforts (which we often take for granted) with those around us, that we earn the right to impose our will on others. No, we cannot mend the world's ills by ourselves; however, as slave, scientist, and inventor George Washington Carver (1860-1943) observed, "When you do the common things in an uncommon way, you'll command the attention of the world."

There is a way you can tell whether your well-meant gestures reach the right target(s). Although there is no clear-cut method or procedure to follow, there are subtle clues you may look for when dealing with panhandlers.

> 1) Good hygiene is seldom a priority for the truly indigent. Look for unwashed necks or dirty fingers; however, if clothing is filthy or torn but the person's skin underneath appears clean and washed, chances are you are probably being scammed.

> 2) Look at the quality of the person's sneakers. People down on their luck can't afford good footwear, nor, for that matter, iPhones.

> 3) Real beggars seldom ask for help. They tend to look at you *only* when they notice you are looking at them.

> 4) Those who are truly poor are generally thin looking and on the lean side.

> 5) Many tote their prized possessions along with them wherever they go.

"A man who shows me his wealth is like the beggar who shows me his poverty; they are both looking for alms, the rich man for the alms of my envy, the poor man for the alms of my guilt." (Ben Hecht, 1894-1964)

"The manner in which a gift is given is sometimes worthier than the gift itself." (Pierre Corneille, 1606-1684)

Compass to Guide You at Work

- It is not essential that you come in early and stay late—the important thing is why?

- "Flipping burgers is not beneath your dignity. Your grandparents had a different word for burger flipping; they called it opportunity." (Charles Sykes)

- "A wrongdoer is often a man who has left something undone, not always the one who has done something." (Marcus Aurelius)

- Don't focus on money but on doing a good job; the money will come eventually.

- "Show me a man who cannot bother to do little things, and I'll show you a man who cannot be trusted to do big things." (Lawrence D Bell)

- The man who watches the clock will always remain 'one of the hands'.

- The best way to find out if a man has done what he was supposed to do is to advise him how to do it. He will not be able to resist boasting how he's already done it without being told.

- "Trust him not with your secrets, who, when left alone in your room, turns over your papers." (Johann Kaspar)

- Don't say, "Everything happens for the best." This seldom happens. It is better to say, "I do hope some good can be derived from this."

- "If you get to thinking you're a person of influence, try ordering somebody else's dog around." (Will Rogers)

- Don't fret over yourself too much. Ninety percent of your co-workers aren't interested in your opinion anyway.

- "It doesn't matter how strong your opinions are. If you don't use your power for positive change, you are, indeed, part of the problem. (Coretta Scott King)

Traditional company department stances:

Sales & marketing: Yes, let's go for it!

Finance: No, hold on there, the projections are all wrong!

Legal: Wait, let's review these papers more carefully!

Personnel: Guys, we need to document everything first!

Engineering: It is not our problem and it does not concern us!

Manufacturing: Darn, we need more floor and storage place!

Top management: Who will be held accountable, if this fails?

Mistakes on the job:

When employees make mistakes, it is crucial that everyone understands how it happened and how to prevent it from happening again. Shaming people because of an error is not constructive. It invariably leads to resentment. When things go wrong, don't harp endlessly upon it. It wouldn't hurt the boss much if he or she were to step forward and absorb some of the blame as well. By owning up, others in the group may be inclined to do so too. Though the boss is blameless, it is nevertheless one way he or she could persuade others to share in the responsibility freely. Do not worry about absorbing blame yourself. It is the constructive and courageous approach of a genuine leader. The blame you willfully put on yourself isn't going to hurt you one bit. On the other hand, even a small amount of undeserved blame you place on another may be deeply resented. No matter who's to blame, don't rub it in. It's all about helping another to save face and to learn from the experience.

"The search for someone to blame is always successful." (Robert Half). And Judith Martin, aka Ms. Manners, noted, "Allowing an *unimportant* mistake to pass without comment is a wonderful social grace."

Event	Those in charge say, they are ...	But they consider their employees.
When it takes a long time to finish something.	Being thorough	Slow
When something doesn't get done.	Too busy	Lazy
When success happens	Deserving	Lucky

Author Jeffery J. Fox, author of the bestseller *How to Become a CEO*, offered the following morale-building statements that could be used when interacting with subordinates. Practice saying them more frequently, and of course be sincere when you do so.

- "Please and thank you." (The more often, the better)

- "You remember John Doe in our sales department, right?" (Say this when introducing someone from your work team to a superior.)

- "That was a first-class job you did."

- "I appreciate your effort."

- "I hear nothing but good words about you."

- "I am glad you are on the team."

- "I need your help."

- "You certainly earned and deserve this."

- "Congratulations."

- "You showed initiative" or "You've got a good memory."

While praise is warm and desirable, it is also something that must be earned. For example, an impulsive hug received from a child. Praise that is unbefitting or tactlessly bestowed is never really appreciated. However, imagine how motivated a subordinate might feel if his or her boss were to say, "I can't think of a better person than you to finish this job." Know that people have a way of becoming what you encourage them to be, not what you nag them to be."The meanest, most contemptible kind of praise is that which first speaks well of a man, and then qualifies it with a 'but.'" (Henry Ward Beecher,1813-1887)

Individual recognition is just as important as salaries, bonuses, and promotions. People, whether they are engineers, store clerks, or pastry chefs, yearn to be creative. They want to identify with the "brownie points" associated with their profession or organization. When an individual provides either more comfort, better service, or an engaging experience for others, the most welcomed reward is an acknowledgment that he or she has made a difference and it is worth mentioning. This is especially true when received from an unexpected and respected source.

Delegation:

General George S. Patton said, "Never tell people how to do things. Tell them what to do and they will surprise you with their ingenuity." When you give people jobs to do, take care and tell them what, when, and why you want it done, but do not take the challenge out of it by telling them how. Let them figure it out for themselves and grow in the process. A manager might say what he/she wants is too crucial or important to delegate. While that might be so, that manager may still choose to delegate with close supervision. That manager may start by asking the subordinate what he or she thinks is the best approach. Once given the green light, the subordinate is requested to check in with you before implementing any changes. Leaders who delegate wisely are the ones who develop capable subordinates. It is also a sign that those leaders are ready to move ahead. The manager who has the right to boast seldomly does so because he already knows it's not the whistle that pulls the train, it's the engine.

Employees are increasingly being asked to do more and to do it autonomously. Rewards and recognition provide an effective low-cost way to encourage higher levels of performance. However, rewards that come weeks or months later do little to motivate employees. If management's expectation is for the employee to repeat the thing worthy of their applause, recognition should come soon thereafter.

Asking an employee to participate or become actively involved is always a good starting point, but consider these other forms of recognition too:

- Offer a deserving employee a change of job title.

- Provide the employee with better furnishings, space, equipment, etc.

- Volunteer to do another person's least desirable task for a day.

- When you reward people with food, know it's something they'll use.

- Make a photo collage of a project that shows all the people who've worked on it (from development through completion), and have it displayed as a proud example of collective effort and achievement.

"The man who knows how will always have a job. The man who knows why will always be his boss." (Ralph Waldo Emerson)

Compassion

You have been given life. Your purpose and path in this life will be drawn on a map created by you.

ILLUSTRATION 1 (From Clara Null, *Humor for Preaching & Teaching*)

> *"It was one of the worst days of my life. The washing machine broke down, the telephone kept ringing, my head ached, and the mail carrier brought a bill [for which] I had no money to pay. Almost to the breaking point, I lifted my one-year-old to his highchair and leaned my head against the tray and began to cry. Without a word, my son took his pacifier out of his mouth and stuck it in mine." (Page #33)*

The above story proves even babies know and have learned how to express feelings of compassion.

ILLUSTRATION 2 (From the book "Words for all Occasions" by Glenn Van Ekeren)

> *"World War II devastated Europe, and the fight was on to pick up the pieces and go on with life. Undoubtedly, the saddest sight was the numbers of children who had been orphaned. Many were without clothes and were starving on the streets. Their present existence was unfortunate, and their future looked hopeless. Early one foggy morning, an American soldier was making his way back to his base when he spotted a young boy with his nose pressed against a bakeshop window. The little boy's hunger was quite evident as he watched every move the baker made in preparing the day's goods.*
>
> *Taken in by the emotional sight, the soldier pulled his jeep over, got out and quietly approached the boy. There was a silent plea etched on the boy's face.*

Suddenly, the soldier's heart felt heavy. He asked the boy if he would like one of the tasty morsels. Startled, the boy replied, "I sure would!"

The soldier made his way inside and purchased a dozen pastries for the young boy. Stepping back into the chilly morning air, he smiled as he approached his also-smiling friend. "Here you are, son." As he turned to leave, he felt a little tug on his coat. He looked back and heard the little boy ask softly, "Mister, are you, God?"' (page #346)

It is not an uncommon sight today to see men and women begging for money as they tote around signs with the words *Hungry and Homeless*. Then, there are others who use a more direct approach and ask, "Ma'am, can you spare a dollar so I can get something to eat?" No doubt, there are tricksters among them, and each time you give, you're never sure your gesture will succeed as you intended. When you are in doubt and cannot decide, allow your compassionate side to prevail. Why? Because one of the greatest burdens an individual may bear is the knowledge that no one cares or wants to understand. Don't become another callous statistic in their life. Indeed, only a few may be truly deserving, but even if your call is wrong, you have nevertheless given a good account of yourself.

ILLUSTRATION OF COMPASSION AND JUMPING TO CONCLUSIONS.

Notty was enjoying his daily stroll through the neighborhood when a slightly intoxicated street bum approached him and asked for some "change" to buy something to eat. We'll call him Lenny.

Notty: "You say you want food, but where do you sleep at night?"

Lenny: "Oh, I sleep at a shelter."

The man produced some sort of shelter ID.

Notty: "If you're hungry, I will buy you a sandwich, but I won't give you money."

Lenny: "Sir, I don't want a sandwich. I much rather a plate of rice and meat."

Notty: "OK let's go get a slice of pizza instead. There is a store right over there."

Lenny: "But mister, they sell really good rice at the Chinese restaurant across the street."

Notty gave in, and they both walked over to the restaurant.

Notty: "It's chicken and rice, you wanted right?"

Lenny: "No, I want Hunan beef with rice."

Notty: "No! That'll cost too much. You'll have to settle for the chicken."

Lenny: "Ok! Ok! Whatever you say."

Notty paid for the meal and left Lenny to wait for his free meal. As Notty glanced back to have a last look at Lenny, he could clearly see an expression of disbelief still planted on Lenny's face.

Although he felt proud of himself afterward, Notty wanted to make sure everything ended well. So, after he departed, he circled back three minutes later and stationed himself across the street to observe the events through the restaurant's glass exterior. As he peered in, he noticed there were no customers inside. How could the man have obtained his meal and left in such a short time, he wondered? As he surveyed the surrounding area, he caught a glimpse of the deceitful bum a block away with several of his buddies, joking among themselves. There was no food in sight nor bag containing it. Dismayed and feeling betrayed, Notty gestured to Lenny to come over to where he was standing to reproach him for his deceit."

Notty: "Where is the food? Didn't you tell me you were hungry?"

Lenny: "Oh! I told another guy to pick it up for me, over there."

Lenny pointed in the direction of the restaurant as he struggled to explain *himself.Clearly,he was caught red-handed.*

Notty: "Why are you lying? What was so pressing that you couldn't wait and pick up the food yourself?"You cancelled the order after I left and pocketed the refund, didn't you?"You know, it's guys like you who create doubt in the minds of others and prevent them from giving to those who truly need help."

Lenny: "No Sir! No Sir! It is still in the restaurant. I'll go get it now!"

Notty stood his ground and looked on as Lenny walked toward and into the restaurant. He just wanted to hear what Lenny would say to wiggle himself out of the mess he created and then leave afterwards. But lo and behold, Lenny exited the take-out restaurant with a bag that appeared to be his meal. He walked up directly to Notty and asked if he would like to share some of the food with him. Notty declined. Lenny then proceeded to explain why he behaved the way he did. As it turned out, he didn't want to share his food with his loser buddies. He arranged with the restaurant to pick the food later at a more convenient time and after he had ditched his deadbeat friends.(to eat it alone or perhaps with his family.)

As Notty turned and began to walk away, he had to look back and smile when he heard Lenny say out aloud, "You're sure you don't want any?"

A poem by Emily Dickinson (1830-1886)

If I can stop one heart from breaking,
I shall not live in vain;
If I can ease one life the aching,
Or cool one pain,
Or help one fainting robinUnto his nest again,
I shall not live in vain.

"Whether one believes in a religion or not, whether one believes in rebirth or not, there isn't anyone who doesn't appreciate kindness and compassion." (Yamamoto Tsunetomo)

Compromise, but Consider This Too!

From the time we are little children, we are taught to please others. As we grow older, we may recognize that we're sacrificing honesty and sometimes integrity by trying to get along. Often, people talk about the middle of the road as if it were the more acceptable position, but former British Prime minister Margaret Thatcher had another perspective. "Standing in the middle of the road is dangerous because you can get knocked down by traffic from either end."

No doubt, government decisions, human benefits, and bargaining are all prefaced on compromise and exchange. However, you should consider these kinds of accommodations you make when you do compromise.

- "A compromise is an agreement between two parties to do what each feels deep down is the wrong way to go." (Lord Edward Cecil, 1867-1918)

- "To compromise simply means that you are prepared go down a tiny bit lower than the limit you have set yourself." (Joyce Meyer)

- Consider a couple who decided to compromise while out shopping for a living room rug. Neither could find an equally appealing design and ended up buying a piece that neither would have purchased on his or her own.

- "A compromise is the art of dividing a cake in such a way that everyone believes that he has the biggest piece." (Ludwig (Erhard, 1897-1977)

- " Compromise in colors is grey." (Edi Rama)

- "Compromise makes a good umbrella, but a weak roof." (James R. (Lowell, 1819-1891)
- "It is the weak man who urges compromise - never the strong man." (Elbert Hubbard)

Former CEO of Avis Car Rental Robert C Townsend, (1920-1998) made the following observation. He said, "Compromise is usually bad. It should be a last resort. If two departments or divisions have a problem they can't solve and it comes up to you, listen to both sides and then pick one or the other. This places solid accountability on the winner to make it work. Condition your people to avoid compromise."

Indian nationalist Mahatma Ghandi concluded, "A 'No' uttered from the deepest conviction is better than a 'Yes' merely uttered to please, or worse, to avoid trouble." Compromise is known to squelch dissent but becomes very wrong when it means sacrificing principle.

Every man carries with him the world in which he must live. His decisions should consider how much he is prepared to bear or give up.

Conscience & Guilt

ere is a retelling of a Native American story. Your conscience is like a little triangle in your heart. It acts like a pinwheel. When you are good, it does not rotate, but when you are bad, it turns around and its sharp edges cut and cause you pain. If you keep on being bad, the edges eventually wear down, and as the triangle spins again, it doesn't hurt anymore.

In their book titled *Conscience*, authors Andy Naselli and J.D.Crowley advanced the following thought: "Feeding excuses to your conscience is like feeding sleeping pills to a watchdog. Eventually, you become so used to the watchdog's silence that its presence no longer affects you." It is a sad truth, however, that many people tune out their conscience when money begins to talk. Essayist and critic Logan Pearsall Smith expressed the same concept this way: "Most people sell their souls, and live with a good conscience on the proceeds." Often, in order to tranquilize the inner conflicts that sometimes develop, they medicate themselves with an assortment of pills and thrills, then go on living like their yesterdays were never part of their life.

So feel blessed when your conscience hurts, and be worried when it doesn't. When it hurts, it is a sign you have done something wrong that needs to be repaired. "Happy is the man who renounces anything that places a strain on his conscience." (Islamic proverb) A bad conscience may be compared to being close to a bee hive. You may not see the bees, but their buzzing makes you anxious and puts you on high alert. It's like the baby that must go to sleep before you can, and an inner voice that always reminds you someone else may be looking.

ILLUSTRATION: (From *God's Little Devotional Book*)

> *A mother was helping her son one day with his spelling assignment, and they came to the words "conscious" and "conscience." She asked her son, "Do you know the difference between these two words?" He thought about it for a moment and then replied "Sure, Mom! Conscious is when you are aware of something, and conscience is when you wish you weren't." (pg. # 281)*

"Guilt: The one gift that keeps on giving." (Erma Bombeck)

Guilt is a way of generalizing a single bad action or feeling you have and projecting it onto another person. It is a vicious circle that works like this: You do something unkind or destructive to another that you immediately know is wrong. The guilt you feel soon becomes distressingly painful, and you look for relief. Enter rationalization—the mind's solution to help you deal with your mental conflict. You say to yourself, "If only she had not done so and so, I wouldn't have done this or that." Soon, you convince yourself of this storyline, and, it becomes your defense and justification. In the end, you successfully free yourself of the internal anguish and transfer it outside yourself. The other person now is the one at fault and must explain or defend him or herself for *provoking you*. Of course, the accused person, in defense of your assault, may then do or say something that injures your self-esteem. By this time, the initial guilt you felt is a long-lost memory, and you are now consumed with defending your reputation against those scoundrels whose sole purpose is to debase you. Your character has been tarnished, and it's now up to you now to clear your good name and set things right again.

ILLUSTRATION: of displaced guilt (From *Wisdom Tales* by Heather Forest)

> *As two Zen monks walked along a muddy rain-soaked road, they came upon a lovely woman attempting to cross a large mud puddle. The elder monk stopped beside the woman, lifted her in his arms and carried her across the puddle. He set her gently down on the dry edge of the road, as the younger monk discreetly admired her charms. After bowing politely to the*

woman, the two monks continued down the muddy road. The younger monk was sullen and silent as they walked along. They travelled over the hills, down around the valleys, through a town and under forest trees. At last, after many hours had passed, the younger monk scolded the elder. He said, "You are aware that we monks do not touch women ! Why did you carry that girl?" The elder monk turned, smiled and said: "My dear young brother, you have such heavy thoughts! I left the woman alongside the road hours ago. Why are you still carrying her?"(page # 39)

"All people know the same truth. Our lives consist of how we choose to distort it." (Woody Allen)

Corporate Shenanigans

The administrative processes associated with change:

1. Wild enthusiasm
2. Disillusionment
3. Total confusion
4. Search for the guilty
5. Punishment of the innocent
6. Promotion of the non-participants. (Arthur Bloc)

Trivia, Truth or perhaps both?

- Have you ever noticed within a corporation, those who are the least capable and/or knowledgeable are always the most vocal and find themselves up in the front row, advocating for changes to the original proposal?

- Neither automation nor computers will ever replace man. Why? Because neither is able to kiss-up to the boss at a moment's notice.

- "For a real quick energy boost, nothing beats having the boss walk in." (Robert Orben)

- For your own good, be warm and friendly with your boss's wife. He may not be swayed by her opinion, but she makes him look at you in a different way.

- "If a problem causes many meetings, the meetings eventually become more important than the problem." (Hendrickson's Law)

- "Those who make their dress a principal part of themselves, will, in general, become of no more value than their dress." (William Hazlitt)

- "Influence is like a savings account. The less you use it, the more you've got." (Andrew Young)
- It is not the number of people employed in the business that makes it successful, it is the number of people actually working.
- "It is not who you know, but sometimes what you know about who you know that counts." (Mrs. C. Lowe)
- "The bearing of a child takes nine months, no matter how many women are assigned" (Frederick Brooks). Translation: More manpower only affects costs, not progress.
- No matter how glamorous a job may seem at first, after six months, it is just another job.
- "If enough data is collected— anything may be proven by statistical methods." (Hiram's Law)
- "The average executive is lazy, indifferent, and frequently dishonest." (H. T. Rowe)
- The biggest idiot can sometimes ask a question that the smartest person would not be able to answer.
- "After learning the tricks of the trade, many of us think we know the trade." (H. Jackson Brown)
- "Experience teaches you that the man who looks you straight in the eye, particularly if he adds a firm handshake, is hiding something." (Clifton Fadiman)
- "The man whose authority is recent, is always stern." (Aeschylus)
- "The more you know, the more you think somebody owes you a living." (Will Rogers)
- "The most powerful person in a company spends most or all of his or her time in meetings and signing documents." (Murphy's Law)
- "When people you greatly admire appear to be thinking deep thoughts, they probably are thinking about lunch." (Douglas Adams)
- Wicked people are always surprised when they learn that good people can be more clever than them.

- "No matter what happens, there's always somebody who knew it would." (Lonny Star)
- When a boss exclaims, "Our company is like one big happy family," there is a good chance many of the hires are his relatives or the children of his better friends.

It has always been and always will be the same in the world: the horse does the work, and the coachman is tipped.

Criticism: A Practical Approach

Before you criticize anybody, ask yourself three questions:

- **How do I feel about offering this criticism?** Does it give me pleasure or pain? If part of you is looking forward to it, hold back. Your motives may not be sincere, and your listener will probably respond defensively in an attempt to rebuff your insinuation. If it pains you to criticize, then by all means do so, because then your motives will be more sincere, and chances are you will use words that convey your thoughts in a more caring and personal way.

- **Does my criticism offer specific ways to change?** The goal of any criticism is to leave the person you are attempting to criticize with feeling that they are being helped.

- **Are my words threatening and demoralizing?** To find fault is easy—to do better is difficult.

When criticizing, avoid words like "always" (e.g., "You have always been selfish") and "never" (e.g.,"You never think about anybody but yourself"). Replace them with "often" and "hardly." The words "always" and "never" demoralize the person who is being criticized and, of course, their natural reaction is to deny everything. Also, be particularly careful and avoid saying those same words to children. Their egos are especially vulnerable, and such rebukes can result in feelings of worthlessness. If a child tells a lie, don't call him or her a liar. Being called a liar is a label that the child must wear, and it stains the ego much deeper than the lie itself.

If you are on the receiving end of criticism, ask this question to the person chastising you: "What would you like me to do?" Concentrate on finding out what your antagonist wants from you, and perhaps a solution may present itself. Also, consider leaving an escape hatch so that your provoker may gracefully swing over to your side without losing face if he or she should change their mind.

ILLUSTRATION:

A drunk got into a bus and staggered over to a seat beside a priest. He sat for a few minutes looking at the priest, who was reading the Bible. Then without any provocation, he let loose with a barrage of insults at the innocent priest.

Drunk: "I am not going to heaven because there is no heaven!"

The priest ignored his callous comments, kept his head lowered, and continued reading his book. The boozed-up man, not getting any attention, decided he had to try something else. He inched himself closer to the priest and poked his face closer into the book's open page. This made the priest even more uncomfortable, but he managed to keep his focus and remain calm.

It soon became clear to the priest that no one aboard was going to step in or help him defuse the situation, so he turned the page on his open book and the drunk immediately withdrew. But the drunk felt an obligation to continue on with his abuse, however now in an even louder tone.

The drunk bellowed, "I'm not going to heaven because there is no heaven. So, what do you say to that, Padre?

Priest: "Then, go to hell if you must, but for heaven's sake be quiet about it!"

Those words were enough to shut the drunk up. He picked himself up and relocated to an empty seat at the back of the bus.

Generally, when we criticize another, we've already decided the other person is guilty and worthy of our reprimand. Here is an example: Joan flushed Jack's cigarettes down the drain. Jack retaliated by accusing Joan of always trying to control his life, but the truth was she was always looking after his best interests. When she flushed the cigarettes, she was actually trying to help him live up to his commitment to quit. So before judging a person's actions, first try to understand their motives. When we know and understand a motive, we are less likely to be judgmental. Unfortunately, when we jump to conclusions, we often conclude other people's intentions are bad, and those false perceptions shape our attitude toward them.

"If it's very painful for you to criticize your friends—you're safe in doing it. But if you take the slightest pleasure in it, that's the time to hold your tongue." (Arthur Miller,1923-2010)

Many of our critical assumptions are prefaced on past experiences. Consider a car accident witnessed by two people from different vantage points. Ever notice how each person's perception and interpretation of an incident differs sometimes? The reason why this is so because we normally identify with those things that are more important or closer to our hearts. Initially, we are unable to absorb *all* the finite data present in that split-moment and end up discarding or discounting a number of them. Second, people make decisions based on their constitutional makeup. For example, an artist and a scientist may both witness a parade before them and "experience" it from different perspectives: the artist from a creative or scenic angle, and the scientist from a collaboration of various laws and physical processes. In either case, impressions and opinions are governed by their likes and dislikes or what works better for them.

We all have different stories to tell about the world. We assimilate information and measure that info against our internal mirror of how things should be. We erroneously believe each pair of eyes sees the exactly the same thing(s), and when there is a difference of opinion, the other side is clearly mistaken. It is then our moral obligation to set them right, and we feel justified in doing just that. It occasionally happens in our haste to restore normalcy, we communicate our differences of opinion in unflattering ways and which we later come to regret.

So knowing all of this, what are we to do? We must never forget there are always two sides to everything. We all know the opposite of love is hate, but the middle ground is indifference. That is a terrible state to be in. Instead of trading accusations back and forth, it would helpful if we could introduce a series of "and" statements in our exchanges, e.g, "I understand how hurt you are *and* I understand that you think I should have been more upfront with you *and* however bad things may be right now, I do not want to do or say something that I might regret later."Looped "and" statements humanize you and may open doors. They also serve to weaken your risk threat and encourage dialog.

> "Many people believe in 'law and order', as long as they can lay down the law and give the orders."

Decision-Making

When confronted with two competing courses of action, follow the one that will bring you the most happiness. Psychologist Dr. Joyce Brothers (1927-2013), expressed that notion this way, "Trust your hunches; they are usually based on facts filed away in your subconscious mind." William Shakespeare in his play *Measure to Measure* described the same concept as follows: "Go to you bosom: Knock there, and ask your heart what it doth know?"

Hesitation when making a decision and feelings of uncertainty have one similar characteristic in common. In each case, it may feel like walking through a dark tunnel without a flashlight and though you may see faint reflections of light out in the distance, you are tempted to go back through the darkness from where you began. During those times when you find yourself stuck, truthfully ask yourself the following two questions and be guided by them: (1) Does it make sense? (2) Is it fair?

Here is another suggestion. Jot down on a piece of paper all the "yes" or "in favor of" arguments on one side of the page. On the back side, list all the "no" or "against" arguments. Try and be arbitrary, spontaneous, but thorough when listing the pros and cons. Put the list away and return to it later (from six hours to several days—the longer the better). On your return, assign a numerical value (between 1 and 10) to each item, with 10 being the highest (either for or against). Tally the scores on each side of the page and lean toward the side having the bigger numerical advantage. Should both scores be equal after the count, revisit the weightier items on the front and reverse side and assign an incremental fraction on those items only. For example, if you initially assigned a score of 7, you may change it to 7.1 or 7.2 or 7.3, etc., based upon your perception and level of importance. Re-total both sides, and again take the course suggested by the result with the larger score.

If you can wait before making an important decision, wait until early the following morning. After a night's rest, your thoughts are clearer and more logically structured. French historian and writer Voltaire advanced this thought, "The man who, in a fit of melancholy, kills himself today, would have wished he had waited a week."

Whether you are fretting about buying a new home, relocating, losing your job, retiring, getting divorced, setting up a business or filing for bankruptcy, just tell yourself that big decisions have a way of making themselves. Swiss poet and critic Henri Amiel (1821-1881), observed, "The man who insists on seeing with perfect clearness before he decides, never decides." Don't exhaust yourself with "what if" scenarios because, as writer Rita M. Brown acknowledged, "A peacefulness always follow any decision, even a wrong one."

People will say, "I don't know what the best thing to do is." Rarely will someone say, "What's the *right* thing to do?" The "best way" implies compromise. The "right way" implies clear conscience. Doing the right thing involves sacrifice or upholding some time-tested standard or principle and unlike the "best thing", may turn out less gratifying and even alienating. Within this context, you should decide which works better for you.

In the central place of every heart, there is a recording chamber, and as long as it continues to receive messages of beauty, hope, and courage, it remains hopefully alive and echoes the promise of tomorrow. When the wires are all down and the heart is covered with a blanket of pessimism and icy cynicism, isn't it reasonable to think the decisions made then may reflect the same despair?

ILLUSTRATION:

A young woman complained to her mother about how hard her life was. She said she did not know if she was going to make it, and she was on the verge of a nervous breakdown. She was tired of the daily struggle of living because when one problem was solved, a new one arose. It seemed that instead of things getting better, problems just reset themselves with no end.

The mother asked the daughter to sit at the table and close her eyes. She then placed before her daughter a carrot, an egg, and a teabag.

She asked her to feel each item and describe it to her. The young woman felt the carrot and noted it was half stiff but bendable; the egg she immediately recognized to be hard-boiled; the teabag was moist and warm and felt like a wet cotton pouch. The daughter said, "Mother, what is the point of all this?" The mother requested she open her eyes and look at the three items on the table. She explained that each of the three had faced the very same adversity: boiling water; however, each had reacted differently to it.

The carrot had been stiff and hard, but after being subjected to the boiling water, it had softened and was easy to break into pieces. The egg's thin outer shell had protected its liquid interior, but after sitting through the boiling heat, its insides were toughened. The teabag was unique, however. Being immersed in the steaming water, it soon changed the water's appearance and imparted a distinctive aroma.

The mother then asked her daughter, "Which one of these items describes you, my child? When faced with adversity, do you respond like the carrot, the egg, or the teabag? Are you the carrot that appears strong, but when adversity strikes, you become weak and lose your strength, or are you like the egg, which starts off with a soft heart and becomes hard when the heat is turned up? Or are you perhaps like the teabag—your true strength and value is revealed when the heat is turned on?

The fact that we permit other people's judgments (or what we perceive to be their judgments) to influence our thoughts and actions is one of the main reasons why we have so much difficulty making decisions. Philosopher and writer Elbert Hubbard (1856-1915) admonished the seesaw way people often make decisions. He pointed out, "Parties who want milk should not seat themselves on a stool in the middle of a field in hope that the cow will back up to them." He prescribed grabbing the 'bull by the horns' and going for it.

Women's right activist Susan B Anthony (1820-1906) captured the essential essence behind our existence in this beautiful observation. She wrote, "Sooner or later we all discover that the important moments in life are not the advertised ones, not the birthdays, the graduations, the weddings, not the great goals achieved. The real milestones are less prepossessing. They come to the door of memory unannounced—stray dogs that amble in, sniff around a bit, and simply never leave. Our lives are measured [and best remembered] by these."

> *"Decide promptly, but never give any reasons. Your decisions may be right, but your reasons are sure to be wrong." (Lord Mansfield)*

Dependency & How It Causes Unhappiness

*I*n their SMI audio presentation *Beyond Success and Failure,* Willard & Marguerite Beecher made a few intriguing observations that shape our attitude and ultimately determine the level of our personal happiness. Here are three of them.

- Dependent people, when approached by others, always appear helpless. Know that all situations rooted in dependency result in disapointment because sooner or later, others refuse to carry us on their backs *unless* they're compensated well for the ride. No wonder the dependent person feels disappointed and betrayed when the stroking subsides. Eventually, those feelings of distress are transformed and find expression as rage and sometimes deep resentment.

- In a way, dependent people are no different from alcoholics, addicts, and gamblers. It isn't so much that these people are in love with their addicting agents, but they can't imagine living without the good 'brownie points' they've grown accustomed to receiving from 'pals' who share their same interests. Their whole social life is made up of others who've made the same conformist mistakes as they have. What better way to feel good about oneself than to compete with others where the bar is already set low and the odds of coming out "on top" are realistically much better?

- Imagine a horse is let loose on a roadside; it begins to graze immediately. If he sees a clump of grass, he starts to eat it. While nibbling at that he sees another clump a few steps away and he reaches for it ...

and then another and another. In no time, he is hundreds of yards away from where he first started, with no thought about tomorrow. What is important is that he enjoys the process. His moment-to-moment fulfillment is its own reward, and he has no dependence on anything at the end of the day to pay him for his efforts. Truly innovative people gravitate toward the grazing principle to lead them into new pastures or discoveries."

We don't have the privilege to preview the consequences of our actions, but if we could recognize that half of our troubles come from wanting our way and the other half comes from having it, we may be able to avoid the traps we set for ourselves. How can we guard against this? Perhaps, televangelist Joel Osteen was on to something when he said, "Don't do anything that you wouldn't feel comfortable reading about in the newspaper the next day."

It is either "total denial" or "total acceptance" that controls and governs our feelings of insecurity. With respect to total denial, our competence is somewhat questioned and the only way to keep our identity safe and secure, is to deny the incoming stimulus. For example, "I have more experience than you, and therefore I am more qualified than you." Denial is a reaction to a perceived threat, and the response is almost always to challenge, negate, and dilute the criticism, e.g., "The reason why you hate me is because you're jealous of me. Contrarily, with regard to total acceptance, the response we receive from other people may define us. As an example, we may interpret negative vibes as a confirmation of our true identity, e.g., "I believe Jackie and Sara are avoiding me because I didn't participate in their charity event and they probably think I'm selfish and not as committed as them." Total acceptance forces us to interpret 'perceived' impressions as an endorsement of the truth."

We fear judgment so much that we allow it to control our reason, our identity, and our freedom to be honest. The values we use to pass judgment aren't so much our own values, but rather the beliefs and opinions of others whom we hold in higher esteem. Since our reputation and future rests in their hands, we must do all we can to prevent them from knowing too much about us because once they recognize our dependence on them, it is more than likely at some point "down the road" they'll abandon or throw us away.

According to motivational author Dale Carnegie, the reason why birds and horses are happy (apart from mating rituals) is because they aren't trying to impress other birds and horses. Too often, human beings are "on stage" and performing for an audience. But after our little show is over, we await feedback from those present, wanting to know whether they were impressed with us or not. Within this context, it is easy to identify conceited people. They seem to have a perpetual need to validate their value or importance before others.

A great deal of what we see depends on what we are looking for. Don't overwhelm your conscious mind with the whys, whens, and hows. Decisive actions in life are often those unconsidered actions. Televangelist Billy Graham made the following comment about courage and its contagiousness. He said, "When a brave man takes a stand, the spines of others are often stiffened."

"Instead of worrying about what people say of you, why not spend time trying to accomplish something they will admire." (Dale Carnegie)

Destiny

When you are comfortable, you tend to forget you are going to die soon, and you may think that peace of mind comes from things like good health, the behavior and attitude of those around you, or the obtainment of more wealth.

Know that at any juncture in your life, you do end up serving three lords, i.e., your money, your body, and your standing in the community. Journalist & Author, Don Marquis made this poignant observation: "Fate often puts all the material for happiness and prosperity into a man's hands just to see how miserable he can make himself with them." Philosopher, Arthur Schopenhauer (1788-1860) offered a more fateful answer. He said, "Whatever fate befalls you, do not give way to great rejoicing or great lamentation. All things are full of change, and fortunes may turn at any moment."

If you hope to experience joy in this life (and perhaps another beyond this one), provide for the happiness and comfort of others. Do it within your own means and in your own way. Shape your destiny by becoming mindful of the following temptations.

- Sudden displays of temper and anger.
- Spending too much time worrying about things outside your control.
- Being overly sensitive or quick to put meaning to unkind words or acts.
- Talking too much or perhaps too readily.

Historically speaking, the following were the common sources of ruin and they remain true to this day.

- A king is ruined by bad advisers.

- A son or daughter by overindulgence.
- A business or farm by neglect.
- An honorable man by the company he keeps.
- An opinion fueled by prejudice rather than fair judgement.

Businessman and author Harvey Mackay shared this thought, "People will seldom let you down if they understand that your destiny is in their hands and vice versa." We should also consider the truth contained in these words by French poet, Jean de La Fontaine (1621-1695) who concluded, "A person often meets his destiny on the road he took to avoid it."

Famed cosmologist and physicist Stephen Hawking made this intriguing re-mark about fate. He said, "I have noticed even people who claim everything is predestined and we can do nothing to change it, look before they cross the road."

... something else to consider:

Ruts are easy to fall into and hard to get out of, so pay attention to your hab-its as they may keep you too complacent. We should be bold and coura-geous when making decisions because according to H. Jackson Brown Jr., author of *Life's Little Instruction Book*, "Twenty years from now you will be more disappointed by the things you didn't do than by the ones you did do."

It makes no sense to give the appearance that you are putting your best foot forward when you are subconsciously dragging the other one. For example, showing up regularly at your place of worship, talking a whole lot about love, cooperation, and compassion, and incorporating those principles only to those from your own faith. Instead of blaming, complaining, or waiting for that perfect moment, take action right now with the tools you have at your disposal. If tomorrow truly matters to you, do not echo the attitudes of the lazy. You already know those people can dazzle you with their thoughts and ideas but seldom, if ever, do they ever execute upon them.

"Those who depend on the merits of their ancestors [should] search the roots of a tree for those fruits which the branches ... produce." (Isaac Barrow) No doubt we should all be proud of the accomplishments of our ancestors, but ask yourself this question: If it were possible to meet them today, would they be proud of who we are, or what we've become? On the topic of ancestry, former US President Abraham Lincoln remarked, "I don't know who my grandfather was; I am much more concerned to know what his grandson will be." Don't brag about your ancestors, instead, give your descendants something to brag about.

A man once said, "Inside of me are two dogs. One is mean and evil, and the other is good and loving. And the mean dog fights with the good dog all the time." When he was asked which dog wins, he reflected a bit and then replied, "The one I feed the most." (Native American tale)

"The methods that help a man acquire a fortune are the very ones that keep him from enjoying it." (Antoine Rivarol)

Doubt

o what do you do when you can't make up your mind? Well, you should do something, anything, so long as you don't sit still. Action puts fear to flight and builds self-confidence. As humorist Sam Levenson (1911-1980) puts it, "It's not the sugar that makes the tea sweet, but the stirring." And even if you were to mess up along the way, you should start over and try again or do something different. "The most likely way to reach a goal is not to be aiming at the goal itself, but at an ambitious goal beyond it."(Arnold J Toynbee). For instance, let's say you are studying to become a lawyer and feeling a bit apprehensive about an upcoming exam, think about after you have graduated. Then, envision your friends/family seeking your counsel and putting their full trust in you. The less you worry, the clearer you are able to think.

If you want to achieve something important, the first steps may be daunting and frightening. However, when you dare to make that first move, anxiety and fear dissipate in the name of action. People who take those first brutal steps aren't any stronger than the rest, however when they conjure up a 'teeny weeny' bit more confidence in themselves, they find themselves in motion and before they know it , they're in a much better place than they were in before.

Contrarily, if you suspect someone is not being genuine with you, do not distress yourself by exploring the merits of what they've expressed nor waste your time with counter arguments .Change the subject and plan your next move. People like these have to live with themselves—you don't.

In his Simon & Shuster audiobook presentation: Principle-Centered Leadership, Dr. Stephen Covey suggested it's better to encourage people to do their own thinking than follow pre-planned "maps" and arrive at the same unexciting results.

ILLUSTRATION:

"Once Columbus was invited to a banquet where he was assigned the most honorable place at the table. A shallow royal court advisor who was meanly jealous of him abruptly asked, "Had you not discovered the Indies, are there [no] other men in Spain who would have been capable of the same enterprise?" Columbus made no reply but took an egg and invited all present to make it stand on its end. They all attempted, but in vain; Columbus then tapped it on the table, denting one end, and left it standing. "We could have done it that way!" the advisor accused. Columbus replied, "Yes, if you had only known how. And once I showed you the way to the New World, nothing was easier than to follow it."

When in doubt, consider the words of 20-year law professor, influential author & Ethics Institute president, Michael Josephson.

- ◆ What matters is not what you bought, but what you built.
- ◆ What matters is not your success, but your significance.
- ◆ What matters is not what you've learned , but what you taught.
- ◆ What matters is not how wonderful you are, but how many were encouraged to emulate your example.
- ◆ What matters is not only that you be remembered, but by who and for what?
- ◆ "Be bold but be smart. Don't be afraid to fail or [feel] intimidated by the possibility of criticism or ridicule in pursuing your important goals, but don't take foolish risks either, especially where the upside is small and the downside is serious."

When we dwell in anticipation of 'tomorrow', we usually forego the pleasures of today. So, pay attention to what you do today. To get you started, consider these two suggestions: First, 'mind your own business'. Second, play fair. Doing these two things will place you on a path toward a brighter tomorrow.

> *"Pay no attention to what the critics say. A statue has never been erected in honor of a critic." (Jean Sebelius)*

Education

"Education is what remains after one has forgotten what one has learned in school." (Albert Einstein). It is only thing in the whole world people are willing to pay for and not get. It means developing the mind, instead of suffering the memory.

ILLUSTRATION:

> *Once, a frail young man approached boxer Muhammad Ali and mentioned to him that he could not decide whether he should continue his schooling or go out into the world and seek his fortune. Ali responded, "Stay in school and get an education. If they can make penicillin out of moldy bread, surely they can also make something out of you too!"*

The following words were spoken by Jahan Sadat, the wife of former Egyptian President Anwar Sadat.

> "When you feel discouraged or simply lazy, as is bound to happen sometimes, remember the millions of people in the world who have not had your privilege. Remember the poor and obscure lives of those countless millions who suffer from every sort of deprivation and frequently find themselves the unwilling victim of wars, and a variety of cruelties, perpetuated by man on man. Isn't it significant that the first bid for self-realization, among the poor and downtrodden, is to assert their right to education?"

Former Secretary of Education William J Bennett made these remarks in a speech soon after he was confirmed in his government post.

> "We should want every student to know how mountains are made, and that for most actions, there is an equal and opposite reaction.

They should know who said, "I am the state" and who said, "I have a dream." ... they should know a bit about how a poem works. ... they should know the place of the Milky Way and DNA in the unfolding of the universe. ... In certain places in America, there is a great zeal to remove certain things from study. Let us match that zeal for exclusion with a zeal for inclusion."

Author Otto Kleppner made the following comment on education. He determined, "The purpose of all higher education is to make men aware of what was and what is; to incite them to probe into what may be. It seeks to teach them to understand, to evaluate to communicate." And writer and poet Samuel Johnson, (1709-1784), expounded further on this by adding "The supreme end of all education... is the power to tell good from bad, the genuine from the counterfeit and to prefer the good and genuine to the bad and counterfeit."

ILLUSTRATION:

A teacher was giving a history lesson to her fourth-grade students. She said, "Our first US President, George Washington, not only chopped down his father's cherry tree, but he also admitted to doing it. Now, does anyone know why his father did not punish him?" One of the students jumped up immediately and blurted out, "Because George still had the axe in his hand."

Some other thoughts on the subject of education:

- "Do not say the people must be educated when all you only mean is refreshed, soothed, put into good spirits or kept away from viciousness." (John Henry Newman)
- "Nine-tenths of education is encouragement." (Anatole France)
- "The highest result of education is tolerance." (Helen Keller)
- "Education is hanging around long enough, until you've caught on." (Robert Frost)

- "Do you know what's the difference between an education and experience? Education is when you read the fine print, experience is what you get when you don't." (Pete Seeger, 1919-2014)
- "Teachers open doors, but you must enter by yourself." (Chinese proverb)
- "As is the teacher, so is the school." (Victor Cousins)

Never forget: IQ is less important to a man's image than his "I will."

Encouragement & Inspiration

The following inspirational story was described in the June 1994 issue of the magazine, Bits & Pieces:

> *"For many years, Monterey, a California coastal town, was a pelican paradise. As the fishermen cleaned their fish, they flung the entrails toward the pelicans. Over time, they grew fat and lazy. Eventually, another use was found for the discarded entrails, and there were no longer snacks for the pelicans. When the change came, the pelicans made no effort to fish for themselves. They waited around and grew gaunt and thin. Many starved to death, for they had forgotten how to fish. The problem was solved by importing new pelicans from the south. Those birds were accustomed to foraging for themselves. They were placed among their starving cousins and the newcomers immediately began stalking the fish. Not too long after, their hungry cousins followed suit and their famine was ended." (page # 17)*

Without that guidance, the old flock would have perished and just like the old pelicans, we may sometimes feel dispirited and need a small injection to remind us of our own capabilities. All that's required are a few words of encouragement or perhaps a slight push and before we know it, we too will take to the skies.

ILLUSTRATION: (James Keller Priest & TV Producer, 1900-1977)

> *One day, the Devil decided to go out of business. His tools, being for sale, were put on display; Malice, Jealousy, and Pride were soon recognized by most of his prospective customers. There was one worn, tiny, wedge-shaped*

tool bearing the highest price, however, which seemed difficult to identify. 'What is that?' someone asked. The Devil replied, 'Oh, that's Discouragement. It is my most valuable tool. With it I can open many hearts, for few know it belongs to me and with it I can pry into any person's mind.'

People don't fail, they just give up. There are no hopeless situations but there are only men and women who have grown *hopeless*, and therefore we should devote more time to inspire and encourage them. The greatest enemy of man is not disease, but *despair*. Author and preacher Charles Swindoll added "Courage is not limited to the battlefield or the Indianapolis 500 or bravely catching a thief in your house. The real tests of courage are much deeper and much quieter. They are the inner tests, like remaining faithful when nobody's looking, like enduring pain when the room is empty, like standing alone when you're misunderstood.""Know that the true radiance of light is best appreciated by those who having struggled alone, emerge step by step from the own private darkness."(Karsh)

You are only as good as those with whom you associate. Surround yourself with people who inspire you. Why would you want to be around individuals who drag you down? Anyone who makes you feel worthless, anxious, or distressed is wasting your time, and perhaps making you more like them. Cut them loose! You no longer become the master of your destiny when you measure your successes by comparing them with others. Of course, you may not be able to ignore how terrible you feel when others react adversely toward you, but one thing is for sure: you are never as good or as bad as they say you are.

Maxwell Maltz (1899-1975), author of the 1961 bestseller Psycho-Cybernetics, made the following comments in his audio presentation, "If you don't understand and accept life as it is, you will keep wishing for something else and never get it. The next chapter in the cycle of life must be written anew by each of us. People who say that life is not worthwhile are saying that they have no personal goals that are worthwhile."

Depending on how you live your life, it can be bitter or better—you must decide for yourself! And former CEO and chairman of General Electric, Jack Welch added, "Control your own destiny, otherwise someone else will." Do not forget, whatever you do, do it well and then some—that "then some" is what counts.

"Live each day as you would climb a mountain. An occasional glance toward the summit keeps the goal in mind, but many beautiful scenes are to be observed from each new vantage point. So climb slowly, enjoying each passing moment; and then the view from the summit will serve a more rewarding climax for your journey." (Bishop Fulton J. Sheen)

"If we are not our brother's keeper, at least let us not be his executioner." (Marlon Brando)

Failure & Dealing with It

*T*here are two benefits of failure. First, if you do fail, you'll learn what doesn't work; second, failure provides you with an opportunity to try a new approach.

No matter how much effort you put into something, you will make mistakes. And it's the lessons we learn from our mistakes that count. No child learns to walk without falling; no writer or salesperson escapes rejection. Who learns a foreign language faster, a person who studies endlessly before attempting a conversation, or the person who jumps right in and makes a lot of errors in the process? Former CEO of IBM Thomas J Watson (1874–1956) commented, "If you want to increase your success rate, double your failure rate."

Former German chancellor Konrad Adenauer asserted the following: "We all live under the same sky, but we don't all have the same horizon."If we must wish for something, it is better *not* to wish for things to be easier, but rather to wish that we can do better than we expect.

Too often we're in the habit of blaming others for the bad things that happen to us rather than the situations that caused them. When we say things like, "Why on earth did I ever hook up with such and such a person?" we are essentially reducing the probability of reconciliation and attributing all the negative feelings associated with the current emotional conflict to the other person. When we engage is such banter, we insinuate the current troubles are the result of a deliberate act(s) of the other party and whose sole goal is to sabotage the relationship. This is seldom the case—if at all.

There are children of the world who live in filthy huts because they have no other choice. There is no water, nor soap, and some do not have hands to wash. They don't know about milk and cookies, only stale scraps and hunger. They do not take naps because it is too dangerous to close their eyes. Their teachers are not conscientious academics with backgrounds in child psychology, but indifferent instructors called fear, pain, and misery. They tell stories of monsters—but theirs are real. When we compare our world and life to theirs, doesn't it make sense to invest more in repairing the cracks and dents in our own relationships? We will still be far ahead of the game, but more importantly, we will share a bond with a much bigger global community, one that has learned to adapt to the unwelcomed intrusions in their lives and still awaken the next morning and begin all over again.

The children described above are not in need of our sympathy; rather, they want our muscles. Author Robert Fulghum in his audio presentation of, *It Was On Fire When I Lay Down On It* expressed that same conclusion this way, "The old wild-west wagon driver who wrestled with his horses as he climbed a steep hill didn't need people to cheer him on. What people like him needed was best conveyed when he hollered out, 'Those who're going with me, get out and push, those who aren't, get out of the way.'"This too, should be our attitude. We should offer our 'muscles,' when it is appropriate, and be what we wish others to become.

"If someone listens, or stretches out a hand, or whispers a kind word of encouragement, or attempts to understand a lonely person, extraordinary things begin to happen." (Loretta Girzartis)

We should never let our difficulties become an excuse to do nothing. Theologian Dietrich Bonhoeffer expressed this notion as follows: "Silence in the face of evil is itself evil: God will not hold us guiltless." And within this same context, Italian politician Antonio Gramsci (1891–1937) came to the following profound conclusion: "If you think about it seriously, all the questions about the soul and the immortality of the soul and paradise and hell are... only a way of seeing this very simple fact —that every action of ours is passed on to others according to its value, of good or evil, it passes from father to son, from one generation to the next, in a perpetual movement."

No one can become strong without struggle, adversity, or difficulty. When we overcome obstacles, we find out we possess strengths we never imagined we had. It is only through pain and facing hardships head-on that we learn and grow. In general, there are two ways we can meet any difficulty. Either we can accept the challenge, or we can alter ourselves. The sad truth, however, is that most people abandon that journey because to do either is far too daunting.

When the troubles of the world descend upon you, and you feel like you are on your last leg, consider engaging in some type of physical activity (walking, jumping, shopping, mopping)—i.e., any event that takes your mind off your worry for a brief moment. Studies have shown that activity increases the number of blood vessels nourishing the brain and that extra nourishment enhances brain activity. Some of those benefits include improved mood, sleep, thinking skills, and memory recollection.

Clergyman, author & lecturer Preston Bradley (1888-1893) put it this way : "I've never met a person — I don't care what his condition—in whom I could not see possibilities. I don't care how much a man may consider himself a failure, I believe in him, for he can change the thing that is wrong in his life any time he is ready and prepared to do it. Whenever he develops the desire, he can take away from his life the thing that is defeating it. The capacity for reformation and change lies within."

Man's perennial desire is to be well-thought of. One way he goes about accomplishing this is his reluctance to say no. We should cultivate an ability to say no to those activities that we do not have the time for or talent or interest in. If we learn to say no to these things, then we will be able to say yes to other things that matter the most—and we won't have to devote so much time apologizing afterward.

We are all capable of making extraordinary things happen. All we need to do is follow our hearts! The following opinion was expressed by hockey player Brad Brown. He said, "There are no extraordinary people, only ordinary people who do extraordinary things with what they've been given."

Life is like a cow pasture. If you walk through it with your head down, you will certainly avoid the manure, but you will never find the gate. The perception that success spoils people by making them vain or egotistical is not true. In actuality, it is failure that makes people cruel and bitter. How you treat failure is your choice, for it can become a weight or give you wings.

In summary, re-evaluate the decisions you've made and consider more deeply the possible **long-term** damage to yourself and others. If you decide to leave the past as is, then going forward, make an earnest attempt to be honest with yourself and those around you. Don't add or build on the mistakes of the past. If you embrace your darker side by admitting your errors and mistakes, it's very likely you'll expose yourself to judgment and trial. But over time, the shame associated with it will subside. You will no longer be beholden, nor will there be a need to "nurse" your secret(s) further. Imagine what it will be like to be able to walk, talk, and express yourself freely without having to consciously guard each word that comes out of your mouth. Think of the peace you'll feel by not having to hide or lie anymore.

It is true that no matter how much you care, it is hurtful when others choose not to return that kindness. Know that the outward expressions on our faces bear the hidden truths of our hearts. It is to your advantage to stand tall and resolute before another than to remain angry and frustrated in secret.

> *"Those who want to rid themselves of their past think they can do so by beginning all over again. But, the only way to rid yourself of your past is obtain a new future out of it." (Phillips Brooks)*

Faith and Non-Belief

*D*ifferences of opinion and interpretation of doctrinal verses will always divide a faith. Each religion will not admit to the fragmentation that exists among their flock and those who are brave enough to acknowledge them may end up downplaying those differences as minor or of little significance. They may declare there is only one supreme being or that we are all brothers and sisters in faith. The fact remains, however, that neither party is likely to be present at the other's place of worship, and if by chance one does show up, it is merely to show interfaith kinship. To do otherwise is considered blasphemy and labeled a traitor among one's own congregation. Described differently, belief is much like a toothbrush— everyone has his own and would never consider using another's.

ILLUSTRATION: The following is a re-telling of a story by Dr. Benjamin Alexander and excerpted from the book, Wit & Wisdom.

A medical student once dissected a dead body and then questioned his instructing professor, "How can religious people say a soul exists when I opened up every single organ of this body and found absolutely no evidence of it." The following exchange ensued:

Professor: "When you opened the brain, did you find an idea?"
Student: "No."
Professor: "When you opened the heart, did you find love?"
Student: "No."
Professor: "And when you dissected the eye, was vision seen?"
Student: "No."
Professor: "Because some things are not seen or proven conclusively to exist, is no reason to conclude that they do not."
Student: "But Professor, with all due respect, I looked for and found no soul."
(page # 176)

The above argument can go and on, with neither side conceding an inch. It is pointless to try and persuade a person who is heaven-bound of another opinion. It is equally pointless to convince a non-believer about providence. A secular person may say, "Produce a piece of scripture dictated and signed by God," and the believer will present his sacred text as irrefutable proof. The believer's creed forces him to lean in the following direction, "If there is no God or Heaven, then there is no persuasive reason to be moral." The non-believer's creed is, "If God doesn't like the way I live, then let him tell me, not you." In this life, a man or woman may or may not actively seek paradise or reward, but regardless whether true or not, when a person does good for good's sake, a valid stake and claim has been placed upon it. There is no refuting that. Know that people who always argue and debate religion are of the same opinion before and after. Catholic Priest, Thomas Aquinas made this comment, "For those who believe in God, no explanation is needed; for those who do not believe in God, no explanation is possible."

Seldom has there been true unity among any religion's followers for any sustained period of time. Why is this? Because sooner or later a few privileged persons will use their power to influence and deride another's version of the truth, sowing the seeds of distrust and creating division among the group. Many souls fail to find God because they want a religion which will remake society, without remaking themselves. (Bishop Fulton J Sheen)

ILLUSTRATION SHOWING HOW WE RATIONALIZE OUR FAITH.

In ancient Iraq, there was once an exceptional drought. The elders decreed that prayers be offered to end the continuing distress. The Christians, the Jews, and the Muslims each dutifully offered their supplications, but to no avail. Only the idolaters did not participate. But because they were also suffering from the effects of the drought, their chieftain agreed to participate and held a grand sacrificial event. During the ritualistic ceremony, the skies opened up and huge raindrops began to pound the over -parched soil. Later, to explain the turn of events, the three Abrahamic faiths offered the following explanation: "The Almighty refused our requests to prolong the pleasure of listening to our prayers, but once he witnessed the abomination of the infidels, he sent the rain to put an end to their loathsome tributes."

ILLUSTRATION ABOUT FAITH: (Told by Senator Lawton Chiles of Florida)

There is a story of a man who accidentally fell off a cliff. As he was falling, he stuck his hand out and was lucky to grasp a branch sticking out from the side of the mountain. It was shaking and dirt was falling off the roots. He knew the branch wasn't going to hold him for too much longer. He cried out, "Help" Help!" ... but there was no reply. He shouted, "Is there anybody up there, please help me?"Finally, a voice said, "I AM HERE."

He said, "Who is there?'The voice: "It is I, the Lord, have faith!"Man said: I do have faith."The voice: "Then let loose!"

The man thought about it and then exclaimed, "Is anybody else up there?"

Motivational author, Dale Carnegie suggested people are prone to do what others are doing, believe what others believe and accept without question the testimony of others whose knowledge they trust.

ILLUSTRATION:

A new husband watched his wife prepare her first turkey and noticed she chopped a few inches off the bird's bottom before placing it in the oven. He asked her why she did that, and she explained it was the way her mother taught her. They decided to call her mother, who admitted to cutting the inches off as well, but could not offer a reason why, except that her mother before her did it that way. Of course, a call was subsequently made to grandma, who acknowledged she did indeed slice off a few inches but added it was only because her baking pan was too small and by slicing off a few inches, she was able to fit the whole bird into the pan.

Light-hearted observations about faith from both sides of the aisle.

- A religious leader standing before members of his sect decided to instruct them on the difference between fact and faith. He said, "It is a fact you are all sitting here before me. It is also a fact I am standing here speaking to you, but it is faith that makes me believe you are listening to what I have to say."

- Corporate trainer Zig Ziglar said, "I know a lot of people who don't go to church because they say, 'they are a bunch of hypocrites down there.' I say, 'Come on down anyway, there is always room for one more' ... but then I say, 'If a hypocrite stands between you and God, is the hypocrite closer to God than you?'"

- A little girl masked her mother : "How did the human race appear?" Her mother replied, 'God made Adam and Eve and they had children and that's how mankind was made.' Later that day, she asked her father the same question and he answered this way, " Many years ago there were monkeys and from them,the human race evolved." Confused by the conflicting answers, she approached her mother for a clarification. Her mother responded, " Well, darling it's very simple. I told you about my side of the family and your father told you about his."

- If you say, "God, why me?" when the bad things happen in your life, to be fair, you should also say, "God, why me " when the good things happen?" (Arthur Ashe, 1943-1993)

- Words for those who want to suggest that 'goodness' is not the property of the faithful or the religiously inclined–**only**.

   (i) "You don't have to be a cow to know what milk is." (Abigail Van Buren)

   (ii) "You don't have to step in manure to know what crap smells like." (Texas Bix Bender)

- The believer asserts: Science is like watching God at work. The non-believer asks: What happens next when fear knocks at the door, faith opens it, and there is nothing there?

- This amusing anecdote was related by entertainer and comedian Bob Monkhouse. "One goldfish says to another goldfish, Do you believe in God? The other goldfish replies, 'Of course I do, who do you think changes the water?"

- After several months of little or no rain, a rural farming community decided to hold a prayer meeting to ask God's blessings for much-needed rain. On the day of the event, everyone gathered but seemed more preoccupied with socializing than sticking with the agenda. As the pastor stood up front and struggled to obtain the attention of all in attendance, his eyes descended upon a thirteen-year-old girl who sat quietly in the front row with a red umbrella lying beside her. She was silent, but her face could not hide her excitement and anticipation. That sight of Faith made the pastor's heart smile briefly, for he realized the crowd had come to pray for rain, but she had come to see God answer.

- For centuries, people believed Aristotle was right when he said that the heavier an object was, the faster it would fall to the earth. In 1589, over two-thousand years later, Galileo summoned some learned professors to the base of the Tower of Pisa to disprove that theory. He climbed to the top and pushed off a ten-pound weight and a one-pound weight, both at the same time, and while each load landed at the same time, the learned professors denied what they had just seen; despite clear-cut, infallible, physical evidence, the power of conventional belief remained the same. So is it too sometimes with old opinions and beliefs.

- Perhaps the words painted on the door to Hell may be "deserved" and on the door to Heaven, "Well deserved."

- We've all heard religious organizations assert that all denominations are welcome at their services, but undoubtedly what they probably mean are "tens" and "twenties." And as French historian and philosopher Voltaire noted, "When it is a question of money, everybody is of the same religion."

- Scientist: "You know God, we can replace limbs and organs, and it seems we don't need you anymore." God replied, "OK then, let's have a contest and make a human being." The scientist agreed, reached down, and grabbed a handful of dirt. But God stopped him midway and said, "No, No, No! Get your own dirt."

- A man posed the following question to an Irish Bishop: "What was God doing *before* he created the earth?" The Bishop answered: "He was creating hell and damnation for people who ask that question."

Visit any Shinto temple in Japan and you may see this: A simple stand from which hangs scores of wooden plaques with a colorful image on one side and densely scribbled Japanese characters on the other. Each plaque is covered with personal pleas to the gods for assistance and support in times of hardship and distress. Why is it necessary to know this? No reason really. But what is important to know is that regardless how one perceives ultimate truth or purpose in life, that belief is predicated on whether an idea or solution works for you or not.

Footnote to all:

We should allow every man the right to chart his own destiny. Nothing is more upsetting to a believer or non-believer than a hammering or a questioning of the truth behind his or her faith or non-faith. Recognize this: If a man has no need for God in his life, he should be afforded the same respect and courtesy as the one who does. To reconcile these opposing perceptions concerning belief and non-belief, French Catholic priest Abbe Pierre (1912-2007), offered the following opinion, "What really matters is not the difference between those who believe and those who do not believe, but the difference between those who **care** and those who do not."

> *"The world will be more impressed by a demonstration of our faith than by a description."*

Flattery vs Praise — Character vs Reputation

*F*lattery is vague, ill-defined, and sometimes confusing. It may leave the flattered person wondering to themselves "Why?", "How?" or "In what way?" The recipient does not know what he or she did to deserve the recognition and therefore is not in a position to repeat its performance. Flattery praises one for what he or she is and not for what he or she did or accomplished.

Genuine praise on the other hand, does not create that confusion. When you proceed to praise someone, you are forced to find a reason for the praise. Praise requires deliberate thought and perhaps admiration from the sender. In return, what the receiver hears are finite and specific reasons in support of the compliment received. Praise congratulates a person for *what he or she does.*

Flattery	Praise
Reverend Bill, you are the nicest preacher we've ever had.	Reverend Bill that was an inspiring sermon. We can always use more like that.
Tom, you are the best salesman in the company.	Congratulations, Tom! This month you had the most sales in the entire district.
Ms. Jones, you are the most beautiful admin assistant working in this building.	Ms. Jones, your files are always so neatly organized, and you know how to find almost anything. I'm so glad you are with us.
George, you are the smartest guy I've ever met in my life.	George, that suggestion of yours was an outstanding idea. It'll save us much time and many unnecessary man-hours too.

"Beware the flatterer; he feeds you with an empty spoon." (Cosino De Gregrio)

A person's reputation is what is generally believed about him or her. Therefore, a reputation may be either positive or negative depending upon how that person impacts or influences you. A person's character, however, is a collection of one or more distinctive qualities that defines and distinguishes that person as a unique individual. The virtues associated with character are generally more glowing and enduring.

Reputation	Character
It doesn't take too long to establish a reputation as an "expert: A man only had to make three or more correct guesses consecutively and he's one. (Dr. Peter J Lawrence,1919-1990)	May take years to develop. One has to knock off huge chunks of selfishness and only then does character begin to emerge.
Recommenders: Neighbors, relatives, servers, other acquaintances. Also, those who are indebted to you.	Recommenders: Food delivery people, etc. or those your five (5) senses tell you need help.
If you are a doctor, it is built upon the number of eminent men you've treated or who died under your care. It is not made in times of crisis.	It requires no endorsements. And is more concerned with 'utility' than 'jewelry'.
"A reputation once broken may possibly be repaired, but the world will always keep their eyes on the spot where the crack was." (Joseph Hall)	It is like a fence that cannot be made stronger by whitewash.
It is like a tree's shadow, or what you imagine it to be.	It is the tree or what you imagine it to be
It is seeming.	It is being.
May be obtained by actions that takes you 'all the way to the top, however it can be smeared or ruined by just one error or mis-step.	It is not a gift. It is a personal victory and cannot be taken away from you.
It is transient. It may change and is often manufactured.	It is always developed and grows over time.
It is what men and women 'think' of you whenever you are in the spotlight. It may also be what's written about you on your epitaph.	What people, God and the angels 'know' about you.

ILLUSTRATION:

A contractor wanted to bribe a government official with a brand-new sports car, however the official objected.

Government Official: "Sir, common decency, my reputation, and my basic sense of honor would never permit me to accept such a gift."

The Contractor: "Well, let's do this, I'll sell you the sports car for a hundred dollars. What do you say?"

The official, with a big smile planted on his face, replied, "Ok, I'll take two."

 "Be more concerned with your character than your reputation, because your character is what you really are, while your reputation is merely what others think you are." (John Wooden)

Forgiveness

*D*o not accept apologies that are qualified by a list of reasons or excuses (i.e., things that suggest it is not the apologizer's fault). The apologizer's sorrow and sincerity is the thing that matters. Additionally, when someone hurts you and you say, "Forget it," often, you only say that to be free of disturbing memories and not because it provides you with peace of mind. The hurt remains alive in the dark recesses of your mind and manifests itself in future thoughts and behavior. Former American diplomat and UN Ambassador Jean Kirkpatrick observed, "We have war when at least one of the parties to a conflict wants something more than it wants peace."

Indian mystic, Sadhguru made this observation: "Have you ever noticed even if you throw filth at a flowering plant, fragrance will still come from it?" Although plants and trees aren't bothered by the foulness placed before them, humans tend to be far less tolerant. German poet and writer Heinrich Heine may have better captured the essence of the human reaction to transgression when he said, "People forgive their enemies only after they are hanged."

In spite of all the disappointments and obvious unfairness that surrounds us, we should not lose faith in tomorrow. Artist/Philosopher, Elbert Hubbard said, Do not lose faith in humanity; there are over a hundred million people in America who have never played you a single nasty trick."

ILLUSTRATION: (Taken from *The Sourcebook of Wit & Wisdom.*)

According to a traditional Hebrew story, Abraham was sitting outside his tent one evening when he saw an old man, weary from age and journey, coming toward him. Abraham rushed out, greeted him, and invited him into his tent.

There, he washed the old man's feet and gave him food and drink. The old man immediately began eating without saying any prayers or words of thanks. Puzzled by his lack of respect, Abraham asked him, "Do you not worship God?" The old traveler replied, "I only worship fire only and reverence no other God." When he heard this, Abraham became incensed, grabbed the old man by the shoulders and threw him out of his tent into the cold night air. When the old man had departed, God called on his friend Abraham and asked where the stranger was, Abraham replied, "I forced him out because he did not worship you." God answered, "I have suffered him these eighty years, and although he dishonors me, could you not have endured him one night?" (pg.# 163)

Some thoughts on forgiveness:

- ◆ "He that cannot forgive others breaks the bridge over which he must pass himself; for every man has need to be forgiven." (Tomas Fuller)

- ◆ "Always try and forgive your enemies—nothing annoys them as much." (Oscar Wilde)

- ◆ "The weak can never forgive, for forgiveness is an attribute of the strong." (Mahatma Gandhi)

- ◆ "Forgiveness is not for the other person, forgiveness is for you." (Bill Ferguston)

- ◆ To say, "I can forgive, but I cannot forget is only another way of saying I will not forgive." (Henry Ward Beecher)

- ◆ "Everyone says forgiveness is a lovely idea, until he has something to forgive."(C. S. Lewis)

- ◆ "Children begin by loving their parents; after a time, they judge them; rarely, if ever, do they forgive them." (Oscar Wilde)

- ◆ "When you hold resentment toward another, you are bound to that person or condition by an emotional link that is stronger than steel. Forgiveness is the only way to dissolve that link and get free." (Katherine Ponder)

If someone is rude to you but you just can't bring yourself to forgive him or her, you may consider saying the following: "I'll forgive your rudeness, I know you are just being yourself."

   "It's far easier to forgive an enemy after you've got even with him." (Olin Miller)

Games of Chance

Winning the lottery is dangerous to your well-being. Many lottery winners claim that five years later, their lives are in tatters. The lottery winner enjoys his bonanza only for a little while before he is consumed by excesses and not too long after, his marriage and health are compromised. As soon as people acquire great wealth, they feel an inner pressure to project an image of success all the time and accomplishing that requires a constant outlay of cash. Once the cash dries up, the appeal associated with that notoriety and good fortune melts away and is quickly forgotten. Renowned Roman-educated scholar Quintilian (35AD -96 AD), observed almost two-thousand years ago: "Nothing is more dangerous to men than a sudden change of fortune."

One of the dangers in pursuing a quick, easy fortune is that you get attached to the process and can't give it up easily—even if it is making you miserable. In a way, you find yourself working for a lord in whom you have little faith. As you continue gambling, your enjoyment factor wanes but your anxiety level scales upward. The pursuit of wealth is never the problem, but it is the attitude after a loss or win that often dictates the extent of one's joy or misery.

If you must visit a casino, go there for fun and not to return home rich. Should you play the slot machines, be mindful that the total payouts are pre-determined, but the frequency of those payouts are absolutely random. Betting establishments set machines situated near the casino entrances or in high-trafficked areas to pay out more, with the sole purpose of enticing onlookers. Always remember, casinos operate on the premise that *you* will lose more than they will ever have to pay out.

The deck is also stacked against you regarding state lotteries. The odds of winning the New York state Lotto are 22 million to one. The odds of winning the Mega million is 300 million to one. You have a much better chance of getting struck by lightning in any state with odds of one million to one. Your chances of winning at horse racing aren't too great either. The horse of your choice is a winner and can run like hell, until you bet twenty "bucks" it can.

Here are a few observations on the topic of luck:

1. Luck is like aiming at nothing in particular and hitting it with remarkable precision.
2. There is a Swedish proverb that goes: "Luck never gives; it only lends."
3. "Nothing is as obnoxious as other people's luck." (F. Scott Fitzgerald)
4. "Good luck in most cases comes through the misfortune of others." (Jackie Stewart)
5. "The world is a mere succession of fortunes made and lost; lessons learned and forgotten and learned again."(Rich Cohen)

This is something you may want to think about : If you had one hundred million dollars and decided to spend (without fail) $1,000 each day, for a full 100 years (from mathematical perspective), you would conceivably use up only about 37 million dollars, leaving behind assets of at least 63 million. Makes you wonder who'll benefit the most from your windfall, after you die, doesn't it?

Footnote: Never put one dollar more, than you can afford to lose.

"Winning is overrated. The only time it is important is in surgery and war." (Al McGuire, 1928-2001)

Genererosity & Kindness

ILLUSTRATION:

One day, a mother returned home after visiting her doctor and was so exhausted afterward that she went straight to bed and was soon fast asleep. Later in the afternoon, her eight-year-old daughter returned home from school, and since the place was so very quiet, she went straight to her mother's bedroom, opened the door, and saw her mother resting peacefully. Aware that her mother wasn't feeling well that morning, she decided to unfold the nearby blanket and began tucking it around her. Suddenly, her mother stirred and realized immediately what her daughter was attempting to do. She pulled her daughter closer to her and, in a low whisper, spoke into her ear, "It wasn't too long ago that I was tucking you in and now, look at you, you're tucking me in." Without missing a beat, her daughter replied, "Mommy, please! I'm all grown up now; isn't it my turn now?"

Some years ago, an American journalist was sent to China to cover a story in one of its remote provinces. While there, she saw a frail Catholic sister cleansing gangrenous sores on the bodies of wounded soldiers. The journalist remarked, "I wouldn't do that for a million dollars. "Without pausing from what she was doing, the sister humbly remarked, "Neither would I."

The point of the above story is that we are always ready to quantify our situation in a monetary context ("Not for a million dollars"), as if money is the only barometer against which everything should be measured. Those who truly serve seldom, if ever, broadcast their contributions. That shouldn't prevent us, however, from occasionally offering humble recognition to those who do. Everywhere, if you look closely enough, you we will see them at work. And how can you recognize them? They are the folks whose daily acts of devotion and sacrifice are something you would never consider doing yourself on a daily basis.

Generosity is rooted in character, not withdrawals from bank accounts. It is limited only by our perspective. A man found an impoverished elderly woman living in a tiny shack with dirt floors and no running water. He asked, "What would you do if someone came along and offered you five hundred dollars? What would you do with it? The lady looked up, pondered a bit, and then replied, "I guess I'd give it to the poor."

In her book, *Little Ways of Caring*, author Marjabelle Stewart wrote, "When you are generous with someone else, the good feeling inside you expands until it bursts and touches those around you." (Page 63)

ILLUSTRATION:

A father was teaching his sixteen-year-old daughter how to drive. Along the way, the teenager motioned another driver to go ahead of her. That driver took advantage of the opportunity but did not bother to acknowledge the girl's courtesy. "I'll never do that again!" she exclaimed. "Yes, you will," bellowed her father. "A kindness or courtesy is not done with the expectation of receiving some recognition after it. You should practice goodwill because it is the decent thing to do."

As members of society, we should not cease being benevolent when we encounter people who are undeserving of it. If we don't make a total commitment to whatever we are doing, chances are we'll look to bail out the moment our boat springs a leak. We should fashion our lives just like water. It is flexible and immensely powerful, but it is also yielding and can adapt to every possible circumstance. It just keeps changing form, and its shape is determined by that which surrounds it. Put it in a cup, and it becomes cup-shaped. Dump it into a little stream and it will soon assume the shape of a river. It needs no receptacle of its own and harmonizes with all things, never imposing its will upon that which envelops it.

Kindred thoughts

- English poet Henry Wordsworth,(1770-1850) observed, "The best portion of a good man's life: his little, nameless, unremembered acts of kindness and love."

- We cannot always return an act of kindness to the person who bestowed it, but we can pay back that debt by helping another. Why? Because a kind act freshens everything around it and leaves gladness and hope when it departs.

- If someone were to pay you ten cents for every kind word you spoke and collected five cents for every unkind word, would you be rich or poor? Many people have a tendency to pray high but give low. Archbishop Fulton J. Sheen said, "Never measure your generosity by what you give, but rather by what you have left."

- Actress and author Marlo Thomas said, "My father said there were two kinds of people in the world: givers and takers. The takers may eat better, but the givers sleep better."

The story below is a satirical tale; the words expressed by each party are factual and true. In real life, these exchanges are played out in many intriguing ways, and they almost always end with the same selfish attitude. As we grow older and perhaps become wiser, we will come to realize that being stingy is the common contributing factor behind most of our sadness and loneliness. What a difference it would make if we could preview the ill feelings we create from our selfishness.

ILLUSTRATION:

A highly successful businessman was once asked to make a substantial donation toward an urgent charity appeal. The businessman listened and then answered with the following response: "I can understand why you approached me. Yes, I do have a lot of money, and yours is an important cause, but are you aware that I have a lot of financial obligations that I have to consider first?

"Did you know my mother needs twenty-four-hour nursing care?" "No, we didn't," came the reply. "Did you know my sister is struggling to raise a family of eight on her own?" "No, we didn't," came the reply again!"Did you know I have one son in a drug rehab clinic and another doing voluntary work overseas?" "No, we didn't."

"Well, since I am not planning on giving any of them one penny, what makes you think I'm going to give you guys anything?"

ILLUSTRATION:

A teacher once asked her students to tell her the meaning of the word "loving kindness." One boy stood up and said, "Well, if I was hungry and someone gave me a piece of bread, that would be kindness, but if they put a little jelly on it, then I think that would be loving kindness."

American Rabbi Samuel H Holdenson made this wonderful symbolic statement of the true meaning of kindness when he said, "Kindness is the inability to remain at ease in the presence of another person who is ill at ease; the inability to remain comfortable in the presence of another who is uncomfortable; the inability to have peace of mind when one's neighbor is troubled."

There may be times when you will be sorry about something you said. You may be sorry that you stayed out too late or left too early. You may be sorry about something you lost or can't get back, but you'll never be sorry when you were kind.

On making it to the summit, your first move should be to turn around and offer a hand to the person behind you.

God's Probable Facebook Page

- "The only people with whom you should try to get even are those who have helped you." (John E. Southard)

- "Everyone wants to live on top of the mountain, but all the happiness and growth occurs while you're climbing it." (Andy Rooney)

- "Men occasionally stumble over the truth, but most of them pick themselves up and hurry off as if nothing had happened." (Sir Winston Churchill)

- "The greatest way to live with honor in this world is to be what we pretend to be." (Socrates)

- "That man will never be unwelcome to others who makes himself agreeable to his own family.".(Platus)

- "Blessed are those who give without remembering and take without forgetting." (Elizabeth Bibesco)

- "The man who does what he pleases is seldom pleased by what he does." (Philemon)

- "Death is not the greatest loss in life. The greatest loss is what dies inside us while we live." (Norman Cousins)

- "The only thing necessary for the triumph of evil is for good people to do nothing." (Edmund Burke)

- If what you are speaking is the truth, you do not have to choose your words so carefully.

- Much of the illness in the world is caused by an obsession with competition and acquisition. Forsaking your health to make money and then losing your money to restore your health is a waste of life.

- Purge yourself of prejudice. If you manage to make it to heaven, you will discover it is not the exclusive property of one denomination.

- "What you don't see with your eyes, don't invent with your mouth." (Jewish proverb)

- "Sometimes it's not the people who change; it's the mask that falls off." (Haruki Murakami)

- If you try to be like them, who will be like you?

- My concern is not about your ability. It is about your availability.

- "The greater a man is in power above others, the more he ought to excel them in virtue. None ought to govern who is not better than the governed."(Publilius Syrus)

- "There is only one religion, but over a hundred versions of it." (George Bernard Shaw)

- "An evil deed like freshly drawn milk, does not turn sour at once." (Buddhist Dhammapada)

- "Live as you will have wished you lived when you are dying." (Christian Fürchtegott Geleri)

- "No truth can make another truth untrue." (Ursula K. Le Guin)

It is good that you are either a Jew, Christian, Hindu, Muslim, Buddhist ... but it is far better to be one and show it.

Gossip & Rumor

here are two kinds of rumormongers: those who pass the information along and those who improve upon it. As one dog can cause all the other dogs in its vicinity to bark, so can one person encourage a whole group to engage in gossip. Ask yourself the following question if you feel an urge to participate in gossip: "Is the thing I want to say to another something I wouldn't want to commit to on a piece of paper?" If the answer is yes, then don't do it. More people are overrun by gossip than by vehicles, so don't add your name to that list of people.

ILLUSTRATION: (From a 1946 Readers Digest article by Constance Cameron)

> One day, when I was about eight, I was playing beside an open window while Mrs. Brown confided to my mother a serious problem concerning her son. When Mrs. Brown had gone, my mother, realizing I had heard everything, said to me, 'If Mrs. Brown left her purse here today, would we give it to anyone else?' 'Of course not,' I replied. Then my mother said, 'Mrs. Brown left something more precious than her pocketbook here today. She left a story that could make many people unhappy. It is still hers, even though she left it here. So, we should not give it to anyone. Do you understand?' I did, and have understood ever since that a confidence, or bit of careless gossip which a friend has left at my house is his and not mine to give to anyone."
> (page # 226)

ILLUSTRATION:

> "A man walking at night sees a light in the window and says, 'A lovelorn mother is praying for the safe return of her only boy.' A second man sees the

light and says, 'Oh boy! hanky panky is going on up there.'" (Ace Goodman, 1899-1982)

A gossip is a person who feels he or she has an obligation not to lie but knows fully well that the truth will do more harm and damage by its revelation. For he or she knows all too well that people will believe anything whispered to them in hushed tones. Do not assume that gossip needs to be false or evil to be viewed as gossip because there is a lot of truth around us that should not be passed around. Remember as well that (1) Although you are only listening to gossip, you too are engaging in gossip, and (2) Whoever gossips TO you, will gossip ABOUT you.

The greater the potential to damage, the faster the gossip travels, and this is not restricted to one sex. Men gossip as much as women do.

It usually happens that the more demeaning or hurtful a piece of gossip is, the longer it takes for a victim to hear about it. Genevian Poet Jean Antoine Petit-Senn (1792-1870) contended, "It is only before those who are glad to hear it, and anxious to spread it, that we find it easy to speak ill of others."

Here is one way to neither reinforce nor criticize another who wants to share some gossip with you:

ILLUSTRATION:

Judith calls up Ruth to share some "juicy" gossip she heard about Marge, but Ruth was not interested and did not wish to engage further.
Judith: "Wait till I tell you what I heard through the grapevine about Marge yesterday evening."
Ruth: "Yesterday evening I took my kids to the movies. "You should consider taking your children too. It was a wonderful movie."
Ruth's answer connected somewhat to what was said to her but at the same time discouraged a continuation of the intended gossip.

Want to physically visualize gossip? Former columnist Liz Smith painted the following picture, "Imagine news, running ahead of itself in a red satin dress."

The more you tell others that a particular piece of gossip is not true, the more likely they are to believe it. Another columnist Shana Alexander added, "Trying to squash a rumor is just like trying to un-ring a bell."

The following is a summary of statements made by author Susanna McMahon in her book, "*The Portable Therapist.*"

The more unsure we are about ourselves, the more we look for faults in others. "*Let me tell you what he did.*" insures an interested audience. When we criticize others, we may be attempting to excuse our own faults. It is as if we are saying " I'm not so bad, just look at him, he's worse."

No one wants to keep company for too long with people who are always finding fault with others or want to impose their own standards of behavior upon them. Sooner or later those same tale tattlers realize they themselves aren't immune from being judged and criticized.

Since all judgements and criticism implies a demand for perfection, once we recognize and come to terms with our own imperfections, the sooner we'll be able to lay the groundwork to be more accepting and tolerant of others. (pages 128-130)

ILLUSTRATION:

> *A woodcutter was missing his ax. He suspected his neighbor's young son. The boy looked like a thief, acted like a thief, and even spoke like a thief.*
>
> *Two days later the woodcutter located the ax. It was on the bedroom floor, hidden beneath some dirty laundry. When next he caught a glimpse of the neighbor's son, he looked, acted, and spoke like any other boy.*

The moral behind the above story: When looking for a scapegoat, it is easy to find one.

A whispered lie is just as bad as one that's published.

Greed

Nobel prize winner for Literature in 1913, Rabindranath Tagore had this to say on the topic of greed: "The greed of gain has no time or limit as its one object is to produce and consume. It has pity neither for beautiful nature nor for living human beings. It is ruthlessly ready without a moment's hesitation to crush beauty and life."

And writer Jennifer Donnelly made this contribution: "Most of the mess that is called history comes about because kings and presidents cannot be satisfied with a nice chicken and a good loaf of bread." While greediness is defined as an *excessive* desire for food, wealth, and power, what is truly objectionable is not the desire for more wealth and power, but the devious, underhanded schemes devised to ensure an even larger bounty.

ILLUSTRATION: (An excerpt from "Winning by Letting Go:" by Elizabeth Brenner)

> *In India, people have caught monkeys by setting out a small box with a tasty nut in it. There is an opening in the box large enough for the monkey to thrust in his hand, but too small for him to withdraw once he's clutched the nut. When the monkey has grabbed the prize, he must either let go and regain his freedom or keep hold and stay trapped. Most monkeys hold onto the nut, making it easy for the hunters to [round] them up.*
>
> *People have been know to get caught in the same kind of trap. The person who puts the goodies in the box controls the person who grabs it, but [once] we are willing to let go of the goodies, we are free of control."*

So, it is too with greed. You want to possess things, and not too long after, it becomes your primary and only need. Once we are prepared to let go of those "perceived" treasures, we'll be free of controls placed upon us. But just like the monkey, we hang around, thinking it is a matter of time before we too shall prevail.

Here is how contemporary Swiss philosopher Alain de Botton construed the abstracts of obtainment and acquirement. He noted, "We need objects to remind us of the commitments we've made. The carpet from Morocco reminds us of the impulsive, freedom-loving side of ourselves that we're in danger of losing touch. The beautiful furniture gives us something to live up to … all, propaganda for a way of life."

Many of us aspire toward greater wealth with the hope that it will bring with it bliss and contentment, never realizing for one moment that it is the proper performance of duty that propels all and everything. Greek philosopher and mathematician Zeno (495–430 BCE) described greed this way: "The greedy man is like the barren sandy ground of the desert, which sucks in all the rain and dew with greediness but yields no fruitful herbs or plants for the benefit of others." Clergyman Henry Ward Beecher (1813–1887) expressed that same idea this way: "In this world it is not what we take up, but what we give up, that makes us rich."

We should ensure our motives are grounded in deed rather than the image that publicity affords. The thirtieth president of the United States, Calvin Coolidge, asserted, "No person was ever honored for what he received. Honor has been the reward for what he gave."

Canadian journalist and writer Douglas Coupland posed the following question in his 1991 novel, *Generation X*. What might your answer be?

> "After you're dead and buried and floating around whatever place we go to, what's going to be your best memory of earth? What one moment for you defines what it's like to be alive on this planet? What's your takeaway? Fake yuppie experiences that you had to spend money on, like white water rafting or elephant rides in Thailand don't count. I want to hear some small moment from your life that proves you're really alive."

> *The greedy man always wants more. Although up to the chin in water, remains thirsty.*

Grief & Loss

———

For two years, a man grieved over his dearly beloved wife. But when asked what would have happened if he had died first, he replied, "Oh! How she would have suffered." He never thought how his wife's suffering had been spared by his outliving her and for her not having to mourn him. In the same way, when confronted with a situation we cannot change, we should at least consider looking at it from a reverse perspective, i.e., as onlookers and not as active participants. It is no secret that we shouldn't tote our problems around for too long, as they end up hurting us more in the long run. If possible, consider finding someone who is skilled at listening or solving problems of the heart; e.g., a priest, a rabbi, a pundit, an imam—even a wise or understanding friend or good neighbor. More often than not, all we need sometimes is a sympathetic ear.

ILLUSTRATION: (A retelling of the story 'He listened' from *"Stories for the Heart"*)

Author Joseph T. Bayly and wife mourned the deaths of their three children. The first, eighteen days after he was born and after undergoing surgery; another five years later of leukemia; and the third, after his eighteenth birthday and following a sledding accident, with other complications. Each time the wave of grief came ashore, their tears flowed. Later on, Mr. Bayly spoke of his experience, after he had laid all three to rest.

One day I was sitting alone, overwhelmed with grief, when someone I knew stopped by. He spoke to me about God's dealings—why it happened and of hope and promise beyond the grave. My acquaintance spoke non-stop as if his mission was to prevent any feelings of remorse from entering my conscious mind. Throughout his stay, I remained unmoved except to wish that he'd go away. Later that day, another friend stopped by; however, he chose to sit beside me instead of across from me. Mostly, he was quiet and waited patiently for those moments when I had something to say. His spoken words were brief and conveyed more empathy than a sermonizing theme. I was comforted by his presence. When it was time for him to leave, I felt truly sorry to see him go." (page #213)

When in mourning, try as best as you can to focus on the present to keep your spirits alive. Children are uniquely capable of doing this: Observe a child who follows a bug for ten minutes, oblivious to everything around him. When he is tired of doing that, he may start throwing stones at a tree or decide to play with his crayons. Whatever he chooses to do, he is completely lost in the present. The regrets of the past (the falls, the bruises, the cuts) never seem to surface or become an issue. The key to a joyous tomorrow lies with becoming involved and engaged. Like the child, we must cultivate the art of living in the present, for it provides us with purpose and hope for the next day.

We should also remember that after our time to grieve has run its course, we have a responsibility to continue living as best as we know how. Know that the *most welcomed people* in the world aren't those who continually look back upon the trials, sorrows, and frustrations of yesterday, but those who cast their eyes forward with courage, hope, and curiosity.

As adults, we can go about doing that by re-arranging our life in a way that would complement our new future. For example, we could start by moving familiar furniture around and become acquainted with that change; if we have an interest or hobby, we could attempt to find another with whom we can exchange ideas and opinions on that common interest; if at all possible, we should surround ourself with younger kids or disadvantaged individuals who will have greater respect for us and be more likely to hear what we have to say.

Some observations and thoughts on the subject of grief:

- "Sorrow makes us all children again."(Ralph Waldo Emerson)

- "To mourn is to be extraordinarily vulnerable. It is to be at the mercy of inside feelings and outside events in a way most of us have not been since early childhood." (Christian McEwen)

- "People do not die for us immediately, but remain bathed in an aura of life ... through which they continue to occupy our thoughts in the same way as when they were alive. It is as though they were traveling abroad." (Marcel Proust)

- "Grief cannot be shared. Everyone carries that burden alone in his or her own way." (Ann Morrow Lindbergh).

- Grief is unspoken except for those moments at a funeral or wake when it becomes necessary to speak with our tears.

- "In the condition of men, it frequently happens that grief and anxiety lie hidden under the golden robes of prosperity." (Samuel Johnson)

- Do not succumb to the temptation of telling stories of how others handled their loss. People should be allowed to mourn. Concentrate on providing comfort the best way you know how.

Islamic hadith: "Let none of you wish for death because of some harm that has afflicted you. However, if you feel a need to appeal to God then say, 'Oh God, give me life as long as life is better for me, but grant me death should death be better for me.'" (Al Bukhari—Chapter 19 # 5671)

"If you keep a green bough in your heart, the singing bird will come." (Chinese proverb)

Happiness

The ingredients of happiness are so simple they can be counted on one hand.

- "Happiness must be shared, as selfishness is its enemy." (William B Ogden)
- It is quiet, seldom found in crowds and obtainable in moments of solitude and reflection.
- It rests securely on pure goodness and a clear conscience. Religion is not an essential ingredient, but one needs to be guided by basic ethical principles.
- It cannot be bought, and although money may provide a sense of security, it has very little to do with it.
- "To be without some of the things you want is an indispensable part of happiness." (Bertrand Russell, 1872-1970)

Rich people who are unhappy may be worse off than poor folks who are equally miserable. This is because the poor are still able to cling to the hopeful delusion that more money would solve their problems, while the wealthy, who are preoccupied with preserving their wealth, don't have that same psychological assurance. Playwright and author Channing Pollock asserted, "Happiness is a way station between too much and too little." And Mahatma Gandhi described it this way "Happiness is when what you think, what you say, and what you do are in harmony."

Don't fall into the trap of looking at happiness through another man's eye. His perceptions of truth and beauty are not necessarily yours. Consider this, if Jack is in love, he is no judge of Jill's beauty.

Chances are, if all you see in one place is discontent and dismay, then it's unlikely that it'll be different elsewhere. Unless you can find beauty and happiness in your own hometown, what makes you think you'll find it at Niagara Falls?

Rabbi Harold Kushner in his best-selling book,' *When All You've Ever Wanted Isn't Enough* 'posed the following question :"Ask the average person, which is more important to him, making money or being devoted to his family? Virtually everyone will answer family without hesitation. But watch how the average person actually lives out his life. See where he really invests his time and energy, and he will give away the fact that he really does not live by what he says he believes. He has let himself be persuaded that if he leaves for work earlier in the morning and comes home more tired at night, he is proving how devoted he is to his family as he expends himself to provide them with all the things they have seen advertised."

Within this same context, American actor, comedian, and writer George Burns (1896-1996) acknowledged the following: "If you were to go around asking people what would make them happier, you'd get answers like a new car, a bigger house, a raise in pay, winning the lottery, a face-lift, more kids, less kids, a new restaurant to go to—probably, not one in a hundred would say a chance to help people. And yet that may bring the most happiness of all."

"Suppose a bird flies into your window and breaks its wing. You can end its misery and give it a nice burial in your backyard, *or* you can bring it into your house, restore it and then release it when its wing has healed. Which choice will bring you more joy? How do you feel as you watch it fly away? Do you need it to call, send you a card, or visit and say thank you?" (Bernie Siegel)

French judge and philosopher Charles de Montesquieu (1689-1755) postulated, "If one only wished to be happy, this could be easily accomplished; but we wish to be happier than other people, and this is always difficult."

The essentials for happiness are something to do, someone to love, and something to hope for. But to be truly happy, it is necessary to refrain from comparing this moment with other moments in the past.

"Think of a time when you had a really wonderful dream and the sequences flowed uninterrupted. Then you awoke. The sensations and emotions you recalled at that exact moment is what true happiness feels like."(Karsh)

"There can be no happiness if the things we believe in are different from the things we do."(Freya Stark)

Health & the Mind

A ten-year-old girl suffered from persistent vomiting, but lab results revealed no abdominal irregularities. Every medical solution was explored to isolate the cause of distress, but to no avail. Luckily, an innocent conversation with an aunt resulted in an unconventional cure. It turned out that after an incident with her teacher, the little girl wished her teacher would drop dead. Three days later, the teacher did indeed die from a massive heart attack. The child was certain her wish caused the tragedy, and the guilt she felt manifested itself in the form of stomach troubles. After several sessions with a child therapist, it was possible to convince the girl that she was not responsible for her teacher's death, and immediately thereafter her ailment disappeared.

Many of us bury stressful matters in the crypts of our minds, and until we "air" them out, they continue to plague us in unconscious ways. Here is how: When we experience mental or physical agony, stress hormones are released into our body that causes our muscles to tense up. This is a characteristic present in all human beings and is commonly referred to as the fight/flight response. It's a reflex reaction that prepares our body to face the anxiety directly (fight) or retreat to a safer environment (flight). The muscular tension that is produced may be experienced as headaches or cramps, and back, neck, and shoulder pain.

Of course, there are many clinical reasons for ill-health that require further testing and diagnosis, but research has shown that at least 60% of the time an emotional disturbance contributes the most in the escalation of a medical condition. Evidence also suggests mental difficulties upset physical functions and weakens our resistance to infection.

- Forty-two out of fifty patients who complained of stomach pains were literally worrying themselves sick. Emotional upsets affect the flow of hydrochloric acid in the stomach. In a test environment, acid levels soared when casual conversations shifted to (1) the day a man lost his job, (2) a mere mention of an estranged husband, or (3) talk about an impending bankruptcy. In another situation, a woman with frequent colitis attacks recovered the very same day her family forgave her for marrying a man from a different religion.

- Bottled-up anger can send blood pressure skyrocketing. Many deaths after age fifty are related to blood pressure disturbances. Timid and meek people may have fierce resentments smoldering beneath a submissive façade. As an example: During times of industrial peace, a union shop steward noticed frequent spikes in his blood pressure. However, the moment there were signs of unrest out in the field, i.e., a contract violation or a labor impasse, he was quick to rush into the general manager's office and exchange insults with him. Whenever that happened, the release of pent-up emotions always seemed to have a normalizing effect on his blood pressure.

- As we age, we almost never notice that arthritic attacks appear to run parallel with our mental frustrations. Significant muscle tension brought on by stress may cause the cartilage in our joints to squeeze and compress and therefore work harder to maintain their elasticity. The end result is, as we approach our golden years, our faithful joints are now under greater pressure and are more likely to become inflamed. That inflammation manifests itself as arthritic pain.

The old cliché about brides and grooms getting "cold feet" isn't only an expression. It is a genuine physical phenomenon that expresses the conflict between longing for a connection and the fear of responsibility. The mind controls the body in strange ways. Psychotherapy has shown there are links between physical issues like constipation, hemorrhoids, and lower back pain, and the emotional conflict associated with feelings of anger, jealousy, guilt, and disappointment. Once expression is given to those feelings with a "trusted" source, the physical ailments show remarkable improvement.

A patient is a human being full of worries, fears, hopes and despair.Know that our minds have a significant influence on the proper functioning of our bodily organs. It is a mistake for medical practitioners to overlook the mental side of treatment ... but it is not altogether their fault, as they too succumb to those very same pressures. The vast majority of doctors are focused on the clinical side of treatment because their patients have been conditioned to think that lab tests, less carbohydrates, wonder pills, and scanning devices are the symbols of good healthcare. Patients are very protective about discussing their innermost feelings with their doctors, not only because it is embarrassing to "lay bare" one's soul before another, but privacy and self-esteem issues are also affected. To be healthy, you must have a contented mind, and no doctor, regardless of skill or experience, can prescribe a pill for that.

Today, people invest so much time watching what they eat or wishing to eat what they watch, so they can live longer and healthier. Why torture yourself, when life will do it for you anyway? As the late stand-up comedian Redd Foxx put it, "Health nuts are going to feel very stupid someday when they find themselves lying in a hospital bed dying of nothing." His observation mirrored a similar comment by 19th century writer and lecturer Henry Wheeler Shaw (who has been compared to Mark Twain) who observed, "There's a lot of people in this world who spend so much time watching their health, that they haven't the time to enjoy it."

Remember, it's all about moderation without going overboard. Research has shown that people who are happiest are those who have dealt most successfully with the changes in their lives. To accept and adapt to change are skills of a lifetime, and having humility plays a significant role in making that possible.

"The ultimate comfort food is 'soup.' It's a guilt-free, easy to prepare snack that reminds you of mom. Two-thirds of test subjects claimed they felt better about themselves after they slurped soup. (Uncle John's, Ahh-Inspiring Bathroom Reader., 2002)

"It is much more important to know 'what sort of patient' has a disease than 'what sort of disease' a patient has.(William Osler)

How to Respond More Assertively

Here is a transcript of some observations by Susan Coco, from an 1984 audio seminar on assertiveness training.

> The key to avoiding manipulation and feeling guilty is to acknowledge what the other party has said to you. Thank them for thinking of you and then assert what you want to convey, such as, "I'd rather not" or "I do not feel comfortable with this."

> Here is an example: Your boss wants some extra work done. You already have your hands full, and while no one consulted you beforehand, you were selected anyway. It is almost 5:00 p.m., and you want to go home, but your boss comes over and says, "Mary, I would like you to work overtime tonight." Don't say things like, "Well, I worked overtime last week, why don't you ask Jane?" This response will definitely make your boss become defensive. Say instead something like, "Well Bill, I think I would like to help you out with the extra work, but tonight is just isn't good for me. Can I come in an hour earlier tomorrow and help with the work, or can I help you find somebody else who might be willing to stay that hour or two tonight?"

> Always appear willing to compromise. Don't say, "I believe I deserve a raise," say instead, "I'd like to explore with you whether a raise might make sense, and also how you might feel about that. With your permission, I will be happy to discuss with you why I think I deserve one." This introduction not only reduces the stress level for both sides, but gets the conversation off on an even keel. If you're assigned

a job at the last minute and determine you would not be able to finish it on time, say something like, "I don't see any way this work can be done by 5:00 o'clock. If it really needs to be done by 5:00 o'clock, then I want you to know that I'll have to stop working on the ABC project now and make these reports my priority. Is that what you want me to do?" If it is at all possible, avoid "you" statements; use instead "I" statements. "You" statements close down conversation, for example, instead of saying, 'you didn't handle this right,' say, "I didn't like it when we couldn't provide any comfort to this customer." When you make an "I" statement, you are creating an opportunity for two people to comment. Assume you turn in a report to your boss and he says, "This report doesn't make any sense, it has too many errors, etc." Your best response then might be to ask for clarification. For example, "I am not sure I understand your specific criticism. Can you tell me what were the negative points in this report?" After you receive that response, then ask the boss whether there was anything he or she liked about the report?

Should someone point out to you something he or she does not like about you, you can deflect that arrow by saying, "Thanks for telling me, I will think about it." This gives him or her no further grounds to pursue you. You can also turn the conversation around and take the pressure off yourself by saying, "Yes, I know you have been having those feelings. I will think about it."

You should also become aware of the connotations associated with the words "would" and "could." The word "would" suggests a request, but the word "could" looms either as a demand or possibly criticism—so be mindful of these two. Be aware too that in a conversation, the word "yes but" tend to negate everything said before it. Recognize its intent when speaking to others.

If someone is doing something that irritates you or makes you fuming mad, say something like, "Bob, I have something I want to talk to you about in private, but if now is not a good time, I would like to arrange another time very soon to discuss it—because it is important to me." Here is another example, don't say, "Why were you late?" Say instead, "I was quite upset when you came in late this morning."

Here are a few positive ways to re-express negative-sounding statements:

Don't say	Say instead.
Why can't you ...?	What if we ...?
I hate it when ...	Wouldn't it be better if ...?
He always says ...	I've heard him say ...
You must do it this way.	Here is a good idea to consider.
You have to fill out this form.	Can we get some info on this form?
Wait over there.	There's a short wait. Do you mind?
Is this everything?	Anything else we should consider?
Why did you hurt me?	I was surprised by your comment and found it to be uncharacteristic of you.

> *"There are three kinds of person you must not challenge: civil servants, customers, and widows." (Chinese Proverb)*

How We Affect Our Tomorrows

Writer and newspaper columnist Frank Bunker Gilbreth Jr. (1911-2001) composed a list described as *The Seven Deadly Sins*. He wrote it under the pseudonym of Ashley Cooper.

> *Truth, if it becomes a weapon against persons.*
>
> *Beauty, if it becomes vanity.*
>
> *Love, if it becomes possessive.*
>
> *Loyalty, if it becomes blind, careless trust.*
>
> *Tolerance, if it becomes indifference.*
>
> *Self-confidence, if it becomes arrogance.*
>
> *Faith, if it becomes self-righteousness.*

ILLUSTRATION:

> *My grandfather took me out to a fish pond when I was about seven, and he told me to throw a stone into the water. He told me to watch the circles created by the stone and then asked me to think of myself as that stone.*
>
> *He said, "You may create lots of splashes in your life, and the ripples that emanate from those splashes will invariably affect everyone around you. You should live your life so that only good ripples radiate outward. If the ripples you create originate from anger or jealousy, you will send those feelings onto others as well, and you will be responsible for creating them"*

Each of us creates the inner peace or discord that flows out into the world. We cannot build world peace if we are riddled with emotional conflict, hatred, and doubt. We reflect the feelings and thoughts that we hold inside, whether we speak them out aloud or not. Whatever is splashing around inside of us is spilling out into the world, creating beauty or discord. What kind of ripples are you making?

There will always be controversy when you invoke the following words: *best, final,* and *true.* Avoid them if possible. Also, be mindful that most arguments are based on opinions about these two questions:

(1) Who has the most ability?

(2) Who is most needing?

Although some of us may have to work twice as hard as others to accomplish the same things, instead of complaining we should continue to "add value" despite that unfairness. When we give our best, somehow things have a way of working out in ways we least expect.

What good did it do you to be grouchy today? Did your surliness drive any troubles away? Did you cover more ground than you usually do? Did the grouch inside you help make the day less stressful for you? There will always be someone willing to hurt you, put you down, gossip about you, belittle your accomplishments, and judge your being. The reality of those things are no shame to you. The pains they produce are sharp and stinging, but do remember these maxims: what you give, you get; what you send out, comes back; and what you sow, you reap. These have always been the natural laws of life and living. So don't concern yourself too much with getting even with the uncouth. ... just ensure you don't descend to their plane. An anonymous author expressed his view on this subject, the following way: "When tempted to fight fire with fire, remember that the Fire Department usually uses water."

Comedian Buddy Hackett (1924–2003) confided, "I've had a few arguments with people, but I never carry a grudge. You know why? While you're carrying a grudge, they're out dancing." When trust is broken between a couple, the partner who is most disadvantaged may feel betrayed and consider the other unworthy of his or her love. Over time, things may heal and perhaps be forgiven, but occasionally the indiscreet behavior that caused the rift may repeat itself. This time however the party most affected undergoes a ritual change. Now he or she gets upset by the most trivial things and not only that, but is ready for battle at a moment's notice. The aggrieved partner now positions him or herself as the new authority with advice to others on what to look for in their own relationships. As they bemoan their plight to others, wishing for change that seldom comes, they fail to recognize what is more in need of change are certain habits and routines in their own life.

Something to consider:

No bird ever tried to build more nests than its neighbors; no squirrel ever died in anxiety because it failed to lay up enough nuts to cover two winters instead of one ; no fox ever fretted because he had only one hole in the earth in which to hide. However, where men are concerned, many do not mind suffering in silence, as long as everybody knows about it. German states-man, Wolfgang von Goethe re-expressed that sentiment this way: "Some people spend the day in complaining of a headache, and the night in drink-ing the wine that gives it."

> *"Go to the effort. Invest the time. Write the letter. Make the apology. Take the trip. Purchase the gift. Do it! The seized opportunity renders joy. The neglected brings regret."(Max L. Lucado)*

I Want a Divorce!

Psychoanalysts suggests that love results when two people team up, pool their common interests, and stand together against a hostile and sometimes "dog-eat-dog" world. Perhaps this too may explain the psychology behind office romances, as those relationships share the same type of alliances. We all need people we can trust. We also need people who understand and accept us, however in a romantic relationship, much more is required.

What women need and seldom get:

Respect, devotion, and reassurance.

What men need and seldom get:

Appreciation, admiration, and encouragement.

In this context, a woman who wants reassuarance must be prepared to offer in return one or more of the following to her male companion: appeciation, admiration, or encouragement. A failure to reciprocate often results in episodes of bad temper and a barrage of accusations.

Relationship expert, Dr. Ellen Kriedman made this observation in her 2008 taped seminar, *"The Secrets of Making Love Great"*. She suggested that women tend to be more verbal while men tend to be more visual. For example, after an argument, a man would say, "I want to make love to you" because that is his way of saying "I am sorry." The woman, on the other hand would say, "Are you kidding me— get lost?" She wants to hear words like, "I am sorry" or "What can I do to make you feel better?"

An unknown Author capsulized and condensed all the above statements in this single declarative statement: "A woman wants one man to meet her EVERY need. A man wants every woman to meet his ONE need."

No one has the power to reform another; however, when you accept your partner as he or she is, you give them the power to change themselves. The single reason why people undergo psychoanalysis for years is because they have found one human being (the doctor) who accepts them as they are in spite of all their negative, shameful traits. The analyst listens without surprise or moral judgment, and the trust that develops allows for meaningful exchanges. Ever wondered why powerful people surround themselves with "suck-ups"? They serve the same purpose—a constant source of acceptance.

When a man or woman frequently nags, complains, or scolds a mate, it will eventually take its toll. Continual dissatisfaction is like a germ that breeds self- doubt, and, over time and with enough repetition, destroys a person's self-confidence. When a person's self-esteem takes a hit, soon he or she becomes withdrawn and irritable, and is more likely to find fault with the other. The revenge motive is also very pronounced at this time, with the aggrieved needing to get in his or her own "licks" before the argument cools down. Each party pursues this path with the intent of proving the other side wrong—a plan as hostile as the original offense. The eventual outcome :visualize one person later kneeling submissively before the other, after all is said and done.

During a heated argument, each party is usually disappointed with the other and is still reeling from the hurtful things said to him or her previously. In a situation like this, psychotherapist Dr. David Viscott offers this piece of advice. "While angry feelings should be let out and shared with the one(s) who caused them, the best way to express your hurt feelings is by saying, *"You* hurt me or *you* hurt my feelings. If the other person cares, just knowing how you feel will be enough to set matters straight. If however, it doesn't, then you have a problem *no argument can settle."*

An often common occurrence in a distressed relationship is the heavy dependence on false imaginings and then arriving at faulty conclusions based on those imaginings, and then "dumping " on the other person.The following anecdote may help illustrate these two ideas.

ILLUSTRATION : (From the bestselling book, *Aristotle and an Aardvark go to Washington* by Thomas Cathcart & Daniel Klein.)

> *"A young man got a flat tire on a lonely country road late at night. He looked in his trunk and discovered he had no jack. So, he started out down the road looking for a farmhouse where he hoped he could borrow one. After walking a mile or so, he saw a light in the distance but as he approached the house, he began to think, "It's very late and very dark What's this guy going to think when someone knocks on his door at this hour?" The closer he got the house, the more nervous he got. 'He's probably going to tell me to go away. In fact, he is going to yell at me and probably cuss me out." But he felt he had no other choice, so he screwed up his courage, went to the door, and knocked. The farmer came to the door and said, "Good evening. What can I do for you?" and the man shouted, "Listen, mister, you can take that jack of yours and shove it." (page #75)*

"Remembrance" and "acceptance" are words that have little or no meaning during an argument, but it is those qualities during fiery exchanges that guide and control the outcome. Remember, your tomorrows are never guaranteed. What you have today may not be there tomorrow. Are you prepared for that? Mahatma Gandhi coined this statement,"The future depends on what you do today." Acceptance means forgiving and overlooking flaws. When you forgive someone or something, you are ultimately bringing laughter back into your life and freeing yourself of guilt and possibly remorse. Isn't this a good thing? The following story illustrates the power of remembrance and acceptance.

ILLUSTRATION:

> *A little girl unwrapped a beautiful doll given to her by her grandmother. It was such a beautiful doll, the little girl couldn't contain herself and squealed with excitement. "Oh, thank you, grandma, I love it." She played with her doll all through the day, but later that evening placed it in her toy box and pulled out a tattered old doll that she began to cradle in her arms. Its hair had come off, and an eye and one leg were missing. Her grandma, now*

somewhat disappointed, said to her granddaughter, "It looks as though you like this dolly better, dear?" The little girl replied, "Grandma, I do like the beautiful doll you gave me, but I love this doll the most because if I didn't love her, no one else would."

In an argument, Party A becomes distressed when Party B fails to consider his or her point of view and is more preoccupied with responding with hurtful words. Remaining married is learning to live with certain things and accepting them as they are. A divorce may occur when one party says, "I can't live with this anymore" and exits. He or she forgets that while the present discomfort goes away, it is usually replaced by another. This is because "The total amount of evil in any system remains constant." (Issawi's Law of Social Motion) A reduction in one area will always produce an equivalent increase in another (e.g.: if you decrease unemployment, chances are you'll witness an increase in begging or thievery, as the more money in circulation, the larger an audience to fleece). There is always a tit-for-tat arrangement going on. The trick is not to get torpedoed by drawbacks but to find ways to work around them.

Bold & Direct Marital Observations:

An English translation of Surah 49:11 of the Quran says, " O believers! let no man mock another man, who may perhaps be better than he … and do not defame yourself or insult another with nicknames."

Motivational author and lecturer Dale Carnegie expressed a similar sentiment when he said, "Any fool can criticize, complain, and condemn—and most fools do. But it takes character and self-control to be understanding and forgiving."

Know that over time, a spouse who has seen his or her partner make the same mistakes over and over again might lose faith in that spouse's ability to better themselves. If the burdened spouse is certain there is nothing more he or she can do to change the outcome, and it is so deeply disturbing that it affects his or her health and mental capacity, consideration should be given to a temporary separation, if that is feasible.

The most common complaint between husbands and wives is "not being noticed." Many husbands cannot understand why a wife will have hurt feelings because he did not notice her new dress or hairdo. The wife's view of his failure to notice the change translates as follows: "He never looks at me" or "Why should I even bother?"What she sees and hears is,"My husband doesn't consider me important enough to take notice." On the other hand, a man is happiest once these two needs are satisfied: sex and food. Too many men and women fail to recognize that their happiness is conditioned on how their partner feels, when around them.

When things turn sour, some men seem to have a harder time letting go than women do. The woman may cry and pour her heart out to her girlfriends, but soon after she'll get on with her life. The man, however, will call at 3:00 a.m. to say he is only calling to let her know how she's ruined his life and that he'll never forgive her for it. He will then proceed to tell her how much he hates her and what a waste of time she is ... but he also wants to let her know there is still a chance for them, if she is willing to give it another shot.

When your life with another is going badly, it becomes much more difficult to think clearly, to create, to be warm, and even to be courteous to strangers. This happens because our inner disappointment gets externalized and reflected to those around us. Comedian Rodney Dangerfield—in his own way—expressed the lack of warmth in an amusing way: "My wife is always trying to get rid of me. The other day she told me to put the garbage out. I told her, 'I already put the garbage out.' She suggested that I go out and keep an eye on it."

The differences between two people can be wide and far reaching. For example:

Person A	Person B
Enjoys eating out	Prefers to eat home-cooked meals
Goes to bed by 10:00 p.m.	Is a night owl
Prefers soft, light sounds	Likes loud music
Is conservative	Is extroverted
Is always neat and orderly	Lives in a pig sty

Regardless of these differences, when conflicts arise, chances are they existed sometime before. Identifying and solving the underneath or hidden problem requires a lot more effort. For example, partner A may claim partner B is always bossing him or her around and making all the decisions. At the core of their conflict, however, is Partner B's disappointment that Partner A refused to visit his or her parents during the holidays. Remember, once the underlining problem gets addressed, differences will continue to exist, but they won't carry the same weight as before.

If you must seek marital advice, go to someone who has already demonstrated some degree of success. For example, if you want to go into business, seek advice from someone who is already successful in business—not someone who has little or no experience in it. Doesn't it make sense to consider the words of a person who has been married to another for ten plus years than the single mom who has gone through three or four failed relationships?

Sometimes, the best of couples who seem to have everything going for them, file for divorce. As spectators, we have a tendency to speculate on the reasons why. Philosopher and Historian Plutarch (45AD-120 AD), offered the following insight.

> *A Roman divorced from his wife [was] highly blamed by his friends who demanded, " Was she not chaste? ;Was she not fair? Was she not fruitful?" Holding out his shoe [the Roman] asked them whether it was not new and well- made? He then added, " Yet... none of you can tell me where it pinches."*

In the long run, nothing anybody tells you about marriage helps very much. "If it is to last, partners must recognize the difference between 'walking hand in hand' and 'not seeing eye to eye'. These two things must co-exist. After all, isn't that what love is all about?" (Karsh)

⮜ In a marriage, when there is an argument, a good clue of who is more likely wrong is to focus on the one who does most of the talking.

If You ...

- "If you always do what you've always done, you'll always get what you've always got." (Henry Ford)

- If you are ever puzzled how some people can believe some outrageous lies, remember it is because they want to believe them.

- If you are not closer to the Lord today than you were yesterday ... guess who moved?

- "If you are standing upright, don't worry if your shadow is crooked." (Chinese Proverb)

- "If you command wisely, you'll be obeyed cheerfully." (Thomas Fuller)

- "If you create an act, you create a habit. If you create a habit, you create a character. If you create a character, you create your destiny." (Andre Maurois)

- "By all means marry; if you get a good wife, you'll become happy; if you get a bad one, you'll become a philosopher." (Socrates)

- "If you have only one smile left in you, give it to the people you love. Don't be surly at home then go out in the street with smiley 'good mornings' to strangers." (Maya Angelou)

- "If you could kick the person in the pants responsible for most of your trouble, you wouldn't sit for a month." (Theodore Roosevelt)

- "If you live long enough, you'll see that every victory eventually turns into a defeat." (Simon De Beavoir)

- "If you make people think they're thinking, they'll love you; But if you really make them think, they'll hate you." (Don Marquis)

- "If you buy what you don't need, you steal from yourself." (Swedish Proverb)

- "If you tell the truth, you don't have to remember anything." (Mark Twain)

- "If you think nobody cares if you're alive or dead, try missing a couple of car payments." (Earl Wilson)

- "If you treat a sick child like an adult and a sick adult like a child, everything usually works out pretty well." (Ruth Carlisle)

- "If you would know who controls you, see who you may not criticize." (Tacitus)

- Ever notice, if you criticize the beliefs of the religious and you deride the unfaithful for their blasphemy, the religious are usually more offended?

- If you think you are better than another, there is a very good chance you'll treat that person with disrespect and possibly more cruelly.

- "If you want to stand in the shortest line in the world, fall in behind those who think they are overpaid." (Bill Vaughan)

- "If you want a symbolic gesture, don't burn the flag; wash it." (Norman Thomas)

- "If you're yearning for the good old days, just turn off the air conditioning." (Griff Niblack)

- If you are stingy with a small income, it is very unlikely you will be any more generous with a larger one.

- If you see a situation you cannot understand, look for a "financial interest" (either a loss of income or obtaining more of it). If that is not the case, then you should look for a "sheltered" love interest somewhere in the equation. The answer is usually one or the other.

- If blood must be shed, let it be our own blood - Do not take what does not belong to you.

- If a ruler pays attention to falsehood, all his ministers become wicked. (Proverbs 29:12)

- If the Ten Commandments were handed down today, they'd be challenged in court as discriminating against sinners.

- If you cannot feed a million people, then just feed one.

- *If the only prayer you say in your whole life is "Thank You", that would be enough.*

Illness & Convalescence

*O*ften, when illness befalls us, our first reaction is to rail against fate and make jeering remarks about life's unfairness. Sickness may make the mind insensitive and uninterested in important things, like love and learning. But it can also bestow substantive benefits. Just like any momentous experience, illness changes us. How is that? For one thing, we are temporarily excused from the pressures associated with everyday living. We don't have to catch trains, tend to babies, or go grocery shopping. When responsibility melts away, we also tend to become more introspective and self-analyzing. We reflect more on the past as well as the future. We reminisce as well on a number of our earlier life decisions and characterize them for what they were—weak and foolish.

Being sick affords us many hours of "thinking time." And this singular focus may provide us with another opportunity to mend things that need fixing. Illness shakes up our comfort zone and makes us humble. It enables us to throw a searchlight upon our inner selves and discover how often we've rationalized our failures and weaknesses in our work, marriage, and finances. It is only when we are in an incapacitated state and the future does not look so rosy that we find the time to engage in that kind of introspection. Associated Press columnist and author Harold Coffin added, "One often learns more from ten days of agony than from ten years of contentment." The impending shadow of death forces people to get very wise, very quickly.

There is also a spiritual side associated with being sick. An opportunity presents itself to connect with a higher transcendental power. That discovery humbles us as we learn not to take life for granted. Suffering is a cleansing fire that burns away much of the meanness and triviality associated with everyday living. During our illness, we discover that our imagination is more active than ever, and we feel more liberated. Of course, trivial annoyances do continue, but now they don't seem to bother us as much as before.

In his book, *"Prescription for Living"* author Dr. Bernie Siegel writes,

> As a physician, I have seen how people deal with the discovery that they are mortal. When they are diagnosed with life-threatening illnesses, the first thing some people want is a second chance. Before their illness, they may not have been living with any conscious regret or actively searching for a better life. As soon as they are diagnosed, they want to seize missed opportunities, make better decisions and avoid disaster. When made aware of their mortality, they realize they haven't lived their lives authentically and the one thing they want is an opportunity to begin again. But life doesn't work that way. You can't live it in reverse.What is in your rearview mirror is history. (page # 163)

Author Siegel further observed that healthy trees can grow around a barbed wire fence or exist in arid soils. What this suggests is that despite irritation and discomfort, life find ways to overcome. Just like trees, we too should change and adapt in response to the challenges that come our way. He added, "Our bodies know this, but our minds often rebel when change is necessary and choose death over the challenge of life." (page. #199)

The will to live can mobilize the body's natural ability to resist disease. Renowned clinician William Osler suggested that an atmosphere of good humor and cheer can be central to the healing process. When we feel optimistic about tomorrow, our brain is more likely to release chemical substances called endorphins (an internal narcotic without any addictive qualities) that raises our threshold to withstand pain. Some doctors even suggest that cheerful people resist disease better than grumpy ones.What this means is that we can all become actively involved in our own treatment by keeping our spirits up.

Norman Cousins, author of *Anatomy of an Illness,* offered these insights. He wrote,"I have learned never to underestimate the capacity of the human mind and body to regenerate — even when prospects seem most wretched." And French writer Voltaire expressed that same thought a little differently when he said, "The art of medicine consists of amusing the patient while nature cures the disease." However, few will disagree with the conclusion of ancient Greek writer Sophocles, who said, "Sleep's the only medicine that gives ease."

Trials of the bedridden:

At the onset of illness, the attention and care of the whole household is focused on the sick person. As the sickness prolongs, the ailing person who was once understood and treated considerately may begin to feel isolated. This may be because the caregivers have grown accustomed to seeing the patient's pain, helplessness, and confined state, and can now relax their level of attentiveness. Compared to the onset of the sickness, new complaints are no longer addressed with the same degree of urgency. Should the bedridden moan too often, he or she now is likely to annoy his or her caregiver. Choosing not to "rock the boat" and to suffer in silence is not a good option, either, because then the illness is trivialized while the pain and discomfort remains or escalates. Furthermore, the caregiver's reduced attentions may promote feelings of abandonment, and the bedridden could easily drift into a bout of depression.

However, there are some caretakers who allow no antagonistic words or actions to flow through them. They may include wives, husbands, mothers, and children. They do not feel burdened by the suffering of those under their care. Their focus is always to facilitate a recovery and to ease the discomfort of those they hold dear. It is so unfortunate that the majority of people who may get ill, will not have the privilege to experience this kind of 'warm and tender' care. Financial considerations, geographic divides and differing lifestyles (from the caretaker's perspective) all contribute in making this an unlikely probability.

During the convalescent period the 'doting' caregiver who is constant in administering to the needs of the sick and doing what needs to be done without being asked, may derive the greater benefit overall when the patient does recover. Knowing that one's finite actions were significant in providing ease and comfort, is a very gratifying experience. And chances are, it may turn out to be doubly satisfying when others recognize and acknowledge them too, including the grateful patient.

Invariably, the incapacitated may encounter a variety of bedside visitors during their convalescence. They may include:

1. **Health gurus:** These are people who proudly lecture the bedridden about their own diet and healthy lifestyle habits. They swear by them and go into great detail about how they found their miracle cures and of the amazing benefits they've enjoyed by following a prescribed routine. They try to convince anyone who's willing to listen that by following their prescribed regimen, good health and wellness is inevitable. After all, they are living proof that their formula works. But it is insensitive to use this approach. Consider a bedridden patient who is recovering from a serious kidney ailment. Do you think he or she wants to hear how your 6:00 a.m. morning jog or low-carb, garlic diet have helped you achieve a healthier lifestyle? Not very likely.

2. **Sermonizers:** These are people who make sufferers feel like their lives are already over. Since the disabled person may not be leaving their beds in any hurry, what they need is salvation ... and of course, the sermonizers are ready and prepared to deliver it. Their presence is primarily to cleanse the sufferers' souls that are consumed with evil deeds and lay the foundations for repentance and atonement prior to death. As Dr. Thomas A Harris, author of *I'm OK, You're OK*, observed "'True Religion' is an awareness of the presence of God, rather than knowledge of God."

3. **Storytellers.** These are usually comprised of nurses, home aides, or ambulatory personnel. They do not spare "the sick" a single detail of their adventures with other sick patients. They describe in graphic detail all agonies and manifestations of a failing human body. They proudly announce all the unprincipled things they did while caring for previously incapacitated patients.

4. **Martyrs**: These are the ones who suggest that sickness is far more trying on them i.e., caregivers than the patient themselves. They go into abundant detail about their weariness in fetching, mopping, and wiping—not to mention their many sacrifices and commendable actions while taking care of the sick and disadvantaged.

5. **Pretenders**: They include those noisy and obtrusive bedside visitors who make a great show of their sympathy but are always absent when they can be most useful. You know them quite well. They are the ones who would wake up the sick and ask, "Are you asleep?"

In their book, *The Last Dance*, authors Lynne Ann DeSpelder and Albert Lee Strickland wrote, "A nurse who steps into the room, sits down by the patient's bed and displays a willingness to listen is likely to be more effective in providing comfort than the one who breezes in, remains standing and quips, "How are we today?... Did we sleep well?"

Our illness may be a blessing in disguise as we come to realize for the first time those who truly love us and care for us. We are able to witness firsthand what our illness takes from them and what comfort(s) they bring to us. When visiting the sick, do talk about the things that bother you too, but do it in a way that does not accentuate the rift that exists between your life and theirs. Should you pursue that option, consider first whether their physical and mental capacity allows for it. Know that what most sufferers learn soon after the onset of their illness is the virtue of humbleness. They are more attuned and sympathetic about the trials and tribulations associated with pain and discomfort. An anonymous bedridden patient had this to say, "If the thought of my pain comes to your mind, don't hide *your* suffering from me, but know that the length of my illness has given me the wisdom to understand some things a little better."

Former First lady, Nancy Reagan offered this piece of insightful information. She said, " With Alzheimer patients, you have to be very careful of what you say when you're looking at them -over their bed- because once in a while, they understand it."

For those who've reached the "end of the line," the best time to hold on is when we've reached that place where the average person gives up. For others, it's at that moment at the end of the day when a little voice says, "I'll try again tomorrow."

> *"This life is a hospital where every patient is possessed with the desire to change beds; one man would like to suffer in front of the stove, and another believes that he would recover his health beside the window."(Charles Baudelaire, 1821-1867)*

Immigrant Chronicles

The following is French-American author Michel Jean de Crevecoeur's observation of the immigrant population in America over two centuries ago. His written work provides a perceptive glimpse of life in America around 1782. Many of his inferences are still pertinent to immigrants of today.

> *Here in America, immigrants of all nations are melted into a new race of men. He is an American, who, leaving behind him all his ancient prejudices and manners, receives new ones for a new mode of life. He has now embraced a new government that he obeys, along with the new rank he holds. The American is a new man, who acts upon new principles. He must therefore entertain new ideas and form new opinions.*

In 1929, physicist Albert Einstein, speaking at a university in France, said, "If my theory of relativity is verified, Germany will proclaim me a German and France will call me a 'citizen of the world.' But if my theory is proved false, France will emphasize I am a German, and Germany will say that I am a Jew."

Writer and critic Sarah M. Watson said, "My cousin-in-law told me that his ancestors had to leave England for stealing sheep. They went to Holland but had to leave for practicing their religion. So, they came to America, where they could steal sheep and practice their religion.""A starving Haitian who has spent every cent he had, even mortgaged his family's future, and has just to set foot on American soil is a greater patriot than the millionaire who lives in Scarsdale, NY, and complains that the government is taxing him far too much for his twenty-room Victorian [mansion.]" (Kevin B.Todd)

The following was excerpted from the book Strange History :

> *"When the Black Plague devastated Europe, many people assumed it was caused by witchcraft. And cats,with their glowing eyes and night-prowling*

habits were thought to be tools of witches. Result: Thousands of cats (and several women thought to be witches) were slaughtered. Scientists later determined the plague was transmitted by the fleas that lived on rats. Had all those cats not been slaughtered, they might have been alive to kill all those rats, which could have vastly reduced the death toll of approximately 30 million people.' (page #270)

So why is it necessary to know this piece of history? Well, the vast majority of immigrants are housekeepers, janitors, health aides, kitchen staff, agricultural workers, and laborers—many of whom work for minimal wages and in less than ideal environments. Sure, we should have stronger borders and restrictions on who can enter the United States, but before we decide to reduce the "cats," let's make sure that there are enough 'replacements 'willing and available to continue the job (under the same conditions) before we limit or restrict their numbers.

Barak Obama, the 44th President of the United States offered this sober opinion regarding America's illegal immigration problem. He said, "I think the American people have a generous instinct. They understand that we're a nation of immigrants. But, if those folks are going to live in this country, they have to be put on a pathway to citizenship that involves them paying a fine, making sure that they are at the back of the line and not cutting in front of people who applied legally to come into the country.

Political scientist, Zbigniew Brzezinski,(1928-2017) and counselor/advisor to two former US presidents, expressed this opinion: "What makes America unique is the rest of the world learns what is in store for them by observing what happens in the United States." It's no wonder so many people want to be part of it.

A good man was granted one wish by God. He said to God, "I would like to go about being decent and polite to all, without knowing about it." So, God granted him his wish. It was such a clever gesture, that God made it a choice available to all human beings ...and so it has been to this very day. (Yes, we do have differences of opinion on how to approach and do things, but do we have to abandon decency and politeness in the process?)

> ✍ *Here is an interesting comment and observation by American singer Erykah Badu: "Don't judge someone, just because they sin differently than you."*

Indifference

The foremost English preacher of his day, Sydney Smith (1771-1845), expressed these words, "It is the greatest of all mistakes to do nothing because you can only do little." To know what is right and not do it is just as bad as actively doing wrong. The person who stands neutral usually stands for nothing. It doesn't do much good to put your best foot forward if you are dragging the other one. And within this context, columnist Dave Barry reasoned, "A person who is nice to you but rude to the waiter is not a nice person." This idea was expressed in the Buddhist Dhammapada, the following way: "Even a dog distinguishes between, being stumbled over and being kicked."

ILLUSTRATION: (From the book of Wit & Wisdom, 1996)

One Sunday morning after services, a parishioner told the priest that he felt there was a lack of friendliness among members of the congregation and that people were reluctant to greet one another in church. Agreeing, the priest said that he had devised a plan to change things. During the services the next Sunday, the priest described the situation to the congregation and said that the following Sunday we would have a brief pause to allow parishioners to turn to those seated behind them and greet them with a friendly 'Hello'. After the service, one parishioner turned around to the woman behind him and said, "Good morning!" She looked at him in shocked indignation [and replied],"That doesn't start until next Sunday!"(page # 163)

American blues musician and composer W.C. Handy (1873-1958) arrived at the following life conclusion, "Life is something like this trumpet. If you don't put anything in it, you don't get anything out...and that's the truth."

The following wonderful observation was expressed over one hundred years ago by Baptist minister F. B. Meyer (1847-1929). He described the essence of character as follows:

> "The supreme test of goodness is ...not what we are when standing in the searchlight of public scrutiny... but our attitude when we are called to sentry-duty in the grey morning, when the watch-fire is burning low. It is impossible to be our best at the supreme moment, if character is corroded and eaten ...by inconsistency, unfaithfulness and besetting sin."

At a very early age, doctor, philosopher, and humanitarian Albert Schweitzer, (1875-1965) understood his calling in life. He maintained it was to remind people they must *not* regard their lives as belonging to themselves alone. He stated, "Whatever you have received more than others in health, in talents, in ability, in success—all this you must not take to yourself as a matter of course. In gratitude for your good fortune, you must render in return some sacrifice."

The kindest thing you can ever do for your children is to treat your own mother or father with extraordinary respect. Pastor Billy Graham verbalized that same sentiment this way, "A child who is allowed to be disrespectful to his parents will not have true respect for anyone." Contrarily, it's worth noting too, the criticisms children level at their parents, ultimately come back to them as regrets.

The following is the opinion of South African cleric Desmond Tutu on the subject of neutrality. "If you are neutral in situations of injustice, you have chosen the side of the oppressor. If an elephant has its foot on the tail of a mouse and you say that you are neutral, the mouse will not appreciate your neutrality."

"More good things in life are lost by indifference than ever were lost by active hostility." (Robert Menzies)

Insecurity

Here are three of the most common fears people experience:

- The fear that they are not qualified or competent enough.
- The fear they aren't perceived as "good" because of a disconcerting thing they've done.
- The fear they are not worthy of love.

Each of us is a complex mixture of positive and negative qualities. But chances are, we're somewhere in-between "I am perfect" or "I am worthless". Perhaps we may feel apprehensive about an upcoming meeting because a previous action of ours may not have been motivated by good intentions or we may have lied or withheld info. Either way, we persevere and look for opportunities to reinforce our safety and fear concerns. When we relinquish some of our pride and admit to ourselves that we may have directly or indirectly contributed to the situation, we lay the groundwork for reconciliation. To be humble is not thinking *less of yourself* but rather thinking of *yourself less*.

Ever notice a little child who is distressed because it is temporarily separated from its mother and then sees her again? Consider this familiar scenario. At a doctor's office a mom is in the examining room and her three-year old is outside in the waiting room with a relative. The toddler is usually well-behaved and content, if sufficiently distracted, but the moment the little tyke spies its mother coming toward him or her, there is an outburst of tears and outreached begging arms. This happens not because of any physical discomfort, but because of a longing to be hugged and cuddled by the one who will provide the greatest safety and comfort. So, it is too with whiny whiners. Their whining conveys the same meaning as the baby's pleading gestures; however, their need is not a physical hug but an emotional hug—a longing to know their feelings and/or thoughts are taken seriously.

Kids have a much better chance of growing up normal if there is consistency in their parents' attitude toward them. Confusion results when parents see-saw back and forth by being too liberal and then too strict. Writer Marcelene Cox conveyed this concept as follows: "A child should not be denied a balloon just because an adult knows that sooner or later it will burst." Too many parents are guilty of over-parenting and then wonder later, how is it their kids turned out the way they did.

Feelings of insecurity and immaturity share a common bond, i.e., a lack of self-confidence. Columnist Abigail Van Buren, aka Dear Abby observed, "Maturity is the ability to do a job whether you're supervised or not; finish a job once it's started; carry money without spending it; and the ability to bear an injustice without wanting to get even." These are lessons that should be taught in all schools.

When children are estranged from their parents, deep within them there is a hunger for home and for mommy or daddy to come after them and not behave in ways that suggest they have no interest. Instinctively, children also know their mother's love is like a fabric that never fades, though it may be drenched in waters of grief and sorrow. Writer Philip Roth declared, "When he is sick, every man wants his mother ". And theologian and philosopher Søren Kierkegaard noted, "A son is like a mirror in which the father beholds himself. To the son, his father is a mirror that reflects him in time to come."

If you want to appear more self-confident, think how those people behave and try and emulate their mannerisms. Don't worry that you lack their sophisticated knowledge. Just make sure you exercise good judgement along the way, and you'll be perceived as smart. Once you embark upon that journey, you will notice a change in your mood, and you'll feel a lot more confident about what you do and say.

A man judges the disposition of others by his own fears. For example, if he himself is a deceiver, he fears deception.

Jealousy & Hate

"People who treat other people as less than human must not be surprised when the bread they have cast on the waters comes floating back to them, poisoned." (James Arthur Baldwin, 1924-1987)

There are far more well-behaved and decent civilians among us than we think. Renowned seventeenth-century poet and author Charles Caleb Colton said this: "We hate some persons because we do not know them; and we will not know them because we hate them."

Here are the stages before resentment sets in: First, you are deeply disappointed in the other party's failure to meet your desired expectations. Second, you are angry at yourself for being so naïve and trusting. Then, to obtain relief from these conflicting feelings, you take matters into your own hands, going to great lengths to slander and/or tarnish the offender's motives or intentions while you disparage those with whom he or she is most friendly.

It is indeed a challenge to hear of an enemy's success without becoming jealous. Jealousy always breeds resentment, and resentment often manifests itself in the form of anger and/or hatred. It is reasonable to feel cheated when we give away far more of ourselves than we receive in return. However, we need to recognize that despite all the precautions we may take to avoid disappointment, it will at some point make an appearance in our lives. How well we handle those trials then will depend on how much hate and ill-will we've brought along and not shed.

Research suggests that 75% of the total population harbors feelings of jealousy, and 50% of the time that jealousy is experienced within the family unit. French Renaissance philosopher Michel Montaigne (1533–1592) theorized, "Only a few men have been admired by their own households."

While we may not all want to rob others of their special moment or glory, we do sometimes feel cheated and denied the grace bestowed upon them.

As we look outside our own doorsteps and witness what appears to be seemingly perfect marriages, doting sons and daughters, neighbors with the brand-new vehicles, friends and acquaintances journeying to island resorts or taking luxury cruises, we ask ourselves,"Why them and not me?" Our egos and self-esteem do take a hit, but in the same vein, we fail to recognize that 'all that glitters is not gold'. Yes, the parents of your best friend may visit his or her home more often than yours, but those visits may not be as gratifying as when your parents come over. Once you understand that you can preach a better sermon with your life than with your lips, you won't be too disappointed in yourself. For those fighting a losing battle with their diet and weight, consider what doctor and author Jonathan Miller had to say about that. He postulated, "People are so busy lengthening their lives with exercise and healthy living that they don't have enough time left over to enjoy them."

Because something "appears" a certain way does not make it so. Sometimes we are ahead, and sometimes we are behind. The trick is to focus on the blessings we do have and enjoy them as best as we can. We always seem to notice those who are 'better off than us' and unleash on them. Seldom do we consider the much larger group i.e., 'those who are a lot worse off than us.'

French philosopher Jean Rostand (1894-1977) proposed the following: "We spend our time envying people whom we wouldn't wish to be." How does that work? Well, when we compare ourselves with others, we usually end up feeling jealous toward them. We want what they have, but we never consider that to be like them we'll also have to take ownership of other aspects of their lifestyle i.e., their values, opinions, and prejudices. To do that, would mean to deny our own identity.

This is the conclusion of Greek philosopher Plutarch (46 CE-119 CE) on the subject of jealousy He said, "If you hate your enemies, you will contract such a vicious habit of mind that it will break out upon those who are your friends, as well as those who are indifferent to you." We should all keep this in mind!

    "Jealousy is no more than feeling alone against smiling enemies."
(Elizabeth Bowen)

Job Interviewing Tips

*P*rospective employers say these are the qualities they generally look for:(1) a good work attitude. (2) dependable skills. (3) initiative.(4) adaptability. When preparing for a job interview, it will be to your advantage to customize your answers to accommodate these concerns.

Here is one employer's description of his hiring process.

> *"When a recent graduate or student comes to me for a job, I don't ask him what he knows. I don't ask him what his grades were. I don't care what clubs or organizations he belonged to. I simply give him a hypothetical set of circumstances and ask how he would respond. Those who identify the problems but not the opportunities, I send them on their way, with my best wishes. Those who see the opportunities, but not the problem, I send them right behind the first. But those who are able to recognize the problems and opportunities before them, I offer the position on the spot."*

Your very first words and actions during an interview set the tone for the remainder of the interview. If you begin with a clownish disposition, it will be difficult to switch gears later on without appearing awkward. If you want to be taken seriously. set that tone at the beginning of the interview.

ILLUSTRATION:

> *A salesman knocks on a door; a housewife answers, and the salesman says, "I hate to bother you, ma'am. I promise not to take up too much of your time. "Immediately he is setting the tone where the housewife can only act out the role of a person who is bothered and whose time is being wasted.*

If you know others have interviewed before you, you can break the interviewer's boredom by saying something like this: "Gee you must get awfully tired of interviewing for this position. What do you do to break the monotony?" The interviewer is likely to appreciate the question, and who knows, you may end up scoring a point or two.(The idea is to come with something that connects the interview with a feeling most of us can identify with)

"If you can present valuable information or perform an amazing feat when others least expect it, you will greatly increase the impact of your accomplishment. Feigning ignorance, then showering others with facts, can come in handy during job interviews, contract negotiations or oral exams—anytime you want to manipulate another person's opinion." (Perry Buffington).

If you wait expectantly for your interviewer to ask questions and dutifully answer them, you have done nothing to distinguish yourself from the dozens of other applicants. When the list of probable candidates is long, boredom is bound to creep in. Know that your chances of success are directly proportional to the degree of pleasure you derive from your accomplishments. Therefore, if you are interviewing for a job that you don't care much for nor have the ability for, face that fact squarely, and save yourself the regret and disappointment that is sure to come. Of course, available jobs aren't customized to meet our needs and preferences. If you are not qualified for a position but nevertheless get hired anyway, you will regret you accepted it later.

If you are fortunate and 'land' the job of your choice, at the end of your first day as you make your way home you begin to wonder, "What was I thinking when I accepted this job?" Here's a suggestion to help deal with that:

Think of work as a complex jigsaw puzzle. When you dump a thousand pieces onto the table, it looks like a jumbled mess and an overwhelming impossibility. But if you start by finding the edge pieces, looking for the corners, sorting by color, slowly but surely the bigger picture begins to take shape. If your work environment feels like a five-thousand-piece puzzle, start small and break down big projects into smaller manageable ones. When you concentrate on the immediate task at hand and then move on to the next, the sense of accomplishment you feel will propel you onto the next plateau and perhaps challenge you to do bigger and better things.

Internationally known theme park entrepreneur Walt Disney once remarked, "Do what you do so well that those who see you do what you are doing are going to come back to see you do it again and tell others that they too should see you do what you do." If you can manage this small task, chances are you will be called upon to do bigger tasks, and there is a very good possibility recognition and other rewards may follow.

"In an age short on craftsmanship and long on shoddiness, anything done well, for example, laying bricks, playing games, or writing an essay should be admired." (Author unknown) So, within this context, what can you possibly do? Well, perhaps you could begin an assignment a half-hour ahead of its proposed commencement time—if possible. Or if an opportunity presents itself, be the person who says, "I must do something," instead of the one who says, "Something must be done."

One of the major reasons why the first person interviewed for a position is frequently *not* hired, is because after several interviews the interviewer tends to forget the first person. If given an option to choose a day and time for an interview, pick a Wednesday and opt for the last appointment slot.

FUNNY ILLUSTRATION:

> General Manager: *"Young man, I have selected you for this job over dozens of other applicants. You should regard this as a clear vote of confidence in your ability and training. Work hard and make an outstanding career of it."*
>
> Applicant: *"Thanks, Dad!"*

> ~ *"Every job is a self-portrait of the person who did it. Autograph your work with excellence." (Author Unknown)*

Jumping to Conclusions

*I*f your purpose is to change another person's mind, shut them down, or even vent your feelings rather than tell them how insensitive or irresponsible they've behaved (and thereby make the situation more unpleasant), it would be more prudent to respond with questions like, "What makes you say that? or "When did I make you feel that way?" With leading questions like these, you stand a much better chance of altering the tone and direction of a conversation and steering it in a more fertile direction.

In any type of disagreement or quarrel, the better approach is to listen for clues about what is causing the other person to feel uneasy about you. The idea behind this is to see how the other person's opinion or conclusions make sense within the context of *their* world. An understanding of what is provoking them, along with our own knowledge and experiences, is like a reservoir we can tap into to make more educated decisions. However, this cannot be made possible unless we find ways to unlock the shut doors. Admittedly, we are all deeply prejudiced by our own opinions and are forever preoccupied with solidifying or defending them. In most disagreements, when we speak, we always begin from the very spot that provoked our greatest anguish, i.e., "How could you do this to me?"- an opinion that is not easily swayed.

Here are two separate illustrations as described in the book *Difficult Conversations* by Douglas Stone, and Sheila Heen & Bruce Patton on how to go about sounding more conciliatory without appearing accusatory.

ILLUSTRATION A

A teacher talking to a parent: "Your son, Nathan can be difficult in class—

disruptive and argumentative. You've said in the past that things at home are fine, but something must be troubling him. What the parent hears is, "Your son is a troublemaker probably because you're a bad parent who's created a lousy home environment. What are you hiding?"

The better approach would be to re-express the situation in a way that rings true for both parties by suggesting no one is more right or more wrong than the other, but rather that each side has legitimate concerns that need to be aired. Here is one probable way how that might be accomplished:

"I wanted to share with you my concerns about Nathan's behavior in the classroom and hear more about your sense of what might be contributing to it. My thinking is that if a child is having trouble at school, something is usually bothering him at home...and I know you feel that's not true in this case. Maybe together we can figure out what's motivating Nathan and how to handle it." (page #153)

ILLUSTRATION B:

Harpreet and Monisha are a married couple. Monisha is a sales rep for a large pharmaceutical company and spends a significant amount of time on the road. Needless to say, the distance apart has put a strain on the couple's relationship. Described below is a telephone exchange between them:

Monisha: Ok, well, I better get some sleep. I've got a big presentation first thing in the morning.

Harpreet: So, I'll see you on Thursday?

Monisha: Yeah, Thursday night. I should be home around seven.

Harpreet: Ok, Sleep tight ... [silence], I love you!

Monisha: Good night. See you Thursday.

Harpreet hangs up hurt and frustrated. "She never tells me that she loves me" he complains to himself. "Whenever I bring it up, she'll say something like, "You know I love you, so why do I need to say it all the time?"

Harpreet decides it would be a good idea when Monisha returns on Thursday to speak with her, with the hope of understanding how she experiences the issue.

Harpreet: When I say, "I love you," what are you thinking?

Monisha: I'm thinking, "Ok, he is waiting me to say it back to him." So, it makes me not to want to say it then because I feel pressured into it and besides, you know I love you.

Harpreet: Sometimes, I do feel confident that you love me, but sometimes I feel less sure. When you say that I know, how are you thinking I would know?

Monisha: Well, I'm still with you, right?

Harpreet: That's a pretty low standard! Besides, my parents stayed together for years after they stopped loving each other. Maybe that's why I sometimes feel nervous about this.

Monisha: Hmm, I guess. But I have the opposite experience. My parents were crazy about each other and always saying these "sappy" things in front of us. I thought it was so embarrassing. It just seems like if you really love each other, you don't have to say it all the time. You can just show it.

Harpreet: Show it? Show it how?

Monisha: I don't know; like by being kind to each other. Like when I dropped everything and flew to Phoenix the weekend your mom was sick. I did it because I knew how hard it was for you, and wanted to be there to help ..."
(page # 207 & 208)

Of course, real life is far more complicated than this, and just airing things out is no guarantee of success. Know that we all have *differences in preference and/or beliefs.* These differences define us and are acquired through feelings and personal experiences. They are the reasons why we consider some things more valuable or having more weight than others.

When we jump to conclusions, we often end up making regretful decisions. British novelist and critic Arnold Bennett, (1867-1931) surmised "Ninety percent of the friction of daily life is caused by tone of voice." And author Millard Bennett added, "If you get impatient with certain people, *force* yourself to act friendlier to them and before you know it, you'll feel friendlier toward them. It is 'What You Do' that decides how you feel, not 'What You Feel' that determines what you do."

In conclusion, many of our past experiences are stored as memories. They are later reinterpreted as a set of governing rules. Those rules always take the form of what people should or shouldn't do. Be mindful too, at the core of most disagreements are answers to these two questions: Who has the most ability? or Who has the most need?. If you can determine which of the two might be of concern to your partner, you'll obtain a better handle of the situation.

> *"You are not responsible for the programming you picked up in child-hood. However, as an adult, you are one hundred percent responsible for fixing it." (Ken Keyes Jr.)*

Knowledge

*Y*ou should wear your knowledge like you wear your watch: to tell you the time and not as a piece of jewelry for ornamental display. Unlike a grandfather's clock that pronounces the hour on the hour, you should refer to it, only when needed. Don't be like the two hunters who used a canoe to cross the banks of a river and upon arriving safely on the other side, continued onward by foot, still carrying the boat over their heads.

Recognize that stupid sons don't ruin a family; it is the clever ones who do. Here is another eye-opening observation but this time from author, Chuck Goetschel. He said, "Those who know the least, always seem to express their lack of knowledge the loudest." If one is really a superior person, this fact is likely to leak out without too much assistance.

Answer this question: "Why do blind people wear dark glasses?" This is not a trick question, nor an attempt to make fun of the blind. The correct answer is that every blind person is not "totally" blind. More than 75% of individuals who are deemed legally blind have some residual vision. Blindness is the absence of sight and not the absence of light. Many legally blind people are very sensitive to bright lights; hence the reason why they wear dark sunglasses. The dark shades reduce the amount of light reaching their retinas. This is an example of how knowledge can be used to bring awareness when the answer isn't so obvious.

We can tell that knowledge is present when complex ideas and concepts are broken down and re-expressed as simple declarative statements. For instance, eighteenth-century French writer Voltaire said, "Madness is to think of too many things in succession *too fast*, or of one thing *too exclusively*."

Many people sell themselves short by thinking that complex subjects or obscure prose require them to have an intellectual or academic background before those ideas can be understood. But more often than not, it is the person(s) up front doing the talking who are at fault. Speakers often fail to connect with their audiences because they're too focused on relaying their messages using industry slang and falsely believing their audience already thinks and feels as they do.

ILLUSTRATION: (From The Executive Speechwriter newsletter):

> *A four-year-old son was eating an apple in the back seat of the car when he asked, "Daddy, why is my apple turning brown?" His dad explained it the following way: "After you ate the skin off, the meat of the apple came in contact with the air, which caused it to oxidize, thus changing its molecular structure and turning it into a different color." After a staggered silence of about a minute, the son politely said to his father, "Daddy are you talking to me?"*

Ever notice that after acquiring the necessary skills, knowledge, and experience in the field of your liking, your interest in that subject begins to wane soon thereafter? This may happen for one or more of these three reasons:

- There is nothing much else to do.
- There is too much to do.
- Those things on hold, and waiting to be done, have lost their appeal.

Knowledge may bring us pleasure in different ways. For instance, nothing pleases an ignorant man as much as a chance to be involved in something educationally worthwhile—even if it means just handing out pamphlets. Knowledge may mentally fortify us so that we don't take intelligent people more seriously than we should. But regardless of the benefit received, know this: the world cares very little about what a man or woman knows. It is what a person is able to accomplish with what he or she knows that truly matters.

ILLUSTRATION: (An excerpt from *"Wisdom Tales From Around the World"* by Heather Forest)

A wise old monk once lived in an ancient temple in Japan One day the monk heard an impatient pounding on the temple door. He opened it and greeted a young student who said, "I've studied with the wise and great masters and I consider myself quite accomplished in Zen philosophy. However, just in case there is anything more I need to know, I have come to see if you can add to my knowledge."

'Very Well," said the wise old master, "Come and have some tea with me and we will discuss your studies. "The two seated themselves opposite each other and the old monk prepared the tea. When it was ready, the old monk began to pour it carefully into the visitor's cup When the cup was full, the old monk continued pouring until the tea spilled over the side of the cup and unto the young man's lap. The startled visitor jumped back and indignantly shouted, "Some wise master you are! You are a fool who does not even know when a cup is full."

The old man calmly replied, "Just like this cup, your mind is so full of ideas there is no room for anymore. Come to me with an empty mind, and then you will learn something."(Page #41)

ILLUSTRATION:

A motivational speaker implored his audience, "The key to success is to read, read, and to continue reading."

"What should we read? "He was asked.

"Well," responded the speaker, "First, find out what the unsuccessful people are reading ... and then don't read that."

⤳ *"Information is like manure- a little at the right time is a good thing, but pile it up too much and it stinks." (Bill Bonner)*

Language of Feelings

*A*s a rule, when things go wrong in human relationships, each party makes a contribution either directly or in a transient way. We almost always view fault from a singular perspective. Whenever there exists a difference of opinion, the automatic response is either to accuse or assign blame. We see ourselves as decent, innocent victims being taken advantage of by the ungrateful and/or inconsiderate. Quarrels and disagreements are unpleasant experiences because our feelings get in the way. As the other side is preoccupied with explaining or defending themselves, what we hear are pointless mumbo jumbo or phrases that end up infuriating us further. However, our feelings of distress become amplified when our need to convey the extent of our hurt is stifled by the other. As often happens, old unresolved "hurts" have a way of weaving themselves into present encounters in unconscious and sometimes unflattering ways. Sometimes a "loaded" word or name becomes a fuse that sparks a fiery outburst.

The most genuine thing you can do in your struggle to meet others halfway is to portray them in such a way that they would want to cleanse themselves of the false opinion or impression you harbor of them. For instance, you may say: "The idea about you that keeps circulating in my head is that you are rigid and unbending. I know that is an unfair characterization of you, so I am hoping you can help me put things into better perspective." Perhaps someone may say to you, "Oh, you're too sensitive." Admit that possibility, but also ask them to be more aware of your sensitivity in the future.

Dr. David Viscott, psychotherapist & author in his audio presentation, *The Language of Feelings*, recommended that we give consideration to the following three ideas, in all our dealings.

- Accept blame for our actions.
- Do what is possible to repair the damage we've caused.
- Proceed on a path to becoming our best self.

We should stop pretending who or what we are not, because when we live our lives for others, who will live for us? Never forger, no matter how much we may know, how enlightened we are, or how well-read we may be, decency and not intolerance should govern our attitude toward others. Intolerance is simply having all the answers without knowing the facts. Decency is knowing all the facts but refraining from passing judgment anyway. Reflect on this difference.

In personal relationships we sometimes use 'implied hints' to communicate our innermost feelings. One way we go about this, is to state one thing and mean another. For example, let's say a husband wants to spend some cozy time with his wife, but rather than tell her so, he says something like, "I am going to take a shower, O.K Hon, I'll be right back !" Of course, when he returns, she is already asleep or doing something contrary to his romantic plans. It could work in reverse too. The wife may have understood the implied message but let's say she isn't in the mood, she could choose to do one or all of the following: she could yawn wide and long, pretend to be fast asleep or complain how rough and tiring day her day was. British author and speaker, Alan Watts noted, "Behind almost all myth, lies the mono-plot of the game of hide-and-seek." It would have been fine if had said, it pertains to relationships too.

   "The most exhausting thing in life, is being insincere."(Anne Morrow Lindbergh)

Leadership

Former Ford Motor Company automobile executive Lee Iacocca said, "If I had to sum up in one word what makes a good leader, I'd say *decisiveness*." On another occasion he made this follow-up remark, "You can use the fanciest computers to gather the numbers, but in the end, you have to set a timetable and act on it." Entrepreneur John McDonald theorized, "A business executive is by profession a decision-maker, uncertainty is his opponent, and overcoming it is his mission."

A good leader's ultimate goal is to inspire others and encourage their initiatives. He or she experiences the same feelings of loss and discouragement as everyone else but continues to perform and make the job look easy. A true leader draws upon resources from within and denies defeat by giving it his or her all. Great leaders make you feel like both of you are going somewhere together. Author E. M. Kelley expressed it this way. He said, "The difference between a leader and a boss is, a boss says, 'Go,' but the leader says, 'Let's Go!'"

A leader is a dealer in hope. Superior leaders get things done with very little motion. They impart instruction, not through many words but through deeds. They keep their subordinates informed but seldom interfere with the execution of their duties. They are like a catalyst through which things get done, and when they do succeed, they don't seek credit because credit never leaves them. Everyone already knows who is responsible. However, leaders are in the habit of looking over heir shoulders, every now and then to make sure the "arrows" are still pointing in the right direction.

Leaders are not guys who double profits in six months or the mom who can juggle a career, raise five kids, and still bake a perfect turkey at Thanksgiving.

These accomplishments are examples of success, which are often situational and short-lived. True leadership must be for the benefit of the followers not the enrichment of the leaders. Leaders inspire you on a conscious level and make you want to associate with them.

This is US General Colin Powell's perception of a leader: "Great leaders are almost always great simplifiers, who can cut through argument, debate, and doubt—to offer a solution everybody can understand." And business executive Robert C. Townsend added, "If people are coming to work excited ... if they're making mistakes freely and fearlessly ... if they're having fun ... if they're concentrating on doing things rather than preparing reports and going to meetings ... then somewhere you have leaders."

How to make yourself a valuable boss

The department head today who is big enough to consider the problems and suggestions from the point of view of other departments as well as his own will achieve greater heights. There is an unfaltering and crying demand for such employees in the workplace. Author and management consultant Peter Drucker proposed the following: "An effective leader is not someone who is always loved or admired. He or she is someone whose followers do the right things ... is tolerant of diversity in people and are not on the lookout for carbon copies of themselves."

Subordinates, like servants, can sometimes be difficult to handle. If you were to approach them with familiarity, they would sooner or later take liberties outside their boundaries. But, if you keep them at a distance, they will surely start to grumble. Of course, there are the "suck-ups" who are fond of relating the errors and faults of those around them to their superiors. The leader who recognizes the differing manifestations of these office capers, will be hard to manipulate.

An effective leader normally has an open-door policy, and is unlikely to be snobbish about his or her position or success. Interactions with subordinates are seldom hostile, and may include statements like:

- Do you think this procedure will be a better one?
- I am sure you understand this, but I can't figure it out. Can you explain it to me?
- I am sure you can solve this problem in no time at all.
- What's your opinion on this? I'd like to know before we go ahead with it.
- What's your solution to this problem? I know you're an expert in this field.
- Can you help me out with this?
- I need you!

Each of the above statements appeals to an employee's ego and will no doubt make that employee feel important and good about themselves. It isn't money that makes people work harder, it's appreciation!

A few remaining thoughts on the subject of leaders and leadership:

1. Leaders are not born (unless they inherit their parent's business); they are made by themselves.

2. Leading horses to water is management; making them drink is leadership.

3. "The secret of successful managing is to keep the five guys who hate you, away from the four guys who haven't made up their minds." (Casey Stengel)

4. "He who thinks he leads but has no followers is only taking a walk." (John Maxwell)

5. The best teacher is not the one who knows most, but the one who is most capable of reducing knowledge to that simple compound of the obvious and wonderful." (H.L Mencken)

"Mankind is divided into two classes: those who earn their living by the sweat of their brow, and those who sell them handkerchiefs, cold drinks, and electric fans" (Pamela Perry Blaine). Regardless of which group you belong to, if you are fortunate enough and are able to "taste" power, don't be what management expert and author Ken H. Blanchard refers to as a "seagull manager." He explained the meaning as follows: "Seagull managers fly in, make a lot of noise, dump on everyone, and then fly out."

Super rich Wall Street guru, Greg Smith made this insightful remark about leadership in the world of business today. He said, "Leadership used to be about ideas, setting an example, and doing the right thing. Today, if you make enough money for the firm, it is just a matter of time before you will be promoted to a position of influence."

There is only one man better than the man who gets behind and pushes; it is the man who stays up in front and pulls.

Lessons & Advice

- Do not measure yourself against other people. Instead, pick a goal and measure yourself against that and that alone.

- "The saddest thing about betrayal is that it never comes from your enemies."(Anonymous)

- Success is often the result of perseverance. When others give up, leave, or compromise their position, often the last person left is the one who wins. People may be smarter, better connected, or better educated than you, but they cannot win if they are not around at the end. "97 percent of the people who quit too soon are employed by the 3 percent who never gave up." The one thing you should always to do is be the *last* person to give up on yourself.

- Pick and do one thing every day that no one is willing to do (and it may even be small or simple). After a week you will be "uncommon," after a month you will be "special"... and after a year you will be perceived as "incredible."

- Reach out to people who you trust and who want to be part of your life. Then forget all about receiving and focus on providing. There is a good probability they will be there for you when you really need them.

- Success is not how far you got, but the distance you have traveled from where you started. Successful people are more preoccupied with executing their ideas and plans than worrying about the consequences of failure.

- One of the most frustrating things about living to a ripe old age is that when you know all the answers about life and living, no one is interested in what you have to say.

- Have you ever heard this statement before? "If I thought there would have been more money in it for me, I would have been more willing to work harder or do more of this or that." Generally, people expect to be compensated more before they will even consider working harder. Successful people view compensation (financial or personal) differently. They consider it their reward for making a difference. All they need is to be told their efforts will be rewarded, and oftentimes their motivation and steadfastness determine the degree of that compensation.

- There are no degrees of honesty; either you are honest or you are not. Know that parents who are not true with their children are more likely to be untruthful and dishonest with adults.

- "If you would convince a man that he does wrong... do not care to convince him. Men will believe what they see. Let them see." (Henry David Thoreau, 1817-1862)

- "There are two ways of establishing a reputation. One is to be praised by honest people, and the other to be accused by rogues. It is best, however, to secure the first one, because it will always be accompanied by the latter." (Charles Caleb Colton, 1780-1832)

- "Going to church doesn't make you a Christian any more than going to a garage makes you an automobile." (Billy Sunday)

- Caring is a reflex action. If someone slips, you extend your arm and lift them up. If a car gets stuck in a ditch, you join others and help them push. Living and helping go hand in hand.

- "Tomorrow is the most important thing in life. Comes into us at midnight clean. It's perfect when it arrives and it puts itself in our hands and hopes we've learned something from yesterday." (John Wayne)

- "A vigorous five-mile walk will do more good for an unhappy but otherwise healthy adult than all the medicine and psychology in the world." (Paul Dudley White)

- "Free cheese is great, but beware; often there is a mousetrap at the end." (Russian proverb)

- Once you decide to forgive someone, you must commit to letting go of the event, otherwise you haven't truly forgiven.
- "Under all wrongdoing lies personal vanity or the feeling that we are endowed and privileged beyond our fellows." (James Stephens, 1880-1950)
- "One of the oldest human needs is having someone wonder where you are when you don't come home at night." (Margaret Mead, 1901-1978)
- Many of us won't be content with our lot until it becomes "a lot more."
- "There may be people who have more talent than you, but there's no excuse for anyone to work harder than you do." (Derek Jeter)

"Nobody can go back and start a new beginning, but anyone can start today and make a new ending." (Maria Robinson)

Life in Black and White

*K*now that life is like a boomerang. Our thoughts, deeds and words return to us sooner or later with astounding accuracy. The good things we do and say, the unkindness we show to our friends, family, and strangers, all have an uncanny way of coming back to "haunt" us. French missionary Stephen Grellet (1773-1855) made this sobering claim. He said, "I shall pass through this world but once. Any good therefore that I can do or any kindness that I can show to any human being, let me do it now. Let me not defer or neglect it, for I shall not pass this way again."

We are always on the lookout for that one "special thing" that will someday quench all of our anxieties. People change from one faith to another. They may change their diets, hairstyles, jobs, or remodel their homes—each looking for that ideal image, role, or opportunity. But these changes seldom produce the desired effects because soon the joy and jubilation that initially accompanied the change eventually evaporates. As time goes by, everyone will have seen the beautifully remodeled kitchen countertops and living room drapes. The much-hyped garlic diet, when among company now presents an embarrassing bad breath and flatulence problem. That great, new high-paying job, only has two toilets to service a staff of eight. That handsome 'hunk' you married not only has poor hygiene habits, but an interfering mother too.

We have all come to realize in the long run that contentment does not come from obtainment but from being satisfied with what we already have. We should get into the habit of doing more to reinforce our emotional reservoirs than finding new and more exciting ways to extend the pleasures and comforts of the day. Two common thoughts that inhabit our conscious mind when trouble does occur are: (1) Why is this happening to me? and (2) How is my life going to change because of this? The answers to these questions are always hard and may require difficult adjustments. Author and political commentator Thom Hartmann offered this suggestion of how we can increase our emotional reservoir. He said, "The most powerful way to change the world is to secretly commit little acts of compassion. You must behave as if your every act, even the smallest, impacted a thousand people for a hundred generations ... because it does."

This is an excerpt taken from Robert Fulghum's 2004 audio presentation, *All I really need to know I learned in Kindergarten.*

> "You will continue to read stories of crookedness and corruption ... of policemen who lie, doctors who reap what they do not sow, and politicians on the take, but do not be misled. They are news because they are the exceptions. The evidence suggests that you can trust a lot more people than you think and the evidence also suggests that a lot of people believe that."

Don't be misled by those who boast of their contentment. Roman philosopher Seneca observed, "There are no greater wretches in the world than many of those whom, people in general, take to be happy,"

Boasters and liars are close cousins and generally they are the least contented bunch. Their very boasting indicates that they yearn for something that they cannot obtain by their own efforts, acclaim, or recognition.

Know as well when people are mean to you, many times it isn't because they harbor a personal grudge or hatred towards you. It is more likely they are miserable because of something within them. Perhaps, another person may have been mean to them, or something they hoped for did not happen, or maybe there is something they're ashamed of. Being angry at someone else is less painful than dealing with their own internal turmoil. Lashing out works like an emotional release valve. It's so unfortunate that valve is pointed at you.

"Hope is the feeling, that the feeling you have, isn't permanent." (Jean Kerr). Poet and novelist Erica Jong observed, "If every day, I dare to remember that I am here on loan, that this house, this hillside, these minutes are all leased to me, not given, I will never despair. "But do remember, in this topsy-turvy world with all its ups and downs and surprises, it is still a world teeming with goodness and hope. If those commodities were so rare, each day every single newspaper, TV broadcast, or internet posting would make it their front page or lead news story. Helen Keller wrote, "Although the world is full of suffering, it is full also of the overcoming of it."

"Nothing very very good and nothing very very bad ever lasts for very very long." (Douglas Coupland) Sure, life can be unfair (sometimes very unfair), but despite that unfairness, it is important to remember that no one has the right to claim more than he or she is entitled to or worked for. Should you take it upon yourself to remedy the injustice you see before you, here is a word of caution from The Hindu Hitopodesa: "Before you scorn your enemy, find out who are his friends." Heed that advice and you'd be better prepared and less surprised. Writer and TV producer Dennis Wholy offered these other cautionary words. He said, "Expecting the world to treat you fairly because you're a good person is like expecting a bull not to attack you because you're a vegetarian."

If you are kind to people who hate themselves, they'll hate you as well.

Listening

For the person who never seems to absorb anything or who continually repeats himself or herself when talking, you should consider doing this: Listen for any expressions of frustration or pride in the words they speak, and verbally echo those sentiments, as best as you can, back to them. Chances are, by hearing their own words repeated back to them, they'll be flattered enough that they may want to repay that courtesy by being more attentive to what you have to say. Recognize too, if your listener harbors unexpressed feelings or reservations about you, it will interfere with their capacity to truly consider what you are saying. Nobody listens to what another has to say if they're convinced the other person has nothing to add to their knowledge base or is unqualified to do so. This is why it is important when speaking, that you occasionally check your listener's pulse by observing their body language or asking questions.

Author and motivational speaker Mike Moore came up with this easy to remember acronym i.e., **LADDER** to express the essential concepts of good listening.

L. *Look directly at the person speaking to you. This alone sends the message that you are focused and involved.*

A. *Ask additional questions—after the person has finished talking. Try and keep your questions relative to the topic under discussion.*

D. *Don't interrupt. The only time an interruption is acceptable is when you require clarification.*

D. *Don't change the subject. The speaker will indicate when she's finished with her story.*

E. *Empathize with the speaker. Show you're a caring listener. Say things like, "You must be so proud," or perhaps, "I know what you mean."*

R. *Respond verbally and non-verbally. Use head nods and forward leans and phrases like, "Is that right?" or I didn't know that" (if appropriate).*

A person is more likely to win another over with his "ears" than with his mouth. Generally, people who receive counseling don't want advice as much as they want another person to listen to what's troubling them. We all appreciate a sympathetic ear.

ILLUSTRATION:

A teacher asked some of his students if anyone could tell him the difference between listening and hearing. Many of the responses were impressive, but one student's answer stood out from the rest. He said, "Listening is wanting to hear."

Now listen to this!

- A politician will "tip off" his or her true belief by stating the opposite at the beginning of a sentence ... so do not start listening until the first clause is concluded. Always listen for the word "but," after which pay very close attention to what is then said.

- "If you can't get people to listen to you any other way, tell them it is confidential." (*Farmer's Digest*) That'll get their attention.

- For every man who speaks from experience, there is a wife who isn't listening.

- Many speakers have little to say. The trouble is you have to listen and wait until they are finished speaking before you can make that assessment.

- These days, the only people who listen to both sides of an argument are the neighbors.

- "There's nothing like eavesdropping to show you that the world out-side your head is different from the world inside your head." (Thornton Wilder)

- "What Paul says about Peter tells us more about Paul than about Peter." (Baruch Spinoza)

- "Don't judge a man by the words of his mother; listen to the com-ments of his neighbors." (Yiddish proverb)

- The worst thing about growing old is having to listen to a lot of advice from one's children.
- "When a man's wife learns to understand him, she usually stops listening to him."(Murphy's Love Laws)

Compassionate listening:

A little boy was late getting home one day. When he finally showed up, his worried mother asked, "Where have you been?"

The little boy explained, "I stopped to help a friend whose bicycle had broken down."

"But you don't know how to fix a bicycle," his mother said.

"That's true," replied the little boy, "But I stopped to be with him, while he cried."

> *"There are people who, instead of listening to what is being said to them, are already listening to what they are going to say themselves." (Albert Guinon)*

Loneliness

*L*oneliness is not the fault of others but their actions and behavior may upset us so much that we decide to withdraw and brood over it, in private. Days turn to weeks and with little hope of reconciliation our feelings of isolation grow deeper. Soon, we find ourselves adjusting to a new lifestyle but with thoughts of abandonment always at the back of our minds.

Here is how one man expressed his solitude: "I live alone, and sometimes I wish there was another toothbrush in the holder next to mine. I often dine alone and sleep alone. The quarrels I have with myself always confirm my failures. My tomorrows are a replay of my yesterdays."

People decide to marry for many reasons. A motive behind some marriages, is to escape the pain of being single. But after marrying, some do not find the companionship they had sought or hoped for. Instead, they discover two often painful and disappointing realities: solitude and neglect. Russian writer, Anton Chekhov (1860-1904) offered this sobering piece of advice to those contemplating marriage, " If you are afraid of loneliness, don't marry."

The following is a retelling of a parable by Danish philosopher Søren Kierkegaard under the title of '*The illegible letter.*' It describes loss following the death of a loved one.

> *Imagine a man possessed a letter that he believed contained all the happy moments of his life. However, the ink with which it was written was much faded, and many of the words were now in doubt. As he scrutinized the lines with restless anxiety, he found meaning in one line and a contrary meaning in another. This would happen whenever he implied the meaning of obscure words from the few that were visibly clear. Each time he looked at the let-*

ter's contents, the less and less he understood. As the days rolled by, the written words became fainter and fainter, and at one point looked like a completely washed piece of paper. His only comfort were those unannounced moments when tears suddenly appeared and brought with them the memory of a more blissful time.

Never underestimate the cleansing power of a "good cry". Author and theologian C.S Lewis, remarked, " If you've been up all night and cried till you have no more tears left in you – you will know that there comes in the end, a sort of quietness. You feel as if nothing was ever going to happen again." There is an old Jewish proverb that goes: "What soap is for body, tears are for the soul."

Much of the sadness felt by lonely people sprout from an inability to share feelings. When we hide parts of ourselves, we deny others the chance to get to know us. We mistakenly presume they'll not respect us or will avoid us if they knew about our sad condition. Indeed, sharing feelings of solitude may make us feel exposed and vulnerable, but it is still a better option than silently crying alone each day. Feelings of loneliness are nothing to be ashamed of. Each and every one of us experiences it in our own private way.

Famous Swiss psychologist and psychiatrist, Carl Jung expressed the above concept this way: " "Loneliness does not come from having no people about one, but from being unable to communicate the things that seem important to oneself, or from holding certain views which others find inadmissible."

Here are a few suggestions and things to know about loneliness:

♦ People have a way of fixating on the imperfections in their lives. Instead of focusing on changing themselves or circumstances, they should instead focus their attentions on what is already working well in their life (probably activities enjoyed before feeling lonely). Once that happens, the bounce received may provide the motivation to improve on other areas that do require attention. And remember, progress is usually measured in small steps.

- The man who turns his back on his friends and family may find himself facing no one at all. Within this context, the first step in addressing feelings of loneliness may be to share them with those close to you.

- "The thing that makes you exceptional——if you are at all— is inevitably that which must also make you lonely." (Lorraine Hansberry)

- "Some people are severely lonely. All they can do is accept 'single life' as an example of being free and happy." (Anthony Liccione)

- We should reflect on these words by Helen Keller. "Believe, when you are most unhappy, there is something for you to do in this world. Once you can sweeten another's pain, then your life is not in vain."

- "Loneliness is the most universal sensation on the planet. Just remember, one fact — loneliness will pass. You will survive and you will be a better human for it." (Douglas Coupland)

"The miserable state is borne by souls who, despite living a graceful life, received no praise while they lived." (paraphrased from Dante's Divine Comedy, "Inferno" Canto 3, lines 34–36)

Looking for
Mr. or Ms. Right

ILLUSTRATION:

A prosperous young Wall Street broker met and fell in love with a respectable young actress. He frequently escorted her about town and wanted to marry her, but being a cautious man, he decided before proposing marriage he should have a private agency check her background and current activities. After all, as he reminded himself, he had a growing fortune and wanted to protect himself against any possible marital misadventures. The young man, however, requested that the agency not reveal his identity to the investigator who was compiling the report on the actress. Eventually, the investigation was completed and the report was prepared. It concluded that the actress had an unblemished past, a spotless reputation, and her friends and associates were all of the highest character. It went on to say, however, "The only shadow was that she was often seen around town in the company of a young Wall Street broker of dubious practices and reputation."

Things generally come to those who wait, but they are usually things left behind by those who came before. According to songwriter and humorist Kinky Friedman, "Every time you see a beautiful woman, just remember, somebody got tired of her." Often, we postpone our lives until we reach a comfortable weight, have enough wealth, or a more successful career. But as we all know, life doesn't wait for us. It keeps going whether we reach where we want to be or not.

If you cannot find what you like, maybe you can try and learn to appreciate what you already have. Even in a marriage that is a week old, there are grounds for divorce. The trick is to find reasons to remain married and continue on.

Although true love triumphs over all things, we should not overlook the subtle clues we encounter in our pursuit of the ideal mate. Here are a few cautionary observations.

- "Choose a wife rather by your ear than your eye." (Thomas Fuller)
- It is better for a girl with a future to avoid a man with a past.
- "Never marry a man who hates his mother because he'll end up hating you." (Jill Bennett)
- If your dream is to find a caring and supportive wife or husband, the probability of finding such a person at a bar is slim, at most.
- "Never trust a woman whose father calls her 'Princess.' Chances are she believes it." (Wes Smith)
- She who has roses in her garden has roses in her heart.
- Having beauty is a great windfall but know it's a joy only for a while.
- "The more a woman is admired by a man for her achievements, the less easy it is for him to desire her physically, or to have her at all, without fantasizing about someone else." (Irma Kurtz)
- "There are no ugly women, only lazy ones." (Helena Rubenstein)
- "I used to think the worst thing in life is to end up all alone. It's not. The worst thing in life is to end up with people who make you feel all alone." (Robin Williams)
- "There's no such thing, you know, as picking out the best woman: it's only a question of comparative badness." (Platus)
- "Any woman can fool a man if she wants to and if he's in love with her." (Agatha Christie)
- "Women who insist upon having the same options as men would do well to consider the option of being the strong, silent type." (Fran Lebowitz)

- "If a woman tells you she's twenty and looks sixteen, she's twelve. If she tells you she's twenty-six and looks twenty-six, she's damn near forty." (Chris Rock)

- There is an Asian-Indian proverb that goes, "A woman talks to one man, looks at another, and thinks about a third." Writer H. L. Mencken provided the man's perspective. "A man always remembers his first love with special tenderness, but after that he begins to bunch them."

- "Rarely do great beauty and great virtue dwell together." (Francesco Petrarca)

We live in a world where romantic marriage proposals are now televised on stadium screens and social media forums. Movie actress Marlene Dietrich from the 1930's, made this observation on those "Oh, so cute moments." She said, "Tenderness is a greater proof of love than the most passionate of vows." No doubt those publicized displays may cause us to swoon in delight, but Ms. Dietrich may have wanted to remind us they are fleeting moments and lack the depth of more consequential displays of affection. "Tenderness may be likened to an unrehearsed moment that makes your heart want to say, "Oh!" For example, the breath of a sleeping baby as its cheek rests against yours." (Karsh)

Broadcast events lack spontaneity and are almost always choreographed. When a tender moment gets simulcast for all to see, know the participant(s) are more interested in making an impact than delighting in the solemnity of the moment.

The following two controversial statements were made by Austrian educator and psychiatrist Rudolf Dreikurs. How do you feel about his conclusions?

"A great many people fall in love or feel attracted to a person who offers the least possibility of a harmonious union.

"The complaints which anyone now voices against his or her mate indicate exactly the qualities [that] stimulated their attraction before marriage."

> *"When a man opens a car door for his wife, it's either a new car or a new wife." (Prince Philip)*

Management:
Yesterday & Today

*S*uccessful management is all about putting the right people in the right jobs and then sitting on the sidelines in your new role as a rousing cheerleader. Managers who always tell their associates not merely what they want to be done but exactly *how* they want it done are guilty of over management. They rob their people of a chance to use their judgment and initiative.

No boss, no matter how competent, can think of everything alone. Leaders who encourage others to think independently will be rewarded with a lot of good ideas that may surprise them. Most bosses manage from conditions that existed yesterday because yesterday is where they received their training. Yesterday is the storage place of all their accomplishments and successes. However, management is all about tomorrow, not yesterday. The future is concerned about what must be done *now*, not what was done in the past.

Credit and recognition do not come to the man who sets himself above his followers. It comes to the man who stands up valiantly despite the odds and walks with and shields his men as best as he can. A manager with those qualities will always have people who will follow him wherever he goes. However, that doesn't mean that having leadership qualities assures you a position at the top. Consequently, you shouldn't focus solely on the top brass for good examples of leadership. Your friend, a relative, or even your neighbor may already possess the traits of a good manager—don't overlook them.

The following assertion by critic and scholar H. L. Menchen has always been and continues to be the primary motivation behind many of man's actions and decisions. He reasoned, "What men value in this world are not rights, but privileges."

ILLUSTRATION:

> *A king had a torturer who was always able to force a confession. Once, a man was charged with conspiracy, but despite all the torturer did, the man never confessed. Later, the king called the conspirator into his chambers, spoke with him a few minutes, and obtained a confession. Later, the torturer asked the king how he'd manage to persuade him. The king replied, "Oh that was easy. I asked him what he wanted in return for his confession, and he said all he wanted was to change places with you, and I granted him his wish."*

A word of caution: Never work for anyone in a position of authority who feels inadequate about themselves. Such people are perpetually driven by the fear of exposure, and sooner or later they will succumb to the following:

- They will seek advice from the wrong people and act on that advice.
- They will have no qualms about betraying you, especially during times of conflict.
- They will do all they can to avoid taking responsibility.
- They will eventually mess up the entire system and adversely affect many others by their decisions.

When an employee feels included and is able to participate in the decision-making process, he or she is more inclined to contribute to the cause and repeat any good performance for additional stroking. But when this doesn't happen, it is no wonder the person feels he or she is being "used" by management to rake in more profit for themselves. Former Senior VP of Federal Express James Perkins observed, "The way employees treat customers reflects the manner in which they are treated by management."

However, that's not the full story, as it is also a reflection of management's attitude toward its own customers too.

Workplace Survival Tips:

- Don't fight the consensus, and don't resign over policy.
- It isn't a matter of what or who you know, but rather who knows you.
- "Don't talk about yourself; it will be done when you leave the room." (Wilson Mizner)
- "The least productive people are usually the ones who are most in favor of holding meetings." (Thomas Sowell)
- "It is easy to dodge our responsibilities, but we cannot dodge the consequences of dodging our responsibilities." (Josiah Stamp)
- "Those whose approval you seek most give you the least." (Maurice Chevalier)
- "A team effort is a lot of people doing as "I say." (Michael Winner)
- "Don't be irreplaceable; if you can't be replaced, you can't be promoted." (Author Unknown)
- 79.48% of all statistics are made up on the spot, and 40% are meaningless.
- If you want a team to win at high jump, find at least one person who can jump seven feet and not seven people who can jump one foot.
- Experts do not have superior abilities or intelligence over you. What they do is persuade you to do less of this and less of that, all at a hefty price.
- "It's time to question a job or career move when it seems like most energy is devoted to making things appear other than what they really are." (Alan Watts)
- There is a four-word formula for success that applies to organizations and Individuals alike. That formula : "Make yourself more useful" It wouldn't hurt to consider this Amish proverb as well: "Very few burdens are heavy, if everyone lifts."

Seldom is blame the fault of one person. Here is what the authors of the bestseller, *Difficult Conversations,* Douglas Stone, Sheila Heen and Bruce Patton had to say on this subject. "When we blame someone, we are offering them the role of 'the accused,' so what accused people do: they defend themselves any way they can. Given what's at stake, it is easy to see why the dance of finger-pointing usually turns out nasty." (Page#60).

A company may fire an employee because of carelessness or for not being responsible enough. Management may believe that by removing the one who "fouled up" with a new employee it is acting responsibly and restoring order and continuity. However, unless there is a closer examination or review of the structure, policy, and processes in place prior to the firing, there is not much to boast about. We have to recognize that one or more employees may have interacted directly or indirectly with the dismissed employee could have contributed to the firing in their own private way. Blame should not be the sole responsibility of the accused. Others should shoulder blame too for supporting or casting a blind eye on the events that culminated in the dismissal. Good companies recognize that a better tomorrow, depends on the fixes they introduce today.

People do not become evil overnight. Chances are the manager who was cited for being disrespectful to a customer was probably disrespectful before, if not toward customers, then perhaps toward internal staff or outside third parties. Remember, a man's reputation always precedes him. Chances are that an employee's irrational behavior or attitude may have been noticed by other senior personnel, but rather than doing or saying something, it was much easier to look the other way. Those in a position to alter the course of events but chose to look the other way, should be made responsible too. Uttering words like, "It's none of my business" is just like saying, "I know about it, but I've decided not to do anything."

There will always be managers who will sit idly by on the sidelines when a volatile situation escalates. Business consultant, Peter F. Drucker had a few choice words for people like that. He said this, "Rank does not confer privilege or give power—it imposes responsibility.

Your most expensive employees are not those who are the highest paid, but those who are the least productive.

Marital Quips & Observations

- Where there's marriage without love, there will be love without marriage.
- Every chap with money to burn will meet his match.
- Before criticizing your wife's faults, remember they may have prevented her from getting a better husband.
- Some women marry for money and then divorce for love.
- "Men always fall for frigid women because they put on the best show." (Fanny Brice)
- "I have learned that only two things are necessary to keep one's wife happy. First, let her think she's having her own way. And second, let her have it." (Lyndon B Johnson)
- "Love lodged in a woman's breast is but a guest." (Henry Wotton)
- "The trouble with some women is that they get all excited about nothing and then marry him." (Cher)
- The woman we do love is rarely able to satisfy all of our needs, and if we do deceive her, it is most likely to be with a woman we do not love.
- "A man does not look behind the door unless he has stood there himself." (W. E. B Du Bois)
- "Men like to pursue an elusive woman like a bar of wet soap—even men who hate baths." (Gelett Burgesss)
- "Once a woman has forgiven her man, she must not reheat his sins for breakfast." (Marlene Deitrich)

- "To have beautiful servant girls is a threat to good marriages." (Geoffrey Chaucer)
- Marriages are like diets; they can be ruined by a little dish on the side.
- "Every woman is wrong until she cries, and then, she is right instantly." (Thomas C Halliburton)
- "What attracts us in a woman rarely binds us to her." (John Churton Collins)
- Some women work so hard to make good husbands that they never manage to make good wives.
- If my wife has taught me anything, it is, no matter what in the world I am doing— I should be doing it differently.
- "Men prefer the wife of another but love their own sons more." (Georgian proverb)
- "Temptation usually comes in through a door that has been deliberately left open." (Arnold Glasow)
- There would be fewer divorces if husbands try as hard to keep their wives as they did to get them.
- "There is no sweeter pleasure than to surprise a man by giving him more than he hopes for." (Charles Baudelaire)
- "The ultimate betrayal is not a wandering wife, but a wandering wife who tells her lover that her husband doesn't make as much as everyone thinks." (Harry Golden)
- If you want to drive your wife crazy, don't talk in your sleep—just smile.
- "An optimist is a man who marries his secretary and thinks he'll still be able to continue dictating to her." (Michael Hodgin)
- "Before marriage, a man will lie awake all night thinking about something you said; after marriage, he'll fall asleep before you finish saying it." (Helen Rowland)
- "Be kind to your mother-in-law but pay for her board at some good hotel."(Henry Wheeler Shaw)

- "London is full of women who trust their husbands. One can always recognize them; they look so thoroughly unhappy."(Oscar Wilde, 1859-1900)
- Most of the men who rail against women are railing against one woman only.

Comedian Henny Youngman said, "Do you know what it means to come home at night to a woman who'll give you a little love, a little affection, a little tenderness? It means you are in the wrong house, that's what it means!"

By Sophie Tucker:

Age	What a girl wants	*What a boy wants ...*
0 to 18	Good parents.	Good parents.
18 to 35	Good looks.	Sexual adventure.
35 to 55	A good personality.	Earning power.
55+	Cash.	A younger mate.

The world's shortest fairy tale:

Once upon a time, a girl asked a guy, "Will you marry me?" and he promptly replied, "No!" The girl went on to live happily ever after. She spent her spare time shopping, visiting friends, family, and foreign lands too. Her house was always clean, and she was never under any pressure to prepare a meal.

The End

At a seminar on how to find the love of your life, psychotherapist Sunita Singhji suggested the following:

On a piece of paper, list the numbers one through ten. Beginning with numbers 2 through 10, list the qualities or characteristics of your ideal mate. When finished, go back, and write next to number one the following words: "Someone who loves, respects, and admires me, would be/should be:" (This is a snapshot of the one you love or want to win over.)

A newly married couple returned from their honeymoon. As they got off the plane at the crowded airport, the bride said, "Darling, let's make the people think we have been married. The husband said, "OK dear, you carry the bags."

"Love is just a word until someone comes along and gives it meaning."
(Paulo Coelho)

Money's Limitations

Things that money can and cannot buy: by Henrik Ibsen.

What it can buy:	What it cannot buy :
Food	but not appetite
Medicine	but not health.
Acquaintances	but not friends.
Servants	but not faithfulness.
Luxuries	but not culture.
Amusements	but not happiness.
Flattery	but not respect.
Finery	but not beauty.
A bed	but not sleep.
Books	but not brains.

Ever notice whenever you come into some extra cash you weren't expecting there is always some expense 'out of the blue' that completely wipes it out? Also, how a *dollar* can look so big when you take it to your 'house' of worship or donate it to your favorite cause ... but so small, when you take it to the store?

Some other thoughts on the subject of money:

- "All reformers, however strict their social conscience, live in houses just as big as they can pay for." (Logan Pearsall Smith,1865-1946)

- "If women didn't exist,all the money in the world would have no meaning."(Aristotle Onassis)

- "Many speak the truth when they say they despise riches and wealth, but what they really mean is the riches and wealth possessed by others." (Charles Caleb Colton)

- "Every time you spend money, you're casting a vote for the kind of world you want." (Anna Lappe)

- "We know a fool and his money are soon parted, but how did they get together in the first place?" (E. C. McKenzie)

- "The time to save is now. When a dog gets a bone, he doesn't go out and make a down payment on a bigger bone. He buries the one he's got." (Will Rogers)

- "A married man with a family will do almost anything for money." (Charles De Talleyrand)

- "A simple fact that is hard to learn —the time to save money, is when you have some."(Joe Moore)

- "He that is of the opinion money will do everything may well be suspected of doing everything for money." (Benjamin Franklin)

- People who say that money *isn't* the most important thing in the world are usually broke. (Malcolm Forbes)

- Gordon T. Sumner, aka the musician Sting, said, "Cocaine is God's way of telling you you've got too much money."

- Be mindful once you have made a lot of money, the same wheel of fortune that brought it to you, may also take it away from you.

- "Money won is twice as sweet as money earned."(Paul Newman)

- "Money is an abstraction. It cannot of itself buy any pleasure ... because all pleasures, involve skill and love." (Alan Watts)

"Money is only a tool. It will take you wherever you wish but will not replace you as the driver." (Ayn Rand)

On Writing

*Y*ou will do your best writing when you sound exactly like yourself and not an echo of your favorite author/writer. If you care about a subject and feel others should care about it too, then the words you use will be the most compelling. Our audience requires us to be sympathetic and patient teachers. They are hungry, and always willing to let us simplify or clarify things for them. Leo Tolstoy, (1828-1910), one of the best writers of all time, said, "If you asked someone, 'Can you play the violin?' and he says, 'I don't know, I have not tried, perhaps I can,' you laugh at him. ... people always say: 'I don't know, I have not tried,' as though one had only to try, and one would become a writer."

Edward Thompson (1928-2018) a former editor at *Reader's Digest*, offered these tips to help authors improve their writing style.

- Refrain from using words, expressions, or phrases known only to people with specialized interests. For example, a scientist once wrote, "The biota exhibited a 100% mortality response." He could have easily written: "All the fish died."

- Keep your sentences short and avoid long, complex prose. Practice expressing one single idea at a time. See to it that each paragraph deals only with one topic. Including too many will make your reader work too hard.

- Don't waste words telling people what they already know, e.g., "Have you ever wondered how banks rate you as a credit risk? You know, of course that it's some combination of facts about your income, job, and payment history. Say instead, "Many banks have a scoring system."

- Stay clear of "windy phrases" or "puff speak." They are usually elaborate disguises for ordinary words:

Windy Phrase:	Use instead:
At the present time	Now
In the event of	If
In the majority of instances	Usually
Owing to the fact	Since
Feedback	Response
With reference to	About

Here are a few additional tips that may help improve your writing style:

- If a sentence, no matter how excellent, does not illuminate your subject in some new and effective way, delete it.

- Be aware of unclear word combinations, e.g., "John's father says he can't go out Friday." Who can't go out? Is it John or his father?

- One of the things that will help your writing appear more *conversational* is the use of contractions, e.g., "He won't," or "She isn't" instead of the traditional "He will not" or "She is not."

- Bowl people over with the clarity of your thought and use imagery whenever possible.

- "If you want to get rich from writing, write the sort of thing that is read by persons who move their lips, when they're reading to themselves."

- Don't worry for a minute about what anyone else is going to think of you. Write to express and not to impress. Make sure your words sound as if they are coming from a human being and not from an institution or machine, e.g., don't say, "Further notification will follow." Say something like, "I'll keep you informed."

- Dr. Herbert Clark, a psychologist from Johns Hopkins University, discovered that it takes the average person about 48% longer to understand a sentence when it includes negative connotations rather than positive ones. The secret of good communication is positive affirmation. It is not what you won't or can't do that interests people, but what you can *or* will *do*.

ILLUSTRATION:

The famous editor Horace Lorimer rejected a manuscript sent to him by a hopeful author. The angry author later confronted Mr. Lorimer.

Author: "You rejected my story without even reading it."

Horace Lorimer: "How do you know I didn't read it?"

Author: "Because as a test, I pasted pages 16, 17, and 18 together and when the manuscript came back, they were still pasted together.

Horace Lorimer: "Well, let me put it this way. At breakfast, when I open an egg, I don't have to eat the whole egg to conclude it is bad!"

"The most original authors are not so because they advance what is new, but because they put what they have to say as if it had never been said before." (Goethe)

Our Attitude Matters

ILLUSTRATION:

In March 1981, a would-be assassin fired several shots at then-President Ronald Reagan as he and his entourage left a Washington hotel. Reagan was taken to the hospital with a severe chest wound and needed emergency surgery. As he was wheeled into the operating theater, and with a faint smile, he looked around at the team of surgeons with surgical masks over their mouths and said, "Please assure me that you are all Republicans!" About a year later, while giving a speech before an audience, a decorative balloon hanging overhead popped, making the sound of a gunshot. Reagan paused for a second, and without missing a beat, said defiantly, "Missed me," and continued on with the remainder of his speech.

ILLUSTRATION:

A young woman (during a job interview) asked the H/R manager of a prestigious corporation whether she could participate in their well-respected training program. The HR manager, besieged with applications, in a gruff voice replied, "Impossible now, come back in about ten years." The young lady immediately remarked, "Would the morning or afternoon be better?"

When you plant lettuce and it does not grow well, you don't blame the lettuce, do you? You look for reasons it is not doing well. It may need fertilizer, or more water, or perhaps more or less sunlight, but you don't blame the lettuce. The rain doesn't abuse the grass. The ant doesn't curse another because it stands in its way. The worm does not "damn" the plow that severs it. But with humans, the opposite is true. When disappointed with an acquaintance, friend, or family member, the immediate knee-jerk reaction is to retaliate by assigning blame or seeking revenge, often without much forethought. It never occurs to us that plotting revenge allows those who hurt us to hurt us even longer. However, we do have choices, and often it boils down to a choice of attitudes.

In her book *Negaholics*, author Cherie Carter-Scott suggested that almost daily we're bombarded with news about bombings, murders, rapes, droughts, fires, wars, and corruption among our leaders. These are all real and painful realities and do require our conscious attention, but we devote too much time dwelling on the negative aspects of those event(s) while subconsciously discounting the positive. If we want more love in the world, we should first learn to be more forgiving. If we want more competence in our team, we should first improve *our* own competence. If we want more justice, then we should consider the words of Greek historian Thucydides (460 BC–400 BC), who said, "Justice will not come until those who are not injured are as indignant as those who are injured."

The sad fact is that in America there is much complaint with little suffering, whereas in many other countries the reverse is true. The truth is that we are so focused on maintaining our personal comforts and social status that we deliberately ignore traditional values of fairness and common decency. Consider looking at life from these perspectives:

- Whether you drive a BMW or a Honda Civic, the road remains the same.
- Whether you fly first class or economy, the destination does not change.
- Whether you wear a Rolex or Timex, eight o'clock remains eight o'clock.
- "Whether it's winter or summer, people don't notice when they're happy."(Anton Chekov)
- "Whether one believes in a religion or not…. there isn't anyone who doesn't appreciate kindness and compassion." (Dalai Lama)
- "When a man's stomach is full. it makes no difference whether he is rich or poor." (Euripides)

ILLUSTRATION: (From Mary Hollingsworth, in her 2008 book, *"And God Said... Let there be Laughter!)*

> *There once was a woman who woke up one morning, looked in the mirror and noticed she had only three hairs on her head.*
>
> *"Well," she said, "I think I'll braid my hair today." So, she did and had a wonderful day.*
>
> *The next day she woke up, looked in the mirror, and saw that she only had two hairs on her head.*
>
> *"Hmm," she said, "I think I'll part my hair down the middle today. "So, she did that and had a grand day.*
>
> *The next day she woke up, looked in the mirror, and noticed that she had only one hair on her head.*
>
> *"Well," she said, "Today I'm going to wear my hair in a ponytail." So she did and had a fun day.*
>
> *The next day she woke up, looked in the mirror, and noticed that there wasn't a single hair on her head.*
>
> *"YEAH!" she exclaimed, "I don't have to fix my hair today!" Attitude is everything. (page # 264)*

British philosopher and critic Bertrand Russell said, "Few people can be happy unless they hate some other person, nation, or creed." Know that regardless how wonderful or bitter the world is, we all have a capacity to effect change in our own little way. If this endeavor sounds daunting to you, then consider these words of photographer/artist Herm Albright (876 to 194) who said, "A positive attitude *may not* solve all your problems, but it will annoy enough people to make the effort worth it."

> *"People may hear your words, but they feel your attitude."* (John C Maxwell)

Overt Truths

- "Most people have some sort of religion—at least they know which church they are staying away from." (John Erskine)

- "Laziness is nothing more than the habit of resting before you get tired."(Jules Renard)

- "We rarely confide in those who are better than we." (Albert Camus)

- "It is not the employer who pays the wages. He only handles the money. It is the product or service that pays the wages." (Henry Ford)

- Ever notice how many "once-in-a-lifetime opportunities" you can do without?

- "The virtues of hard work are extolled most loudly by people without calluses." (Doug Larson)

- "The poor wish to be rich, the rich wish to be happy, the single wish to be married, and the married wish to be dead." (Ann Landers, 1918-2002)

- "The most effective way of attacking vice is to expose it to public ridicule. People can put up with rebukes ,but they cannot bear being laughed at. They are prepared to be wicked, but they dislike appearing ridiculous."(Jean B. P Moliere)

- "When a lot of remedies are suggested for a disease, that means it can't be cured." (Anton Chekhov)

- "People who want to share their religious views with you almost never want you to share yours with them." (Dave Barry)

- "The wicked are wicked, no doubt, and they go astray, and they fall ... but who can tell the mischief which the very virtuous do?" (William Thackery)

- Ever notice the phrase, "it's none of my business" is always followed by the word "but?"
- "An appeaser is one who feeds a crocodile, hoping it'll eat him last." (Winston Churchill)
- There is something about a long scraggly beard that implies that its owner has no need for advice or direction.
- "If someone tells you he is going to make a 'realistic decision,' you immediately understand that he has resolved to do something bad." (Mary Therese McCarthy)
- "For rarely are sons similar to their fathers; most are worse, and a few are better than their fathers." (Homer)
- "He that first cries out stop thief, is often he that has stolen the treasure."(William Congreve).
- The first thing that captures a man's attention when he sees an attractive woman is whether his wife or girlfriend is around.
- "Most people work just hard enough not to get fired and get paid just enough money not to quit." (George Carlin)
- "When someone hands you a flier, it's like they're saying, 'Here, you throw this away." (Mitch Hedberg)
- Generally, most lawsuits are about revenge.
- "The belief that enhanced understanding will necessarily stir a nation to action is one of mankind's oldest illusions." (Andrew Hacker)
- "If you want to sacrifice the admiration of many men for the criticism of one, go ahead, get married." (Katherine Hepburn)
- "He who helps the guilty, shares the crime."(Publilius Syrus)
- "We can't all be heroes, because somebody has to sit on the curb and clap as they go by." (Will Rogers)
- "You see an awful lot of smart guys with dumb women, but you hardly ever see a smart woman with dumb guy." (Erica Jong)
- "A good reliable set of bowels is worth more to a man than any quantity of brains." (Henry Wheeler Shaw)

- "Nobody speaks the truth when there is something they must have." (Elizabeth Cole Bowen)

- If your older child says, "I didn't ask to be born," consider saying in response, "It's a good thing you didn't, because I would have turned you down."

- "You will always find some Eskimo ready to instruct a [Congo native] on how to cope with heatwaves." (Jerzy Lee Stanislaw)

"A hungry stomach, an empty pocket, and a broken heart can teach you some of the best lessons of life." (Abdul Sattar Edhi)

Perceptions, Conceptions & Observations:

ILLUSTRATION:

A man walked into a UPS store to have his Christmas present delivered to his mother in California. When it came time to pay the shipping costs, he became visibly annoyed, and complained loudly enough for everyone in the vicinity to hear, "You guys are charging me more than I paid for this gift!" The clerk promptly responded, "Maybe you should buy more expensive gifts."

Our sketch of the world drives all behavior from the way we vote, the way we decide, or the person we marry. Consider the following exchange between two mothers as related by Stephen R Covey, in his 2004 audiocassette presentation based on his book, *The 7 Habits of Highly Effective Families.*'

"I can't believe my own child. She recently turned sixteen years old and has become a completely different person. She is so rebellious, ungrateful, and angry all the time. And what's worse, she is messy and least likely to help out with anything." As long as the complaining mother carries around negative perceptions of her daughter, Dr. Covey explained, "chances are she'll continue to behave as she does. This is what is commonly referred as the self-fulfilling prophesy, i.e., 'You say I am bad, well I am going to be bad.'" Each statement the mother has made is a map and underlining image she is carrying around of her daughter. The other mother who was more forgiving and conciliatory responded by saying, "You should make an effort to see things from her point of view and be a bit more positive."

Everyone has special gifts, unique qualities, and characteristics that need expression; however, we are held back by factors that are sometimes outside our control. Just like airing-out a closet is a good idea, so too should we consider giving airtime to our thoughts and talents. Here are four suggestions how we may go about accomplishing that.

1. *Replay in your mind your proudest memories. Then look for a connection between that and the present moment. If you can relate those memories to a current circumstance, then repeat the circumstance..*

2. *Re-examine your motives. Are you quick to embarrass, or throw people away? If so, recognize that those thoughts are counterproductive.*

3. *The hatred of relatives can be most vicious. Those emotions hold you back and never leave you. There is no need to keep lugging that kind of baggage around.*

4. *Leave everything a little better than you found it.*

"People sometimes say, "Time changes things," but you actually have to change them yourself. The quickest way to change a person's behavior is to appeal to his or her perceived role in the community. For instance, as soon as you became a father, a mother, or a leader, you began seeing the world from a different perspective. In that new role, your concerns and considerations became different because your responsibilities and duties changed. Refrain from "knocking" another's behavior or attitude and instead focus on how the responsibilities associated with their *new* role is being challenged by the old ways of thinking. For example, if you say to your mother, "You are a bad mother," that is no way as powerful and effective as saying, "Mom, *I am your child*, and I feel like you are neglecting me." (Stephen R. Covey)

ILLUSTRATION

Queen Victoria and her husband, Prince Albert, had a small quarrel. Prince Albert stormed out of the room and headed straight to his private quarters. Queen Victoria followed him, but upon arrival found his room door shut and locked. She immediately began pounding on it.

"Who is there?" Prince Albert barked."The Queen Of England!" was her

booming response.

The door remained shut, and the pounding became heavier. But two minutes later, the thumping was replaced with a pause and then a gentle tap.

"Who's there?" Prince Albert asked impatiently?

"It is I, dear, your wife."

Upon hearing those words, Albert immediately opened the door and allowed her in.

The lesson here is that one is more likely to have a sustainable conversation when the message is conveyed in a subtle and caring voice.

A few social observations:

- Ever notice, "There are books in which the footnotes or the comments scrawled by some reader's hand in the margins are more interesting than the printed text"? (George Santayana, 1863-1952)
- "Truth needs no defense. It only needs witnesses." (Lenard Larry McKelvey)
- "The government cannot give to anybody anything that it does not first take from somebody else." (Adrian Rogers)
- We are always quick to count others' offenses against us, but seldom do we consider how others suffer because of us.
- Love at first sight seldom happens before breakfast.
- "Women read each other at a single glance."(Antoine Rivarol)
- "Men are like rubber bands. They'll frequently pull away for a time, but they will relax and return. Likewise, women are like ocean waves; they're sometimes caught in low tides, but unquestionably, they will rise and crest again." (John Gray)
- "The loudest boos come from the cheapest seats!" (Babe Ruth)
- "The thing that brings people to wail at a wall, or face Mecca, or to go to church, is a search for that feeling of purity." (Michael J. Fox)

- If you do something of which you are 100% sure and certain to meet with everybody's approval, there is bound to be at least one person who won't like it.

- "At age 20, we worry about what others think of us. At 40, we don't care what they think of us. At 60, we discover they haven't been thinking of us at all." (Ann Landers)

- "You either have to be first, best, or different." (Loretta Lynn)

- Any good-looking person you see who isn't alone will be accompanied by a person of the opposite sex who doesn't appear to be deserving of them.

- "If a man could have half his wishes, he would double his troubles." (Benjamin Franklin)

- "The world has many indispensable people and you can tell who they are by checking the size of their tombstones." (Milwaukee Journal)

- Many of us already know how to tell the difference between right and wrong, but it is always easier to look the other way.

- "What a pity human beings can't exchange problems. Everyone seems to know exactly how to solve the other fellow's." (Olin Miller)

- We generally associate success with intelligence and 'street' smarts, but often, success is no more than a person or group playing by a different set of rules.

Two of the most valuable places on earth and why:

- In someone's thoughts because it is the nicest place you can be!
- In someone's prayers because it is the safest place you can be!

"We first make our habits, and then our habits make us." (John Dryden, 1631-1700)

Persuasion

*I*n his book, *Political Enemies*, Italian philosopher Thomas Aquinas (1225-1274) said, "When you want to convert a man to your view, go over to where he is standing, take him by the hand and guide him. You don't stand across the room and shout at him; you don't call him a dummy; you don't order him to come over to where you are. You start where he is and work from that. That is the only way to get him to budge." Whenever there is a difference of opinion with another, the object should not be to win the argument but to get the other person to change his or her mind by helping them see things your way. You should strive *not* to bring egos into the conversation. Here are a few suggestions how you may go about that and perhaps guide the disagreement in a more promising direction:

- Let the person state their case. Don't interrupt while they are talking, and let that person get off what's on their chest.

- Pause slightly before responding. That shows you are processing what's been said.

- If a person has a point in his or her favor, acknowledge it with lines like, "Yes, I can see why it might appear that way" or "You may be right about that."

- Speak through third-party endorsements. A political candidate's statement that she has integrity and experience does not carry the same weight as when she says, "The League of Upright Citizens endorses my proposals."

- If possible, weave the following two words into your conversation: "if" and "then," e.g., "If you lie down, then you'll feel much better." When you attempt to persuade another, you want to be perceived as supportive and non-condemning. These two words, when used properly, may help facilitate that.

Everyone you meet is trying to make his or her life experience more meaningful. It matters not whether the person is pursuing knowledge, wealth, fame, or recognition, as each wants to experience life a bit larger than it already is. The man who goes to a bar and the man who goes to a place of prayer are both seeking the same thing, i.e., fulfillment, be it peace or serenity. When we knock others for their choices, we're attempting to convince them that our way is the right or better way. Motivational speaker Dale Carnegie theorized, "A man convinced against his will is still of the same opinion."

Here are a few other suggestions to consider :

- You should be vigilant of those who agree with you too readily. Know that lip service quells communication, as its purpose is to shut you down. Contrarily, do not feel too comfortable when the other party adopts a passive role and only offer a series of nods and yeses People who overdo those things aren't truly listening to what you have to say. And don't be swayed by acknowledgments only; seek and obtain feedback in your exchanges. Look and 'take' something from the conversation away with you.

- When you find it necessary to criticize someone, put your criticism in the form of a question. Instead of saying, "You have bad breath," say, "Do you know you have bad breath?"

- "Who" and "Why" questions tend to have two purposes. The first is to find fault, and the other to assign blame. Consider incorporating more "when," "what," and "how" questions in your exchanges. These questions are answered less defensively. For example, when Mike says, "Jane makes me feel very uncomfortable," here are some follow-up questions you could ask:

  When did Jane make you feel uncomfortable?.
  What was the nature of the discomfort? Was it tension, fear, being embarrassed?
  How do you feel now or plan to address it?

- Allow the other person to save face: A person may be willing to concede except for one thing, i.e., his or her lack of credibility following his or her strong opposition. To "cave in" now, is to admit that he or she was wrong. To facilitate a safe exit you could probably say either of the two:

  - "Anybody would have thought the same thing under the circumstances and you didn't have all the facts when you made your decision."

  - " I know you were upset and did not intentionally want to hurt XYZ" or "Don't worry about it, I won't tell anyone."

"We often refuse to accept an idea merely because the tone of voice in which it has been expressed is unsympathetic to us." (Friedrich Nietzsche)

Politeness

"Treat everyone with politeness and kindness, not because they are nice, but because you are." (Roy T. Bennett) Consider too, this African proverb, "Anyone can be polite to a king, but it takes a gentleman to be polite to a beggar."

Dahleen Glanton, a columnist for the *Chicago Tribute*, once wrote a wonderful article titled, "When a man offers a woman his seat on the train or bus, is it an act of kindness or sexism?" She proposed we may want to consider courtesy more in the context of a personal willingness to give above the demands of what is expected of us. The one who sees an opportunity to be kind or polite **and** waits first to be asked or told is not truly being kind or polite.

Author Roger Rosenblatt observed, "If you expect people to demonstrate gratitude for something you have done for them, you are in for a lot of steaming and fuming and wasted hours. Once in a while, someone will actually show thanks for an act of kindness or generosity ... but don't hold your breath. Keep an even keel by having no expectations. Then, on that very rare occasion when someone does show gratitude, you won't have a heart attack."

Honesty is not the most important thing, politeness is. Honesty is to behave in a way that is truthful and fair, but politeness is to recognize when to be big and when to be little. Think of it as the unsaid part of what you truly think. As in competitive events, second or third places don't really count. Only first place matters. Second and third place is just a polite way of saying, "Try harder next time."

ILLUSTRATION:

On a very cold, snowy Sunday in February, only the pastor and one farmer arrived at the village church. The pastor said, "Well! I guess we won't have any service today." The farmer replied, "Heck, even if one cow shows up at feeding time, I feed it." The pastor obliged and did the entire service. As the farmer was leaving, the pastor shook his hands and said, "How did I do?" "It was okay," the farmer replied, "but if one cow shows up at feed time, I don't drop the full load on it.

"When people rely entirely on their intellect, they forget 'how to feel' and they go on rationalizing whatever decisions they make. When people make decisions from their hearts, they speak with a vitality and energy that can be felt even over the telephone." (Bernie Siegel). Know there is a road from the eye to the heart that does not go through the intellect. And while ritual and behavior differ among countries, politeness is the same everywhere.

In this world there are the poor, the middle class, and the wealthy. The wealthy belong to an exclusive club consisting of "movers" and "shakers." But for the poor and middle class, their personal battles and accomplishments forge and shape their identities. The treatment we receive from each of these classes is more a reflection of how they see themselves than how they see us. If it is our mission to leave behind some kind of legacy, we need to recognize the truth behind the words of German architect, Walter Gropius (1883-1969). His message: "If your contribution has been vital, there will always be somebody to pick up where you left off, and that will be your claim to immortality."

P.S. There is a very good chance you'll receive a favorable response when you need help in public by uttering the words, "I wonder if you could please help me?"—Try it, next time!

"No one knows of your honesty unless you give out some samples." (Our Daily Bread, 1991).

Prayer

Things you should be concerned with, when you pray:

- That your neighbor respects you.
- That trouble neglects you.
- That angels protect you.
- That Heaven accepts you.
- That too much prayer is "asking" not "thanking".

Strength in prayer is better than length in prayers. After saying your prayers at the end of the day, get up the next morning and do something to make your prayers come through. Better yet, wake up the next morning and say, "God, what can I do for *you* today?"

ILLUSTRATION:

> God said, "Let's build a better world,"
> I responded, "How, my lord?"
> God replied, "Just build a better you!"

Harold Kushner, Rabbi & Author observed, "People who pray for miracles usually don't get miracles. But people who pray for courage and strength to bear the unbearable and for the grace to remember what they [still] have left instead of what they have lost, very often find their prayers answered."

Ever notice when prayers are offered, people seldom ask for a change of character, but rather a change in their current circumstances?

ILLUSTRATION: (Of one such expectation backfiring)

A cruise ship was sinking fast and the captain shouted, "There are not enough lifeboats for all of us—a few of you will have to remain behind. Does anyone here know how to reach God through prayer? "A number of people immediately raised their hands.

"Good!" said the captain, "You all stay here and pray while the rest of the passengers, find a place on the lifeboats."

World proverbs and other observations about prayer:

- If children's prayer had any effect, there wouldn't be a single teacher alive.(Persian)
- Might never prays. (Bulgarian)
- What men usually ask for when they pray to God is that two and two may not make four. (Russian)
- Good deeds are the best prayer. (Serbian)
- Call on God, but row away from the rocks. (Indian)
- An angry man is not fit to pray. (Yiddish)
- When praying, do not give God instructions—report for duty!
- Those who do not believe in prayer, will make an exception when tragedy strikes.
- Prayer does not change God, but it changes him who prays. (Soren Kierkegaard).

The following humbling prayer, is of unknown origin.

Lord, thou knowest when my day will come, but in the meantime keep me from the fatal habit of thinking I must say something on every subject and at every occasion.

Release me from the craving to straighten out everybody else's affairs.

Make me thoughtful but not moody—helpful, but not bossy.

Keep my mind free of the recital of too many details.

And at the same time, give me wings to get to the point.

Seal my lips on my aches and pains, and as they increase with age, help me to endure them with patience.

I dare not ask for improved memory but for growing humility and composure when my memory clashes with another. Let me recognize the possibility that I may be mistaken.

Keep me reasonably sweet, but not a saint. Some virtuous souls can be quite rigid in their ways and hard to live with.

Help me to grow old gracefully. When I witness those who grow old and sour too, I see the crowning work of the Devil.

Give me the ability to see virtue in unexpected acquaintances and places and to know when and how to speak gracefully of them.

⌒ **"Hypocrites are people who aren't themselves on their day of prayer."**

Prejudice

ILLUSTRATION by Glenn Van Ekeren from his book *"Words for all Occasions"*

"Several years ago, an elderly gentleman tried to make ends meet by selling balloons on a Chicago street corner. His business had its ups and downs. Whenever business got a little slow, the salesman would release a few helium balloons. First, a pink one, then a blue one, and later a white one. Children would notice the colorful array of balloons and business would pick up.

One day, a little black boy sat across the street watching the balloon salesman. He was intrigued with the flying balloons. Toward the end of the day, the boy walked over and tugged on the man's coat sleeve.

Looking [directly at] the balloon salesman in the eye, he asked, "Mister, if you let go of that black balloon, would it go up? "Touched by the boy's sincerity, the balloon salesman looked at the boy and responded with compassion and understanding. "Son, it's what's inside these balloons that makes them go up. [The lesson that may be drawn from this story]: What's on the exterior has little to do with how successful we are. It is the spirit within us [that counts](page # 3)

To say a man is a thief is like saying, "He has stolen and will steal again," which is more a prediction that an assertion of fact. In our world today, the term "Muslim" is viewed by some with the same connotational prejudice associated with the term "Jew." For each, the cycle of distrust continues, and the harm associated with passing judgment is continually re-enforced. Any statement that submerges the true identity of an individual, place, or nation should be viewed as biased.

ILLUSTRATION

Report: Mary Smith didn't come home until 3:00 am last night.

Inference: I bet she was out partying at a club with her boyfriend.

Judgment: She is nothing but a tramp. I never did like her.

A person's knowledge is reflected by that which holds his interest. For example, a soldier will see the world through the eyes of a soldier. Our initial perceptions, reinforced by habit and duty, soon become lifelong judgments of truth and reality. That is why we may end up saying things like, "Right is right," "Black is black," or "Cheap is cheap." Ideas and perceptions about clothes, race, politics, religion, and sex are often inculcated in our early up-bringing and make it impossible for us to discuss those subjects intelligently in our adult life without invoking the prejudice accumulated during our impressionable childhood years. As former US Supreme Court justice Oliver Wendell Holmes Sr., put it, "We are all tattooed in our cradles with the beliefs of our tribe; the record may seem superficial, but it is indelible."

Contrary opinions, when they do occur, are deemed objectionable and must be refuted immediately. To do otherwise is to go against the natural order. Within this context, it is easy to understand why the fear of change and the perceived threat to our cherished sanctuaries promote and encourage prejudicial behavior.

Many enjoy power and prestige within the framework of old institutions, beliefs, and societal norms. And through it, they obtain prized living comforts and financial security. When change threatens those norms, people tend to react in narrow-minded, selfish ways. However, it is *not* healthy to cling to a territorial maps used by George Washington or Abraham Lincoln and say, "If it was good enough for them, it should be good enough for me." Instead, it would be better to embrace the thinking and wisdom of the Washingtons and Lincolns, when they lived. These men were less concerned with who was right or who was wrong. Their policy decisions were prefaced on providing modest benefits and protection to the general citizenry. Their concern was to execute those duties with fairness and equality across the board.

ILLUSTRATION

> *Two brothers are playing in their backyard. One hits a ball, and it crashes through their neighbor's window. Their father later asserts, "Boys will be boys," but the neighbor thinks of the boys as plain, irresponsible, spoiled brats. Each party has classified the event in terms of how he feels about it and would like others to see it too.*

Is there a way then that we could characterize the word "bad" without assigning a label associated with that person? The answer is yes; we can use "index numbers." Polish scholar Alfred Korzbski suggested that if we could get into the habit of indexing our prejudices, we could possibly reduce the harmful effect they may have on our thinking. For instance, let's classify the concept of bad in terms of bad 1, bad 2, bad 3, etc. In this context, the lowest number i.e., bad 1, may characterize your actual feelings in its lowest terms. So for example, bad 1 could mean the injection you received hurt for a few minutes but then quickly went away; bad 2 could mean the injection continued to hurt up to 4 hours after you received it ; and bad 3, could mean the injection was so painful, you couldn't lift your arm up and needed to go home. Someone who assigns a score of bad 4 means 100% bad (if that is possible). Former linguist, professor, and US Senator S. I.Hayakawa in his 1972 book, *Language in Thought and Action"* commented on the above as follows: "This rule, if remembered, prevents us from confusing levels of abstraction and forces us to consider the facts on those occasions when we might otherwise find ourselves leaping to conclusions which we might later have cause to regret."(page 185)

If we can "teach" ourselves to quantify our prejudices more constructively, we'll become less ignorant and more productive, decent citizens. Psychiatrist Abraham Myerson (1881-1948) noted, "The more ignorant the authority, the more dogmatic [i.e., dictatorial] it is. In the fields where no real knowledge is possible, the authorities are the fiercest and most assured and punish non-belief with the severest of penalties."

Just as people do not visit the dentist until they have a toothache, they will not reform abuses by making life more equitable for others until they too become victims. Former US President Richard Nixon, once commented, "A President *may ask* for reconciliation in the racial conflict that divides America ... but reconciliation can only come from the *hearts* of people.""Racism is an issue that white people must address first. Once done, its then the black man's responsibility to reciprocate. Both can't be done together."(Karsh)

Poet and activist James Baldwin concluded, "The power of the white world is threatened whenever a black man refuses to accept the white world's definitions. "To challenge the 'status quo' serves as an open invitation to question your loyalty and patriotism. Lecturer/ philosopher, Ralph Waldo Emerson (1803-1882) had this to say about patriotism : "When a whole nation is roaring Patriotism at the top of its voice, I am [eager] to explore the cleanness of its hands and the purity of its heart."

At the other end of the spectrum and equally troubling is this: Our age cries out for rights: civil rights, women's rights, LBGT rights, gun rights etc., and although these issues continue to provoke much debate, little attention is paid to the figures behind these movements. An unknown but perceptive writer observed: "One trouble with the world is that, so many people who stand up vigorously for their rights fall down miserably in their duties."

> *"Too many of our prejudices are like pyramids upside down. They rest on tiny, trivial incidents, but they spread upward and outward until they fill our minds." (William McChesney Martin)*

Problem Solving Tips:

- Try combining similar problems and deal with them as a group. As a first step, introduce solutions you know have worked before, and consider using them again.

- Understand how the laws of supply and demand work : If supply is low, it's probable prices may increase, and in turn demand will decrease (originating from those higher prices).Similarly, if supply is high, it's probable prices may drop (to 'interest' buyers) and in turn increase demand.(originating from the reduced or lower prices.) However, the basic principles of supply and demand are not restricted to financial matters only. For example, the lesser we feel loved, the greater our resentment toward others; a decrease in faith may result in an increase of doubt ;a decrease in poverty may result in an increase in crime.(i.e., increased opportunities to steal and defraud); and the more education you have, the less tolerant you may become.

- Everything is relative to another. Think "local," but consider the "bigger picture "too. For instance, in a big city, a person might be afraid to go into a park or use public transportation out of fear of getting assaulted. But, in a world of mass shootings and suicide bombings, living in an urban town is a much greater threat and risk to life than the regular street thug.

- Look at both sides of a question: A CFO asks a CEO, "What happens if we invest in developing our people and they leave us?" The CEO replies, "What if we don't and they stay with us to the end?" Always, consider the merits of either side.

- Many problems originate because one party or both want to absolve themselves of responsibility. Someone has to step up and make the first submissive move. From there, there's a chance the other may reciprocate. It's all about "small steps."

- It is true that life is unfair, but we all have to deal with it anyway. Whining rarely levels the playing field. So, commence earnest discussions soon after your anxieties have subsided.

- People are more receptive when they feel they are being taken seriously or when what they say matters. To facilitate this, say things like, "What do you think?" Show interest by helping another finish their thoughts: "By the way, you said there were two things. What was the second?"

- If you do not know what to do, then explore what you 'can do' *to make the situation worse.* Knowing what may aggravate a problem further may help guide you in a more productive direction.

- When pressed, you don't have to wait for approval from others as long as your decision is legal and grounded in good conscience, but avoid quick, sudden decisions. About 50% of the troubles in the world can be traced to saying 'yes' too quickly or 'no' not quickly enough.

- Film director David Mamet, suggested that when you devise a plot scene, you should ask yourself three important questions. He said, "Every scene should be able to answer three questions: *"Who wants what from whom? What happens if they don't get it? Why now?"* Consider asking yourself those same questions regarding your current predicament. The answers may prove illuminating.

"You never change things by fighting the existing reality. To change something build a new model that makes the existing model obsolete." (Buckminister Fuller)

Procrastination & Delay

ILLUSTRATION: (By inspirational author Orison Swett Marden, as described in the February 1997 issue of the magazine, Bits & Pieces:)

> *A lobster, when left high and dry among the rocks, has not instinct and energy enough to work his way back to the sea, but waits for the sea to come to him. If it does not come, he remains where he is and dies, although the slightest effort would enable him to reach the waves, which are perhaps within a yard of him. The world is full of human lobsters; Men stranded on the rocks of indecision and procrastination who, instead of putting forth their own energies are waiting for some grand billow of good fortune to set them afloat. (pg.23)*

The lazier the man, the more plans he has for tomorrow, and tomorrow always seems to end up as the busiest day of the year. "Hard work is really the accumulation of easy things you didn't do when you should have."(John Maxwell) If you are sent to bring something, bring it, but don't return with an explanation of why you couldn't. If you agree to do something, do it, and don't come back with reasons why you didn't. Author and poet Toba Beta pointed out, "There is a lie in between a promise and many excuses."Explanations about how you failed to accomplish something aren't worth a penny. Nobody wants to hear them, nor does anybody care for them.

Former US Secretary of State John Foster Dulles (1888-1959) made this intriguing observation: "The measure of success is not whether you have a tough problem to deal with, but whether it is the same problem you had last year."

Welsh poet and priest, George Herbert (1593-1633), offered this piece of advice, " Do not wait; the time will never be "just right. Start where you stand now, and work with whatever tools you may have at your command and better tools will be found as you go along."

ILLUSTRATION:

> *"A painfully shy man fell in love with a young woman. He had his doubts about her feelings for him and never spoke to her nor found the courage to engage her attention in any way. Eventually, he decided he would mail her a love letter every two weeks, and then after one year he would ask her out for a date. Faithfully, he followed his plan, and at the end of the year he had built up enough courage to ask her out, only to discover she just recently married the letter carrier."*

Don't wait for extraordinary opportunities. Seize common occasions and attempt to make them great. "Where the heart is willing, it will find a thousand ways; where it is unwilling, it will find a thousand excuses." (Arlen Price)."Putting off an easy thing makes it hard. Putting off a hard thing makes it impossible" (George C. Lorimer). In either case, what you're doing is just keeping up with yesterday.

> *Know that success usually comes to the one who acts first. Get into the habit of doing it now and doing it well!*

Purpose of Life

We sometimes act as though comfort and luxury were the chief requirements of life; *however, all that we need to make us happy is something to be enthusiastic about.* Our purpose is to make this life that has been bestowed upon us as meaningful as possible; to live in such a way that we may be proud of ourselves—to act so that some part of ourselves lives on.

Minister and author Norman Vincent Peale (1898–1993) had this to say about getting out of a rut: "Your mind gets bored and tired of doing nothing ... Get interested in something. Get absolutely enthralled in something. Get out of yourself! Be somebody! Do something ... the more you lose yourself in something bigger than yourself, the more energy you will have."

We all want to be happy, however in the pursuit of that happiness, we should also take time and consider the following:

- "Before we set our hearts too much upon anything, let us examine how happy those are, who already possess it." (Francois De La Rochefoucauld)
- "If money could buy happiness, there would be high-priced happiness stores on every block." (Hong & Giannakopoulos)
- "Happiness and intelligence are very rarely found in the same person." (William Feather)
- You can tell a lot about a man by the happiness of his wife and the respect given him by his children.
- "All crimes, all hatred and all wars can be reduced to unhappiness." (A. S. Neil)

- "Happiness isn't something you experience; it's something you remember." (Oscar Levant)
- "Happiness is a way station between too little and too much." (Channong Pollock)

In the world we live in, joy and suffering are inseparable. Some people may have more suffering than pleasure and vice versa, but no one has joy or suffering *all* the time. "The word 'happy' would lose its meaning if it were not balanced by sadness." (Carl Jung)

Because good times do not last forever, a person must appreciate those special moments and at the same time resolve to meet the challenges that difficulty presents. Ever notice the sunshine after a storm is often brighter and more pleasurable than the sunshine following a string of cloudless days? When dark clouds gather in the sky, we must prevail and wait for the bright day to return—for life is a continuous process of getting used to the things we hadn't expected. All of our lives are like this.

ILLUSTRATION: (Author Unknown)

Once a group of 500 people were attending a seminar. Suddenly the speaker stopped and decided to do a group activity. He started giving each person a balloon. Each person was then asked to write their name on it using a marker pen. Then all the balloons were collected and put in another room. The people were then let into that room and asked to find the balloon which had their name written on it within 5 minutes. Everyone was frantically searching for their name, colliding with each other, pushing around others and there was utter chaos.

At the end of 5 minutes no one could find their own balloon. Then, the speaker asked each person to randomly collect a balloon and give it to the person whose name was written on it. Within minutes everyone had their own balloon.

The speaker then began, "This is happening in our lives. Everyone is franti-

cally looking for happiness all around and not knowing where it is. Our happiness lies in the happiness of other people. Give them their happiness; you will get your own happiness."

If we are to make an impact on the future, we need to invest into and positively affect another person's life. The Buddha delivered the following message: "Thousands of candles can be lighted from a single candle, and the life of the single candle will not be shortened. Happiness never decreases by being shared."

"It's great to have two cars and a swimming pool ... but after you've made some money and acquired some things, and after the initial excitement has passed, life goes on, just as bewildering as it always was, and the great problems of life and death once again come to the fore." (Robert Heilbroner) Sooner or later, we re-emerge from our love affair with goods and luxury and realize that obtainment and consumption are not the answers. Keep a steady hand and savor what bounty may come your way. But do take chances. Why? Because when you get older and look back on your life, you'll regret the things you didn't do much more than the ones you did.

At the funeral of the late civil rights leader Martin Luther King Jr., a tape recording was played of a sermon he had given once in which he talked about the kind of things he wanted to be remembered for. This is a transcript of that recording:

> *"If any of you around when I have to meet my day, I don't want a long funeral. And if you get somebody to deliver the eulogy, tell him not to talk too long. Every now and then I wonder what I want him to say, tell him not to mention that I have a Nobel Peace Prize, that isn't important. Tell him not to mention that I have 300 or 400 other awards, that's not important. Tell him not to mention where I went to school.*

> *"I'd like somebody to mention that day that Martin Luther King Jr. tried to give his life serving others. I'd like for somebody to say that day that Martin Luther King Jr. tried to love somebody.*

"I want you to say that day that I've tried to be right on the walk with them. I want you to be able to say that day that I did try to feed the hungry. I want you to be able to say that day that I did try in my life to clothe all [the] naked. I want you to say on that day that I did try in my life to visit those who were in prison. And I want you to say that I tried to love and serve humanity.

"Yes, if you want to say that I was a drum major. Say that I was a drum major for justice. Say that I was a drum major for peace. I was a drum major for righteousness. And all of the other shallow things will not matter."

Author and columnist William Vaughan, (1915-1977) known too by the pseudonym Burton Hillis observed, "I'm not convinced that the world is in any worse shape than it ever was. It's just that in this age of almost instantaneous communication, we bear the weight of problems our forefathers only read about after they were solved."

Despite his pronouncement, we continue to wring our hands in despair, fold them in idleness and perhaps clench them in anger. Regardless how we decide to respond we should not be complicit nor further aggravate the chaos that surrounds us. As 1st century Latin scribe, Publilius Syrus noted. "He who helps the guilty, shares the crime."

About facing the challenges of tomorrow, Calvin Coolidge, (1872-1933), thirtieth president of the United States, advanced this thought, "Nothing in the world can take the place of persistence. Talent will not; nothing is more common than unsuccessful men with talent. Genius will not ... education will not; the world is full of educated derelicts. Persistence and determination alone are omnipotent. The slogan Press On! has solved, and always will solve, the problems of the human race."

"Here is the test to find whether your mission on Earth is finished: if you're alive, it isn't." (Richard Bach)

"The true meaning of life is to plant trees under whose shade you do not expect to sit." (Nelson Henderson)

Raising Your Kids

*A*ll generations of parents believe their kids are smarter than they are. But as parents, they sell themselves short. Parents have something children not only *need* but cannot probably get from anyone else. That thing is called "affection." All small kids want someone to hang onto, a sort of security blanket from which they could swing and return safely. Most importantly, they require someone to speak up on their behalf because they are incapable of representing themselves. They have not lived long enough to be wise about how the world works. There is no way kids can learn how to be made responsible for what is right and wrong without someone to teach them. That is what parents are there for.

Today, it isn't uncommon for a child of three or four years to pick up a foreign language when exposed to it without any formal teaching. Yet, we seem unaware that a child of the same age can also pick up our unconscious attitudes and prejudices without being taught ... oftentimes retaining them throughout their adult lives." In this context, we should heed the words of Scottish physician Andrew Combe who said, "What we desire our children to become, we must endeavor to be before them. "How often do we witness children embarrassing their parents in public, all because their parents failed to set the right example at home?

Despite the changes in the environment from one generation to another, there are some things about all children that transcend time. For instance, if you have three kids, it's possible that you may need to be at two separate school locations around the same time on the same day and every emergency in their lives will happen at the worst possible moment. Raising teenagers is like 'nailing Jell-O to a tree'. But despite these trivial annoyances, there are things that parents can control. Those doing it already know that raising children is a full-time job. What parents sometimes fail to realize is that when they spend *enough time* with their kids, they empower themselves to influence their offspring in ways they never thought possible. Recognize if you bungle raising your kids, it doesn't matter much else what you do.

A few noteworthy parenting tips and observations:

- "Two important things to teach a child: to do and to do without." (Marcelene Cox)
- "Talk to your children while they are eating; what you say will stay even after you are gone." (Native American saying)
- Children won't remember if the house was neat, but they'll remember if you read them stories.
- "Train a child the way he should go and when he is old enough, he will not depart from it." (Torah)
- The easy way to teach children the value of money, is to borrow from them.
- "The fault no child ever loses is the one he was most punished for." (Mignon Mclaughlin)
- "A child needs to be listened to and talked to at 3 and 4 and 5 years of age. Parents should not wait for the sophisticated conversation of a teenager." (Bob Keeshan)
- "If you want your children to improve, let them overhear the nice things you say about them, to others." (Haim Ginott)

ILLUSTRATION: (From The Best of Bits & Pieces, 1994).

"When [a] mother or father leaves [their] child at a day-care center, he or she kisses the palm of their child's hand and the child reciprocates. Then they both close their hands tightly and put the "kisses" in their pockets." If the little girl gets lonely during the day, she can put her hand into her pocket, take out the kiss and put it on her cheek. That makes things easier until one of her parents shows up at the end of the workday."

Faith columnist William D. Tammeus expressed this sentiment: "You don't really understand human nature unless you know why a child on a merry-go-round will wave at his parents every time around and why his parents will always wave back." With young kids, you don't have to list the reasons why they should not hit a younger brother or sister. Just say, "Don't hit!" Parents will enjoy much more success with their kids if they would consider doing the following:

- Say what they mean.
- Mean what they say.
- Do what they say they are going to do.
- But most important of all, "Live so that when your children think of fairness and integrity, they'll think of you." (H. Jackson Brown)

If you give fewer commands to your kids, they're more likely to listen to you when you do have something important to say to them. To illustrate this point, think about the sound of a siren coming from an emergency vehicle. At first, you pay attention to it and are intrigued by the developing events, but if these vehicles pass your location several times during the day, soon you begin to feel indifferent toward them, and although the siren sound does not disappear, it is nevertheless perceived as background noise, not worthy of your attention.

A leader in the field of human behavior and interpersonal relationships, David J. Lieberman in his 1999 video presentation, *Never be Lied to Again*, offers the following practical approach when dealing with a child who you suspect may be experimenting with drugs or alcohol.

> *"Instead of a mother saying to her son, "Jimmy are you using drugs?" she may consider saying, "Jimmy, I know about the drugs; Just promise me you won't use them again until you finish college." If Jimmy is really doing drugs, this method will clearly convey her feelings and also reaffirm her trust in her son's goodness. Despite all the bad and nasty things we do, there is still a deep need to feel accepted. If, however Jimmy is not experimenting with*

drugs, there would be a clear expression on his face suggesting, "What the heck are you talking about, Mom?"

Mothers who have two or more kids often get asked which of their children they like or care for the most. The usual and "safe" answer is almost always, "I love all my children the same." But here is a unique response from one such mother.

> *Researcher: "Do you think all your children deserve full, impartial love and attention of a mother?"*
> *Mom: "Of course, I do."*
> *Researcher: "Well, which of your children do you love the most?"*
> *Mom: "The one who is sick, until he gets well, and the one who's away, until he returns home safely."*

Chances are, you will be proud of your children if you give them a reason to be proud of you. It is hard for children to learn manners when they don't see any at home. Your children are not only heirs to your possessions, they are heirs to your values and character. When teaching smaller children you should focus on the following four-letter words: *duty, work, earn, give,* and *love.*

Decide on a secret code to non-verbally communicate with your children and discreetly let them know what's on your mind. Establish codes for: "Time to split; Let's grab a bite; I am not comfortable here; I'm proud of you." These signals may take the form of a tight hand squeeze, a cough, even a scratch on the forehead. These non-verbal messages could possibly save you unnecessary stress and time.

When disciplining your kids, let the punishment fit the crime. If a tanker spills six million barrels of oil, nothing much really happens, but if a child were to spill a glass of milk, he or she better look out. On the flip side, be mindful of this too: When responsible parenting declines, there will be a need for greater policing,(down the road) to counter it.

Kids sometimes say the darnedest things:

A mother promised her four-year old son that she'd be ready and dressed in about five minutes and after which they'll go out together. Worn out from waiting and not understanding why she was taking so long, he walked up to her and asked solemnly, "Mom, are minutes any longer now than they used to be?"

> *"Likely as not, the child you can do the least with will do the most to make you proud." (Mignon McLaughlin)*

Reading Between the Lines

───

*T*he differences in our relationships should not be as complicated as the maneuvers we invent to hide what's truly going on in our minds. Reading between the lines is a learned skill that allows one party in a conversation to deduce the real and hidden meaning of what is communicated or conveyed. To decipher the intended meaning would require one to have good listening skills, a compassionate attitude, and a genuine interest in the other person. With practice, the rewards can be tremendous.

When a series of choice statements are voiced, the questioner's word order may indicate that which is more important to him or her. We all have a tendency to express our preferences first. When asked, "Do you prefer iced tea or coffee?" You may safely deduce from the order presented, the one asking the question prefers iced tea. Words like "of course" or "well" or "we'll see" are used to hide what a person is truly thinking. Sometimes, these polite words are introduced to suspend further discussion of the current topic.

ILLUSTRATION:

"Of course, once you have some free time, would you look this over and let me know if there are any errors?" (What is truly being conveyed is "What I want is for you to tell me how much you appreciate me and the work I do.")

"Well, it was really nice meeting you." (Chances are, five minutes later they won't even remember your name.)

"About Saturday, we'll see what happens." (The truth is the speaker is not committed to the event on Saturday.)

Other examples of the hidden meaning behind words:

1. *Wife: "I am tired of cooking, so you'll have to settle for a lousy frozen dinner tonight."(In actuality, the wife wasn't as tired of cooking as she was of feeling undervalued.)*
   Husband: "Why don't I make us something, or perhaps we could go out and grab a bite?" (This is the response of a husband who knows his wife and is tactful too.)

2. *Wife: "How did you like the steak I fixed you?" (She is asking, "Did I please you?")*
   Husband: "Delicious, make it again soon!" (Compare this flattering response from the ordinary, "Oh, it was O.K.")

3. *Two people are living together. They are going to some function, and the woman says, "How does my dress look?" and the man decides to be honest and replies, "It looks awful; I've always hated that dress." The more appropriate response would have been, "Why don't you wear the blue one, as it is more becoming on you?" There is a good chance the woman may have just been looking for some reassurance about her appearance but received instead a verbal chastisement of her person. The man in this example was not only insensitive, but far too honest.*

Here are other statements and the hidden fears associated with them:

- "You don't love me" (coming from a spouse). Translation: *Do you?*

- "I hope he doesn't get into that fancy social club. It is full of crass materialistic rich snobs." Translation: *I will never be able to compete with those wives.*

- "She doesn't need a degree. I will love her as much without it." Translation: *Educated women threaten me.*

- "I don't think I should take a three-week vacation so close to month-end. It will be too much of a strain on the staff." Translation: *I don't want to leave the office. My boss may find out how unnecessary I really am.*

- "What's wrong?" (coming from a man). Translation: *What did I do wrong, this time?*

- "We need to talk about our relationship" (coming from a woman). Translation: *We need to talk about what YOU are doing wrong.*

- "Do you think she is pretty?" Translation: *Is she more attractive than me?*

- "I'm always honest, so if you don't want to hear the truth, then don't ask me." Translation: *I will say anything I want, even if it hurts your feelings.*

- "Can you taste this and let me know whether I need to add salt or anything else?" Translation: *Isn't this dish absolutely delicious?*

- "What do you do for a living?" Translation: *What is your economic standing in the community? I want to judge your value.*

- "I prefer a guy with a sense of humor." Translation: *I prefer a guy who can make me laugh, as long as he is also rich and good-looking.* (Joe Carter).

- "Deep down, he's a really good kid." Translation: *I can't bring myself to admit that my child is a mischievous brat.*

- "I don't care what anyone thinks." Translation: *I'm deeply insecure and constantly worry what everyone thinks about me.*

Examples of reading between the lines with teenagers:

- He or she is in a happy, cheerful mood and blushes at the mention of a certain name. (It's quite likely he or she is in love.)

- He or she mopes around, won't leave the bedroom, refuses to talk to anyone, and thinks boys or girls are a big waste of time. (It's likely he or she may have been dumped.)

- He or she says, "I'd rather walk—it's good exercise." (It is possible that he or she may be too embarrassed to be seen in your company.)

Beverly Mitchell, actress and country music singer, inferred the following: "I think the hardest part about being a teenager is dealing with other teenagers, the criticism, the ridicule, the gossip, and rumors." Parents can do little to shield their children from these hurtful experiences. However, what they can do is remind those under their care not to concern themselves much with those who do not like them, but instead they should continue to care for those who do.

"Men are motivated when they feel needed, while women are motivated when they feel cherished."(John Gray)

Reality Checklist

- Don't be too quick to offer unsolicited advice. If for instance, your dentist is rough and crude, don't complain to him that his assistant bruised your mouth while taking X-rays. That may be the least of his concerns.

- "When you teach your son, you teach your son's son." (The Talmud)

- A man who is vulgar before women, is a man who has troubles at home.

- Beware of the man who says, "I don't care about money." He will lie about other things too.

- "You can neither bluff nor impress anyone who isn't paying attention to you." (David Mamet)

- "The handsome gifts that fate and nature lend us, most often are the very ones that end us." (Geoffrey Chaucer)

- Everyone and everything loses its luster and appeal over time. When it's your time, adjust and accept it gracefully.

- "Every quarrel begins in nothing and ends in a struggle for supremacy." (Elbert Hubbard)

- "Never praise a sister to a sister, in the hope your compliments will reach the proper ears and prepare the way later for you. Sisters are women first and sisters afterwards; you will find that you do yourself harm." (Rudyard Kipling)

- Do not wholeheartedly trust anybody who says, "Trust me."

- "Sometimes we're so concerned about giving our children what we never had growing up, we neglect to give them what we did have growing up." (James C. Dobson)

- "Bitter people are not interested in what you say, but what you hide." (Shannon L. Adler)

- "You can't keep people from having bad opinions about you, but you can keep them from being true."(Unknown)

- "An object in possession seldom retains the same charm that it had in pursuit." (Pliny the Elder)

- "The best index to a person's character is how he treats people who can't do him any good and how he treats people who can't fight back." (Abigail Van Buren)

- When someone gives you free tickets, it is unwise to complain to them afterwards about the quality of the show.

- "Never make someone a priority, when all you are to them is an option." (Maya Angelou)

- "There are three faithful friends—an old wife, an old dog, and ready money." (Benjamin Franklin)

- "When a man tells you that he got rich through hard work, ask him, 'whose?'" (Don Marquis)

- "Children rarely want to know who their parents were before they were parents, and when age finally stirs their curiosity, there is no parent left to tell them." (Russell Baker)

- "People with bad consciences always fear the judgment of children." (Mary McCarthy)

- "We are judged by what we finish, not what we start." (Unknown)

- When a person tells you, "I'll think it over and let you know" —chances are, you already know.

- "Right is right, even if everyone is against it, and wrong is wrong, even if, everyone is for it." (William Penn)

- "The more secrets you have, the less happy you're going to be." (Naval Ravikant)

- "The older you get, the more you realize that kindness is synonymous with happiness." (Lionel Barrymore)

- "Never point a finger where you never lent a hand." (Robert Breault)

- "Do not complain about growing old. It is a privilege denied to many." (Mark Twain)

- People who tend to grumble because they didn't get what they wanted usually remain silent when they receive something not earned or deserved.

- Do good not for the credit you receive, but for the pain and suffering you relieve.

- "Test a servant while in the discharge of his duty, a relative in difficulty, a friend in adversity, and a wife in misfortune." (Chanakya)

- "You must never regret what might have been. The past 'that did not happen' is as hidden from us, as the future we cannot see."(Richard Martin Stern)

- There are no degrees of honesty; either you are honest or you are not. Everytime dishonesty wins, it gets harder to convince our kids that honesty is the best policy.

- Here is an important life equation you should never forget:
  Yearnings > Earnings = Trouble

- Say, you are sorry when you hurt someone.

- Don't be envious that the grass is greener on the other side. It is also harder to cut and maintain.

- "He has the right to criticize, who has the heart to help." (Abraham Lincoln)

- "Do not praise an undeserving man because of his riches." (Bias of Priene)

- Know that, respecting other people does not necessarily mean liking them. It means acknowledging that they too, have rights and interests.

- "Ninety-nine percent of the failures come from people who have the habit of making excuses." (George Washington Carver)

- If possible, leave everything a little better after you leave.

- Don't take things that aren't yours.

- "Don't tell your problems to people: eighty percent don't care; and the other twenty percent are glad you have them." (Lou Holtz)

- "Most people when they come to you for advice, come to have their own opinions strengthened, not corrected."(Henry Wheeler Shaw)

- "If you cannot see the bright side of life, polish the dull side." (Christina Dodd)

- "In company guard your tongue. In your family guard your temper. When alone guard your thoughts." (Matt Talbot)

- "Rare is the person who can weigh the faults of others without putting his thumb on the scales." (Bryon Langenfeld)

- "Instead of loving your enemies- treat your friends a little better." (E. W. Howe)

- Leisure is not enjoyed unless it has been earned.

- "Don't be reckless with other people's hearts, and don't put up with people [who] are reckless with yours." (Kurt Vonnegut).

- Live in such a way that those who know you but don't know God, will come to know God because they know you.

- He who takes a stand is often wrong, but he who fails to take a stand is always wrong.

- "The best inheritance a father can leave his children is a good example."(John Walter Bratton)

- The kindness planned for tomorrow doesn't count today.

- Say not to your neighbor, "Go, and come again tomorrow, and I'll give it to you then"—when you have it now." (Proverbs)

- "Let deeds correspond with words." (Platus)

- "Scorn those who follow virtue for her gifts."(The Gita,Ch #2)

- Never cry over spilled milk. Either find a use for it, or invent a better milk carton.

- If you want to be well-liked, never lie about yourself and be careful when telling the truth about others.

"The deeds you do may be the only sermon some persons will hear today." (St. Francis Assisi, (1181-1226)

Reflections of You

"*O*ther people are merely mirrors of you. You cannot love or hate something about another person unless it reflects something you love or hate about yourself." (Sheri Carter Scott). And Sandra Brossman, author of the book, "*The Power of Oneness*" echoed that same sentiment this way, "The traits we tend to dislike in others are usually the traits we do not like about ourselves. Our mission is to discover what we don't love and learn to love it. The people who get on our nerves the most, are among our greatest teachers."

Here are a few illustrative examples:

- If you are selfish, chances are you will be suspicious of others.

- If you are of a generous nature, maybe you'll be more trustful of others.

- If you are honest with yourself, you will not expect deceit from others.

- If you are inclined to be fair, you will not feel cheated by others.

- If you are financially shaky, you'll criticize others for their wealth.

- If you are quarrelsome, your first instinct will be to criticize.

- "If you speak insults, you'll hear them too." (Platus)

- If you are insecure about your weight, you are likely to call others fat.

- If you have a bad attitude, you will be more miserable when you see others happy.

- If you lack patience, you will be rude and unforgiving to those closest to you.

Non-fiction writer Michael E Gerber whom *Inc.* Magazine referred to as, "The world's # 1 Small Business Guru" said, "If your thinking is sloppy, your business will be sloppy. If you are disorganized, your business will be disorganized. If you are greedy, your employees will be greedy...giving you less and less of themselves and always asking for more."

Couples who've lived together for some time may unconsciously acquire each other's negative traits. Listen on to an argument between them and pay close attention to the accusations each levels against the other. It's not improbable, party A's accusation against party B is already a failing of party A.

It is always a good idea to consider when a derogatory remark is made against another that the accuser is not 'excused' from the same scrutiny. For example, greed generally masks itself as criticism. We tend to frown on those who are greedy or want more than they deserve, however we may secretly share those same aspirational qualities. Instead, we choose to criticize the behavior of those who are blatantly obvious. When we too are guilty of the same vice and charge another for theirs, we deflect attention away from our 'ugly' side and protect our good image ... i.e., better them than me.

Within this context scholar and critic H. L. Mencken, added "The man who boasts that he habitually tells the truth is simply a man with no respect for it. It is not a thing to be thrown about loosely, like small change; it is something to be cherished, hoarded, and disbursed only when absolutely necessary."

Now, a bit about them:

If you are still affected by what others think about you, consider these words by inspirational author, Shannon L. Adler.

> *"They will hate you if you are beautiful. They will hate you if you are successful. They will hate you if you are right. They will hate you if you are popular. They will hate you when you get attention. They will hate you when people in their life, like you. They will hate you if you worship a different ver-*

sion of their God. They will hate you if you are spiritual. They will hate you if you have courage. They will hate you if you have an opinion. They will hate you when people support you. They will hate you when they see you happy. Heck, they will hate you while they post prayers and religious quotes on Pinterest and Facebook. They just hate. However, remember this: They hate you because you represent something they feel they don't have. It really isn't about you. It is about the hatred they have for themselves. So smile today because there is something you are doing right that has a lot of people thinking about you."She added, "If you spend your time hoping someone will suffer the consequences for what they did to your heart, then you're allowing them to hurt you a second time in your mind."

People tend to think in opposites i.e., that which is not good must be bad and that which is bad cannot be good. Consider the following: When children are taught History, the first thing they want to know about every ruler is whether he is a "good king" or a "bad king'. At the movies, we root for the good guy and hope the bad guy gets what he or she deserves. What is most attractive in virile men is something feminine and what is most bewitching in feminine women is something masculine. A timid question will always receive a confident answer. We tend to weaken that which we exaggerate. Pain and pleasure like light and darkness, succeed each other.

British writer and speaker, Alan Watts, summed up the above thoughts by saying: "The only thing you need to know ... is this: that for every outside there is an inside and for every inside there is an outside, and although they are different, they go together."

> *"We flatter those we scarcely know. We please the fleeting guest and deal full many a thoughtless blow to those we love the best." (Ella Wheeler Wilcox)*

Relationships

*B*elow is an excerpt from the book *Rules for Aging* by author Roger Rosenblatt and described under the heading, "The Waitress Is Not Waiting for You." The thoughts expressed are familiar to most men and may also be a well-guarded secret.

"A man will be sitting in a coffee shop sipping his coffee ...and a comely waitress has brought him his food. She walks away. He looks up. Suddenly, it comes clear to him [that] all his life he has been seeking that waitress. He hears someone else call her Pam. All his life he has been seeking Pam. Tonight, he will ask her out to dinner and a movie. Tomorrow, they will drive to South Carolina to be married. The day after tomorrow, he will be sick of his drab and deadened life with Pam, but fortunately, will find himself in a coffee shop again where he is served by Chrissie[who has an inviting smile.]

Much time may be saved if he realizes that while he has been waiting for Pam, Pam has not been waiting for him. She has a drab and deadened life of her own, thanks to husband Lou, who after a year-long affair with Chrissie, is about to drop her for Janice [another waitress from downtown.] Pam has eyes for Marty, an insurance executive who has a [similarly] drab and deadened life with Darlene. Chrissie tired of men, hankers for Janice." (page # 96)

The trouble with most people is that when they do decide to change their lives, they attempt to change too many things all at once. If you want to facilitate change, it is better to proceed with small incremental steps. For example, if you want to become a lifeguard, first get used to walking barefoot on the sand, then get accustomed to spending most of the day in bright sunlight. After that, stay in shape and maintain your stamina.

In their SMI Audio presentation *Beyond Success and Failure*, Willard and Mergurite Beecher said, "No relationship is a more rugged test of self-reliance than marriage. People are brought up thinking that marriage is a box-full of goodies ... but the box is empty. There will never be anything in it unless each partner puts something in it. And if they do not want it to be empty, they must 'put in' a lot more than they 'take out' (just like a checking account). Marriage was not designed to make people happy. The empty marriage box has to be filled. Important basic ingredients may include: caring, individual responsibility and a common vision of the future."

Stephen R Covey wrote, "If there is a person you care about, the more you accept him or her *as he or she is*, the safer that person will feel. And in return, you lay the groundwork for that other person to reciprocate and be more accepting of you too. The idea to keep in mind is that what is important to the *one you care about*, must be treated as important by you as well. It is the basic framework for moving forward."

Many troubled marriages have their roots in an unsatisfied want or need. Let's say a wife or girlfriend wants her significant other to rub the soles of her feet. Despite all the suggestions and subtle clues, it does not happen. While the need does not go away, the disappointment associated with it festers like a sore. Partner A feels her need is so very obvious, and for it to remain unaddressed could only mean that Partner B doesn't care for her personal comfort. Soon, Partner A refuses to bring up the subject any longer, and the initial disappointment grows into secret resentment. Meanwhile Partner B, who is on the receiving end of the oftentimes disguised fury, reciprocates to defend his bruised feelings or honor. Of course, Partner A returns fire and the cycle repeats. When the fight reaches such levels, each and every transgression of the other gets free airtime. And the saddest thing is, neither is aware that a simple unrubbed foot was the source of all their troubles.

A world without secrets is impossible. So how does a person go about dealing with it? Couples often ask whether it is a good idea to come clean and disclose everything upfront with their partners knowing fully well that some secrets can be heavier than mountains. The answer to that question is an unequivocal "No." Some things should be left unsaid. However, if a secret must be kept, it should be kept as long as the motivation behind it is grounded in good intentions and no sound reason exists for disclosing it now. Nevertheless, when we decide to keep a matter secret, we should consider the words of author J.R R Tolkien. In the fictional story, 'The Hobbit', one of his characters declared: *"It does not do to leave a 'live' dragon out of your calculations, if you live near him."* In other words, no one has to remind you something is morally wrong. You already know because your conscience tells you. For our conscience to be clear, it can only be made so by its owner.

"The real problem of marriage is not whether John loves Mary, but 'What do we eat?' 'When do we eat?' 'How do we manage our life and those of our children?' 'Should we invest in this stock now or later?' Usually, we choose a partner who is compatible with our own degree of dependency."(Willard & Marguerite Beecher.) What that means is that the person who is not able to walk unassisted will invariably seek another who will allow him or her to hold on. It is possible that the person who is always giving time and money to the less fortunate may subconsciously be trying to reconcile the guilt he or she feels for having more than his or her equal share. Providing comfort to those who are less fortunate is a great conscience booster as it is an efficient way to address conflicts between the haves and the have nots. At a very early age, infants recognize that the act of crying brings adults into service. Babies also soon discover that smiling imprisons the attention of those who excite them.

As many of us approach the last third of our lives, the thought of our impending death may get a little extra play time in our conversations. If a couple were asked what they'll miss the most if their significant other were to pass away, the most common answer may be,"I think making decisions." Many of us — whether we own up to it or not — depend heavily upon our spouse's assistance when it involves spending money and investments for our children's future. Why is this so? Regardless how smart or blessed we are before marriage, it is never enough to prepare us for the role and responsibilities of marriage. The strengths and weaknesses each party brings to the relationship at the beginning, somehow get reversed as the relationship ages. Psychologist and TV personality, (Dr. Joyce Brothers, 1927-2013) may have alluded to this concept when she said, "The best of all possible marriages is a seesaw in which, first one, then the other partner is dominant." So, perhaps,the strong and dominant male figure at the start of a relationship may later assume a more docile role and utter words like, "Ok Hon, if you say so". The soft, hospitable feminine figure is now the ship's commander and in charge of all the major decisions. She is now the go-to person on how, why and when. Within this context, it is easier to understand why 'decision making' might become a problem for a surviving spouse, as original roles need to be relearned.

Three suggestions of how you may go about repairing a fractured relationship:

1. When there is a disagreement or difference of opinion about an emotionally charged issue, agree that no one can defend himself or herself until he or she is able to restate the other person's point of view to their satisfaction. Mimicking or making fun of the other person's words and actions will not do. The speaker must do his or her best to articulate the main point or concern of the listener, and only when the listener is satisfied can the process move forward. The idea is to get past the outward expressions of listening. As speaker and educator Stephen R. Covey observed, "Most people do not listen with the intent to understand; they listen with the intent to reply." Then, once the listener is satisfied with the answer(s) provided, roles are switched and the steps are repeated. Albert Einstein, (1879-1955) made this statement: "You do not really understand something unless you can explain it to your grandmother"—perhaps he was on the same track, way back then.

2. Let's say you are told you had one to six months left to live, but didn't know exactly when you'd die. That night, you have a dream about your funeral. You dream that your spouse is looking down at you in your coffin, and at that same moment you could mystically experi-

ence the same fond memory he or she is having about both of you during a happier time of your lives. You feel remorseful because when you were alive you could have been more caring and considerate, but you weren't. Moments later, you awaken from your slumber, and residual thoughts of your dream linger on. Wouldn't it be wonderful to show your gratitude in "real time" to the person responsible for creating that piece of happiness for you?

3. If you want to get in the last word in a quarrel or disagreement, consider splicing into the conversation the following few words, "I expect you're right." Saying so will ease some of the tension without actually conceding anything. (All you are actually doing is confirming what the other person already thinks.)

You will find, as you look back on your life, the moments that stand out the most are those unrehearsed moments that you've shared and given away to others. Do what you can, for whomever you can, with what you have, no matter where you are. When you make the world tolerable for others, you end up making the world bearable for yourself. Surely,wouldn't this be a finer way to live out the rest of your days?

"Most relationships become stronger after an argument that ends with a heartfelt apology." (Dr. Helen Eckman)

Responsibility

*T*hink of the chap who decides to carry the stool when the piano needs moving. And of those times when he chooses to remain silent, knowing fully well he's at fault, but allow others to take the blame. Later, he may reconcile his inner conflict by looking for a scapegoat (other people, objects, or circumstances) whom he rationalizes as the true culprit(s) and responsible for causing him to behave so badly.

The tendency to shirk responsibility occurs because there is little fear anything terrible will happen. If people were made to suffer the consequences of their words and actions, each would act a lot more responsibly. Take, for instance, a political candidate who pledges to lock up criminals and make the neighborhoods safe again, or the drug manufacturer who implies that by using its green pill, there's a chance you may be able to save your crumbling marriage and become happy again. When each fails to deliver as promised, nothing bad ever happens. It is as if they were never uttered. When people are *not* held accountable for their words or actions, it's no wonder they are able to remain in the background and have a "stooge "step forward and take the heat for them. Satirist Will Rogers (1879-1935) observed, "When drug dealers are caught, the truck drivers are sent to jail while the leaders open up bigger and better enterprises." A victim may feel that once he or she has come forward and stated a problem clearly, things are somewhat better because of it. But that is a false comfort. The hard work commences soon afterwards when someone else must step up and take responsibility for administering justice and making things right again. And by the way, there aren't many candidates out there clamoring for that job because that is not where the money is.

ILLUSTRATION:

A grandfather passing by his granddaughter's room one night spied her kneeling beside her bed and saying the letters of the alphabet out loud. He asked, "What are you doing, my dear?" She replied, "Grandpa, I am saying my prayers, but I am a bit sleepy, so I thought if I just say the letters out loud. God will hear them and put them together for me."

(With regard to the above story, we should be alert and recognize any opportunity to instill a true sense of responsibility in our kids.)

It is not our responsibility to make things better; it's our responsibility to do our best. Of course, there are limits to what one can do. And although we may not be able to make a relationship more intimate, nourishing, or durable, this should not prevent us from at least putting our best foot forward. Disappointed as we may be, our goal should always be to strive and leave no room for regret.

No matter how clearly you express to a teenager how much his or her drinking hurts you, he or she may continue to disappoint you. Or perhaps your partner's constant nagging or blaming makes you want to leave, and although you tell them, they continue anyway. A person with a bossy disposition for most of their life will not cease being bossy because he or she agrees to be more conciliatory. Change often is a gradual process, and each of us must decide how much of ourselves we are going to invest in seeing it through. Know that at the heart of all irresponsible behavior is self-centeredness. So, if things don't "sit well" with you, rather than churning them over and over in your mind, take responsibility for *your* feelings and *act on them*. Perhaps you may regret doing so afterwards, but if your personal safety is not jeopardized and your decision is firmly anchored on principles of fairness and compassion, now is a good time to be who you are. A fault many of us have, was given expression by former US First Lady, Eleanor Roosevelt. She made this remark: "It is not fair to ask of others what you are not willing to do yourself."

Reformist minister Theodore Parker (1810-1860), who inspired speeches made by Abraham Limcoln and Martin Luthur King wrote:

> *"Let us do our duty in our shop or our kitchen, in the market, the street, the office, the school, the home, just as faithfully as if we stood in the front rank of some great battle and knew that victory for mankind depended on our bravery, strength, and skill. When we do that, the humblest of us will be serving in that great army which achieves the welfare of the world"*

Mistakes and repairing them

As may occasionally happen, our well-intentioned gestures sometimes fail to produce the kind of results we expect. For example, when we flatter people we scarcely know, we may end up making them feel uncomfortable. When we go out of the way to please others, give money, or do them a favor, we may end up opening doors of continued service that we may come to regret. And, of course, there is always the reckless blow to the ones we love and care for. More often than not, our innocent words and actions are received differently and may end up causing sadness and distress to others.

Here is a suggested game plan to repair the damage you may have caused.

- Admit your failings, but more importantly, acknowledge the hurt, discomfort, and pain others may have experienced because of your actions or decisions. It is not about you anymore, but about how others feel about you now. You must concentrate on repairing the damage you've caused.

- Remember, the more honest you are about your faults, the more likely people will be accepting of you. Your initiatives should be to provoke a renewed sense of confidence in you. Not only was another hurt by your words or actions, but YOU were hurt too. You need to do things to make yourself feel better too!

- Going forward, your behavior must undergo some change. You must take an active role in re-enforcing the image that you want to protect.

If you continue to maintain old habits, you are only reinforcing the original disappointments. Do not just seek forgiveness by uttering the words "I'm sorry"; you should do something and earn back the trust you've forfeited.

- Of those "not so proud" moments of our lives that we excuse by saying, "Well, I was young and reckless at the time" or "I didn't know better", consider this. What is done is done, but we need to acknowledge and show remorse for the discomfort and pain we've caused others by our selfish behavior. Just as we want others to overlook our past transgressions, we should make an effort and acknowledge the 'hurt' we inflicted upon them too.(Karsh)

If you are successful in doing all of the above, keep the following four precepts in mind as you maneuver through tomorrow's challenges.

1. Know that trials and disappointments indirectly teach you lessons.
2. Have enough determination to finish what you've started or are doing and remain hopeful about tomorrow.
3. "What you don't see with your eyes, don't invent with your mouth." (Jewish proverb)
4. When you say: "I take full responsibility for my actions." Ask yourself, "If not you, then who?"

   "Anybody who gets away with something, will come back to get away with a little bit more." (Harold Schonberg)

Restaurant Dining Tips

*W*hen a food item is not in season but appears on the menu, that's a sure sign you're not getting your money's worth because chances are the food you're eating isn't the freshest or the healthiest—unless the establishment is a super high-end eatery and you know that fresh meat/produce is flown in regularly from 2,000 miles away. Neither is a long-list menu from a *small-sized* local restaurant a good alternative either. It usually means the fish or meat was purchased in bulk previously in a frozen, prepackaged state and kept under refrigeration until ordered by the restaurant's guest.

Always look for the health and hygiene certificate posted at most eatery entrances. The grade is issued by your local or state health department and should reflect the current year's rating. In New York City, each health code violation results in a point against the restaurant. The number of violations, counted as points, are symbolized by the letters A, B, or C. For instance, a restaurant with violations between 0–13 will get an A; those with 14–27 points will earn a B, and 28+ violations or points will earn a C. Those restaurants that receive an A after their initial inspection are re-inspected 12 months later; those with a B after their initial inspection are re-inspected six months later; those with a C are re-inspected four months later. When you see a restaurant with a "pending" grade, that confirms the restaurant did *not* receive an A certification. If the establishment passes a re-inspection, its "pending" grade is replaced with one that reflects its newly assigned letter score.

Don't worry about someone from the kitchen staff spitting in your food because there's usually a bunch of people working together, and once witnessed, that is a "fire-on-sight" offense. However, if you happen to see the cook standing outside the kitchen door looking like he is surveying the dining area, chances are he's been briefed by a co-worker, that a jerk is seated at one of the tables, and it may be you.

When you select a restaurant, choose a place that is usually busy and filled with local patrons. These two factors suggest the food is freshly prepared and tastes good too. Generally, restaurants whose seating arrangements and layouts appear confining tend to sell quality food and offer good service. Do inspect the eatery's washroom—if you are bold enough. Toilets must be clean, and water pipes should not be dripping or clogged. If the washroom has a foul odor or the floor looks like it hasn't been swept in a few days, chances are the kitchen environment may reflect those same hygienic standards.

Then there is the size of the menu. The less extensive it is, the more attention the kitchen personnel will have to lavish on the main and important dishes (a plus for any diner). Contrarily, when an order requires five to eight different menu items for consumption at the same time and sold at *a discounted price*, there is a good probability you may not be getting the freshest food. In a situation like this, ask yourself, "How could management want to prepare a bargain meal for me, pay the wages of two or more kitchen staff, serve it, take a cut in profit and still be happy?"

Consider this too: When the quality of service is poor, it might be a clue of management's perception of its patrons. How's that? Well, besides poor service, it is very likely the wages paid the staff may be on the low side too. What this all means is that the owner is more focused on making a quick profit than offering quality food and a pleasant dining experience. Bad or inefficient businesses tend to get worse over time, but the good ones usually get better, and you may find them still in operation more than a year later.

Don't patronize a restaurant where you have to pay top price for a dish that tastes average when you can buy a better tasting one at a smaller, less expensive eating establishment. Of course, a number of high-end restaurants offer superior service and sumptuous menus, but it is also equally true that people visit these exclusive eating taverns not so much for their culinary delights but for the visibility it affords them and of the opportunity to rub shoulders with people of the same or higher social standing.

Proper restaurant ventilation is an important dining consideration. Although the food may be dainty and affordable, an establishment with poor circulation issues can severely ruin the dining experience despite how great the bread or chicken tastes. Good, efficient air circulation boosts staff morale and guarantees the comfort of all present.

Words that suggest a high-calorie menu:

Loaded, stuffed, creamy, cheesy, gooey, smothered, melted, rich, and velvety.

Words that suggest healthier food options:

Roasted, baked, braised, broiled, poached, seasoned, seared, grilled, spiced, steamed, and sautéed.

"While eating a delicious food, remember the peasants and the workers who made this possible." (Mehmet Murat ildan)

Sadness & Despair

*P*eople feel depressed when they do not feel encouraged, are uncertain, or believe they are not good. Sometimes the depression may be brought on by something in our environment, e g., death in the family or perhaps a debilitating illness.

From a non-clinical perspective, if you want to feel less depressed or disappointed, try watching daytime talk shows. Author Perry Buffington, in his 1996 book, *Cheap Psychological Tricks*, wrote,

> *"Yes! watch a daytime talk show and note all the crazy [and] often depressing lives people are leading. Go ahead and rejoice when you see that your misfortunes are not as extensive as you think and be grateful that your life seems completely stable and extremely happy in comparison to others' situations. Watching a talk show can make you reevaluate your position in life and reassess all the positives in it. When you count your blessings, you may find that your attainments often exceed your expectations. The result is happiness." (pages #2&3)*

Turkish novelist and playwright Murat ildan said, "When you come across a problem in your life, do not always try to solve it; make a long jump like a kangaroo and continue your way! Sometimes problems must be leaped over without touching them!"

ILLUSTRATION:

A little boy was always verbally abused by his classmates. They would make derogatory remarks about how he looked, how he dressed, how he walked, and the meals his mom packed for him. His best friend asked him why he put up with it every time and did nothing about it. He then suggested his friend follow him to a secluded area at the back of the school, where an old trunk lay. The little boy opened the trunk and fished out a smelly old jacket. He threw it in the direction of his friend and suggested that he put it on. His friend, apparently disgusted by what just happened, flung the jacket back at him and said, "Are you crazy, I refuse to let that nasty thing touch my body." The little boy then looked directly at his friend and said, "As you refuse to put on this jacket, so to I refuse to accept the nasty things said about me."

To be aggrieved by offenses of others means you are physically "trying on" the rags they have thrown at you, but more important, remember, it is not what you are called, but what you answer to. Motivational speaker Les Brown conveyed that same thought this way: "Other people's opinion of you does not have to become your reality."

Much of the sadness we feel can be traced back to a failure or series of failures. "Failure can become a weight, or it can give you wings."(Sermon Central) When a baby transitions from crawling to walking, there are many falls; however, despite those failures, the baby is not discouraged but tries and tries again. The baby doesn't say, "Oh, I fell down and because it hurts, I'm not going to try again." And as adults, we too shouldn't give up so easily. When we incorporate the word "try" in our verbal exchanges, we deliberately and cunningly use them to hush the mental conflict we feel when our full commitment is absent or lacking.

Trying can also mean not 'wanting' to do something or not feeling committed enough to do it. Coach and motivational instructor Frankie Picasso illustrates this idea below.

"Sit on a chair and drop a pencil onto the floor. *Try* and pick up the pencil. Did you succeed in picking it up? If yes, *you did not try.* What? Ok, read on! Now, place the pencil back on the floor and try picking it up, but this time don't really attempt to pick it up. The result is the same, *you did not try.*" You see, whether you manage to pick up the pencil or leave it on the floor, you aren't *trying* to do either. It is your commitment and desire that decides the outcome, not your *trying*. Do not confuse trying with conscious effort.

Failure of some sort is usually the source and cause of our sadness, but despite that, failure can be "made right" again through focused effort. A deliberate and coordinated plan of action will have a positive effect on our mood because it will make us feel hopeful about a change in our current situation. If we are fortunate to witness the fruits of our implemented "plan of action," feelings of sadness will subside. Here is a visual example proposed by humorist Kin Hubbard (1868-1930) about reducing our discomfort by being more enterprising: "One of the simple but genuine pleasures in life is getting up in the morning and hurrying to a mousetrap you set the night before." Why so? It's probably because a deliberate plan of action heralds an expectation that brings with it the elimination of a worrisome concern. Anticipation is responsible for 98% of the pleasure(s) we feel, and since worry tends to siphon away our joy, why not engage in things that'll make us feel hopeful about tomorrow? As French emperor Napoleon Bonaparte wisely observed, "Men are moved by only two levers: fear and self-interest."

Described below is an old Hawaiian folklore tale:

> *Each child at birth is given a bowl of perfect light. As the child grows older, he becomes aware of that light and how it appears to flutter at times. He observes that when he becomes envious, jealous or angry, some of the light in the bowl flickers and then disappears. It is as if someone drops a small pebble into the bowl and blocks the light from escaping. If enough stones are dropped in, all the light rays eventually go away and the bowl of light becomes a bowl of stones. The stones do not grow, nor do they move. They just remain there. However, all is not lost. If, at any time, one tires of looking at a bowl of stones, all that needs to be done is to turn the bowl upside down, whereupon the stones will fall out, and the light shines again.*

English dramatist Shelagh Delaney,(1938-2011) made the following insightful observation about love. She said, "You need someone to love while you're looking for someone to love." Therefore, you shouldn't despair when you feel unloved because there are probably countless others—just like you—who feel the same way.

The following was excerpted from the September, 1995 issue of the magazine Bits & Pieces :

> *A psychiatrist once said the most useful concept he discovered when helping people turn their lives around was what he called his "four little words."*
>
> *The first two were If Only! "Many of my patients have spent their lives living in the past, anguishing about what they should have done in various situations. If only I had prepared better for that interview ...' 'If only I had expressed my true feelings to the boss ...' 'If only I had taken that accounting course.'" Wallowing in this sea of regret is a serious emotional drain. The antidote is simple. Eliminate those two words from your vocabulary. Substitute the words Next Time and tell yourself, "Next time, I'm going to be prepared ..." Next time, I'm going to speak out ..." Next time, I have a chance, I'm going to take that class.'"*

Practice this simple technique until it becomes a habit. Never rehash errors you've made ... Simply tell yourself. " Next Time, I'll do it differently." You'll find this closes the door on the matter, freeing you to devote your time and thoughts to the present and the future, instead of the past.

Some well-known historical personalities weren't discouraged by their failings or handicaps, but chose instead to "press-on" anyway. Here are a few and how they overcame their disabilities.

> Albert Einstein was four years old before he could speak and seven years before he could read. Walt Disney was fired by a newspaper editor because, according to the editor, Disney had no original, creative ideas or imagination. Isaac Newton did very poorly in grade school and was a bit absentminded when it came to small, mundane matters. Martin Luther King Jr. received a C+ in public speaking when he was in college. Pepsi Cola went bankrupt three times before meeting with success.

Of course, you may not attain the same level of notoriety as the aforementioned, but nothing prevents you from copying their resolve and desire to overcome. "Notice the difference between what happens when a man says, 'I have failed three times' and what happens when he says, 'I am a failure.'" (S. I. Hayakawa,1906-1992). And to the parent whose child is autistic and feels saddened or apprehensive about that child's future, he or she may well consider these comforting words by French dramatist, Molière (1622-1673) He observed,"The trees that are slow to grow, bear the best fruit."

We are seldom taught by others that pain is part of the living experience. For example, we only tell our teenage sons or daughters that a broken heart can be as painful as a broken arm, after the event has occurred. We should also make our kin aware that each person heals according to his or her timetable. Former US President Teddy Roosevelt made this remark, "Courage is not having the strength to go on; it is going on when you don't have the strength." Psychologist,Timothy Leary, (1920-1996) provided us with this shrewd observation. He concluded, "All suffering is caused by being in the wrong place. If you are unhappy where you are, Move." Sometimes walking away is a step forward.

~ *"The man with a toothache thinks everyone is happy whose teeth are sound." (George Bernard Shaw)*

Salesmanship

ILLUSTRATION (1)

A young salesperson was discussing a lost sale with his manager. The sales representative said, "It proves you can lead a horse to water, but you can't make him drink." The manager said, "Son, your job is not to make him drink ... it is to make him thirsty. Always remember, a customer is not an interruption of your work; he is the purpose of it. What makes a customer return and repurchase an item or service? Well, it's the value you have sold him. If you are successful in leaving a happy memory about your product or service with a customer, he or she is more likely to tell another of their good experience. You will in essence be selling satisfaction and ultimately guaranteeing yourself repeat business."

ILLUSTRATION (2)

A salesclerk in a candy store always had customers lined up waiting for her while the other sales clerks stood around with nothing to do. The store's owner noticed her popularity, and one day asked her what her secret was? She replied: "The others scoop up more than a pound of candy and then start taking away from the top, I always scoop up less than a pound and then add more above it."

ILLUSTRATION (3)

A hot sauce vendor who moves his head from side to side as he exclaims, "You don't want any hot sauce, do you?" guarantees that over 90% of the street traffic will say, "No." But, if he shakes his head up and down and says, "You do like hot sauce, don't you?" he is setting the stage for a more positive outcome. If he were to make a sale and then follow up with a statement like "one or two bottles for you?" he may even gain more and lose nothing in return.

People do not buy matches, they buy fires; they don't buy a new set of golf clubs, they buy a lower score; they don't buy a high-definition TV, they buy hours of entertainment. Never lose sight that you aren't selling things, you are selling benefits. Always phrase your statements so your listener will move toward a favorable buying decision. If you are a car salesperson don't telegraph the message, "I'm here to sell you a car." Consider what might happen if you were to say, "Hey! What do you say we take this beautiful machine out for a test drive?"

Sales statements you should avoid and express differently.

- Don't say, "You will never regret this!" Say instead, "I know you will love it."

- Don't say, "Is that all?" Say instead, "Is there anything else I can help with?"

- Don't say, "You won't consider buying this now, would you?" Say something like, "This certainly is a wonderful value, isn't it?"

- Don't say, "This car handles with ease." Say instead, "This car handles with fingertip ease" (get into the habit of using picture adjectives, i.e., turquoise-green, cushiony-soft, honey-sweet).

A common ploy when selling to others is to introduce artificial deadlines to facilitate the sale. For example, "This offer is for one day only and will be gone tomorrow." It's like the dentist urging a patient to invest in getting his tooth fixed today rather than waiting for tomorrow when things may get uglier and possibly more costly. Recognize that deadlines and generous discounts are introduced to move slow-moving merchandise and/or make room for newer inventory. These sales "gimmicks" are intended to spur an immediate buying decision. Overall, the seller seldom loses, and may even come out better than the buyer who thinks he got a great deal.

Have you ever walked into a store and, after the salesperson comes up to you and says, "Can I help you?" you can tell from the tone in which it is said that they really don't want to, but are only saying it to keep their job?

Good customer service these days is more an advertising slogan than a discharging of it. Author Craig Cochran pointed out that although most companies start out with a strong focus on customers, as the organization grows, management stops looking outward and becomes too preoccupied with internal processes. Bill Gates offered this insight, "Your most unhappy customers are your greatest source of learning." Within this context, if you're a seller, don't be too quick to discount them. Harvard Business School professor Theodore Levitt (1925-2006) contended, "The true purpose of a business is to create and keep a customer, not to make you money."

People have a tendency to deny they are imitators or followers of remarks made by others. They always seek to tell others they are different ...however that is seldom the case. A more successful selling approach may be to have your customer provide a 'yes' answer to either one or more of the following questions. Once you've aroused their curiosity or interest, you can direct the flow of the conversation in the direction you wish, but, make sure you can back up your claims.

- Would you like to increase profits 25%? (Or by whatever amount)
- How would you like to cut production costs in half?
- Want to double the number of your customers?
- How would you like to reduce your utility bills by 20%?
- You want a car with the best safety features and good mileage too, right?

~ *"If stock market experts were so expert, they would be buying stock, not selling advice." (Norman Ralph Augustine)*

Say It Ain't So!

- "A foundation is a large body of money surrounded by people who want some." (Dwight McDonald)

- If a girl tell you "let's stay friends," she won't call ever again. If you call, she won't answer.

- "Executive ability is deciding quickly and getting somebody else to do the work." (Earl Nightingale)

- "An extravagance is anything you buy that is of no earthly use to your wife." (Franklin P Jones)

- "Nobody talks more of free enterprise and competition and of the best man winning than the man who inherited his father's store or farm." (C. Wright Mills)

- "Behind every great fortune, there is a crime." (Honore de Belzac)

- "Guests, like fish, begin to smell after three days." (Benjamin Franklin)

- "The quickest way to make money on Wall Street is to take the most sophisticated product and try and sell it to the least sophisticated client." (Greg Smith)

- "Lawyers spend a great deal of their time shoveling smoke." (Oliver Wendell Holmes)

- "A woman will pay $1 for a $2 item she doesn't want. A man will pay $2, for a $1 item he does want."(Unknown)

- "Go the extra mile. It makes your boss look like a slacker" (Unknown)

- "It's better to be married to one with a good nature than one with a good physique." (Jacqueline M. Carmichael)

- "Wealth—any income that is at least $100 more a year than the income of one's wife's sister's husband." (H. L. Mencken)

- "Humility is a virtue all preach, none practice, and everybody is content to hear." (John Selden)

- "In conversation, the word 'many' usually means *a few* and 'a few' generally means *one*." (Karsh)

- In a fit of anger, when a person says,"I am not saying that", they are saying exactly that. Those words are introduced to limit damage.

- "Just as those who practice the same profession recognize each other instinctively, so do those who practice the same vice." (Marcel Proust)

- "When a lady says 'no,' she means 'perhaps.' When she says 'perhaps,' she means 'yes.' But when she says 'yes,' she is no lady." (Lord Denning)

- "Ten men in our country could buy the whole world, and ten million can't buy enough to eat." (Will Rogers)

- "Men mourn for what they have lost; women for what they ain't got."(Henry Wheeler Shaw)

- The people most preoccupied with titles and status are usually the least deserving of them.

- "Remember that giving any reason at all for refusing, you lay some foundation for a future request." (Sir Arthur Helps)

- "The possibility of a young man meeting a desirable and receptive young female increases by pyramidal progression when he is already in the company of (i) date, (ii) his wife, or (iii) a better looking and richer male friend." (Beifield's Principle)

- "There is nobody so irritating as somebody with less intelligence and more sense than we have." (Don Herold)

- A man's respect for law and order, exists in precise relationship to the size of his paycheck.

- "When a fellow says, 'It ain't the money but the principle of the thing,' it's the money." (Kin Hubbard)

- We spend thousands of dollars on time-saving devices and then work overtime to pay for them.

- "In matters of love, 'Assurances' are practically an announcement of their opposite." (Elias Canetti)

- "People will pay more to be entertained than to be educated." (Johnny Carson)

- "When anyone says they often think something, it means they've just thought of it now." (Michael Faryn)

- "Even with talent, it's who you meet at the right time that tips the scales." (Richard Briers)

- "A man who marries his mistress leaves a vacancy in that position." (Oscar Wilde)

- When someone says, "I don't have time," they're truly saying, "I don't want to."

- "You can know a person by the kind of desk he keeps. If the president of a company has a clean desk, then it must be the executive vice president who is doing all the work." (Harold S. Geneen)

- "People who talk about peace are very often the most quarrelsome." (Nancy Astor)

- "When a woman isn't beautiful, people always say, 'You have lovely eyes, you have lovely hair.'"(Anton Chekhov)

- "It's always the quiet ones who have the two dozen corpses in their basements." (Murphy's law)

- "Almost every wise saying has an opposite one, no less wise to balance it." (George Santayana)

- "Parents forgive their children least readily for the faults they themselves instilled in them." (Marie Von Ebner-Eschenbach).

- If a person says he won't argue with you, it means he won't listen to you after he has had his say.

- "Probably nothing in the world arouses more false hopes than the first four hours of a diet." (Dan Bennett)

- When you find a man usually at a bar drinking, it means he has no wife to go home to, or he already has one and chooses to stay away.

- We live in a world where "sin" is recognized only when we get caught.

- "One of the symptoms of an approaching nervous breakdown is the belief that one's work is terribly important." (Bertrand Russell)

- "Get all the fools on your side and you can be elected to anything." (Frank Dane)

- "Whoever is careless with the truth in small matters cannot be trusted with important matters." (Albert Einstein)

- "When confronted with two evils, a man will always choose the prettier." (Anonymous)

- "The people who are always hankering loudest for some golden yesteryear, usually drive new cars." (Russell Baker)

- "Whenever you hear a man speak of his love for his country, it is a sign that he expects to be paid for it." (H. L. Mencken)

- "Many come to bring their clothes to church rather than themselves." (Thomas Fuller)

- "Beauty without intelligence is like a hook without bait." (Jean B. P. Moliere)

- "When you see a man with a great deal of religion displayed in his shop window, you may depend upon it, he keeps a very small stock of it within." (Charles Spurgeon)

- A generation ago, most men finished a day's work and needed a rest, now they need to exercise before they can rest.

- *"The most difficult battles that you will fight in your life is that between your mind who knows the truth ...and your heart that refuse to accept it." (Paulo Coelho)*

Self—Esteem

*M*any of us have no problem berating ourselves when we mess up, but we allow our many (and more) little successes to go unnoticed. This kind of imbalance is sure to diminish our self-worth over time. In his book *100 Habits of Happy People*, David Niven wrote: "Television changes our view of the world and can encourage us to develop highly unrealistic and often damaging conclusions that serve to reduce our life satisfaction by up to 50%."

Social media, movies, blogs, realty TV shows, each in its own way make people wish they were someone else. American make-up artist, Kevyn Aucoin rightly observed, "Life is too short to spend hoping that the perfectly arched eyebrow or hottest new lip- shade will mask an ugly heart."The key to self-esteem is to know you have a place in this world and no one else can fill it the same way as you can.

Psychiatric studies have suggested that children who were raised but deprived of love at an early age (when they needed it the most), and children who were smothered with an overwhelming amount of affection, grow up emotionally immature. This is because, each child is continually looking for a comforting figurehead who he or she can turn to provide the relief his or her parent was unable to provide or overprovided. Later, the parent figure may take the form of a kindly teacher, an eloquent speaker, a religious manuscript, or political ideology. Whomever we choose to follow, we should structure our lifestyle changes so that they do not conflict with those of our friends, family, and neighbors ...because after all, we will still have to live comfortably among them. There isn't much use talking to God when you aren't on speaking terms with your neighbor.

We all retain conscious and unconscious memories of all those times when we were punished, wronged, or felt bad. The bad feelings we experienced were then inextricably linked with critical judgments made upon us by our parents and teachers (people we depended upon and respected). It's quite possible too we may have been told we were dull, lazy, or even fat, and because we had no way of verifying that truth, it was recorded as a judgment and stored deep within our mind. There is a good probability many of those judgment calls were made by persons charged with providing most of our basic needs. There would be no reason to disbelieve our caretaker's opinions and assessments of us.

ILLUSTRATION:

> A six-year-old boy had been rather naughty. Because his bedroom was next to his parents', it was not hard to occasionally overhear his father praying (his father was in the habit of praying out loud). The father sometimes would pray for his son and mention the bad things he'd done during the day. On one particular night, the boy's mother heard sobbing coming from his bedroom. She entered and asked him what was wrong. The heartbroken boy replied, "Daddy is forever telling God all the bad things I do and never any of the good things, I'm scared God will begin to hate me too."

Often, the feelings associated with our past weaknesses and failures resurface and get free air time in the present, while those of our successes and triumphs remain in exile in the background. In their book titled, *The Self-Esteem Companion*, authors Matthew McKay, Patrick Fanning, Carole Honeychurch & Catharine Sutker pointed out the following.

> "When you feel pain, all you can think about is now. At these times all you want to do is escape There is a technique you can use to combat the bad feelings—it's called anchoring. Anchoring helps you re-experience times when you felt confident and good about yourself. For instance, if you think of your grandmother's love and protection whenever you eat freshly made oatmeal cookies, [she always made them especially for you whenever you visited], then oatmeal cookies are an anchor for you. The cookies are the

stimulus and the feelings of love and safety are your consistent response."
(page 10)

At times when you feel un-loved or are disappointed, by reaching out for an oatmeal cookie you may be unconsciously attempting to "shoo away" those old ill feelings and replace them with more pleasant ones. What better way to feel better about yourself than fond thoughts of Grandma? After all, she already knew how best to warm your heart and make you feel loved. Here is how those authors propose you anchor your good feelings:

"Sit in a comfortable position in a place where you won't be disturbed. Close your eyes and relax your body. Go back in time and picture a moment when you felt successful or especially confident. Notice everything about that time: the sights, sounds, smells, and feelings. Visualize how you looked and how others looked. Hear the confidence in your voice; hear the praise of others. Let yourself feel the confidence and self-acceptance.[As best as you can, try and relive that moment as it was then, including the shadows.] When the images are clear enough to make you feel confident, touch your left wrist with your right hand [or vice-versa, if you are left-handed]. Touch it firmly, and in a particular spot that you can easily remember. You are anchoring your feelings to this [spot] on your wrist. Repeat this sequence with four other memories or fantasy scenes that are [associated] with feelings of worth and self-confidence and bound them by the same slight pressure on the wrist. "(page 11)

Later, when you need to fight a negative feeling, touch your wrist at the an-chored site and hopefully the gentle pressure may work like a catalyst con-necting you with one or more of the finer moments of your life.

Biologists have determined that the bumblebee, from an aerodynamic per-spective, should not be able to fly, but it does anyway. If someone expects little or nothing of himself/herself, it should be no surprise that others will too. If you act as if you are a nobody, the world will take you at your own value.

> *"Men heap together the mistakes of their lives and create a monster they call destiny."* (John Oliver Hobbes, 1867-1906)

Sharing

"*I*t is not what we "take up" but what we "give up" that makes us richer human beings." (Henry Ward Beecher) Often, the things we do for free are the most rewarding. "We are not cisterns made for hoarding, we are channels made for sharing." (Billy Graham)

Those who choose to be selfish and stingy often fail to see the ugliness associated with their actions. Maybe the following may help you conceptualize what it may feel like to be on the receiving end of stingy behavior.

Imagine you are the owner of a tree laden with sweet oranges that is located in the middle of a sun draped orchard. You decide to erect a barbed wire fence around it to prevent anyone from coming close, because it's your tree and you've decided to treat only yourself and family to its bounty. Do you think any of your neighbors and friends would applaud your mean-spiritedness? This is how others receive stingy behavior.

An anonymous writer once described selfishness as a useless wall that is unable to hold one's own joy in, [as it] keeps the world's joy out.

ILLUSTRATION:

One Saturday afternoon, a four-year old girl and her mom went to the movies and were waiting at the ticket line when the small child spied a dime lying on the floor. She stooped down, picked it up and offered it proudly to an elderly gentleman who happened to be standing next to her. Her mother was a bit startled by what her daughter did but chose not to react. The stranger asked inquisitively, "Kid, what do you think I could buy with a dime?" Without hesitation, she glowingly answered," Well... I can buy a wonderful wish with it at the wishing well...and so can you !"

Each day provides us with a new opportunity to offer and share part of our lives and its comforts with others. How can you bring a little more light and warmth into the world today?

Sharing means investing in the comfort of others. English writer and critic Charles Dickens (1812-1870) agreed with this conclusion when he said, "No one is useless in this world who lightens the burdens of another." Of more concern, however, is how long we generally wait before we deliver that relief. There is a Spanish proverb that goes: "He who gives when he is asked has waited too long." Author and pastor William A. Ward, elaborated further when he said, "Feeling gratitude and not expressing it... is like wrapping a present and not giving it."

 Sharing isn't restricted to physical exchanges only. It can also be an idea, a lesson shared, and even a sacrifice.

ILLUSTRATION: (From a Wikipedia article on Rosalie Ida Straus)

Rosalie Ida Straus (1849-1912) was an American homemaker and wife of the co-owner of the Macy's department store. She and her husband Isidor died on board the Titanic. On the night of the sinking, Isidor and Ida Straus were seen standing near Lifeboat No. 8 in the company of Mrs. Straus's maid, Ellen Bird. Although the officer in charge of the lifeboat was willing to allow the elderly couple and Miss Bird board the lifeboat, Isidor Straus refused to go while there were women and children still remaining on the ship. He urged his wife to board, but she refused, saying, "We have lived together for many years. Where you go, I go." Her words were witnessed by those already in Lifeboat No. 8, as well as others who were on the boat's deck at the time. Isidor and Ida were last seen standing arm in arm upon the deck.

When the survivors of the disaster arrived in New York City aboard the RMS Carpathia, many—including Ellen Bird—told reporters of Mrs. Straus's loyalty and fidelity to her husband. Isidor's body was eventually recovered, but Ida's wasn't.

Questions to ask yourself:

- Is someone happier because you passed their way today?
- Did you bring a smile to a haggard face because you chose not to turn the other way?
- Is someone's burden lighter because you provided a lift through a pleasant word, a heedful ear, or a trifling gift?

The following was written by an unknown author and based on Deuteronomy 6:10-12, the fifth book of the Old Testament: (NB: variations of this quote do appear). "We have all drank from wells we did not dig; We have been warmed by fires we did not build; We have sat in the shade of trees we did not plant; We are where we are because of what someone else did."

Isn't it fair therefore that we give something back in return? We are like provisional custodians with an obligation to manage what's given to us, so that it may be passed along better and stronger than when first received. There are no rules or regulations that dictate how those blessings may be returned, so why not be creative as you reciprocate and repay that gratitude?

Here is a thought-provoking observation by Genevan poet Jean Petit-Senn. He said, "At the end of life, we'll find that the only things we've lost were those we tried to keep."

When we give and share, we confirm our goodness before all. Maybe this idea is better symbolized in a statement made by author Michael Isenberg. He said, "When two men share an umbrella, both of them get wet!"

"Nobody has ever become poor by giving." (Anne Frank, 1929–1945)

So, You Are Not Beautiful

*M*ay our happiness be governed by our acceptance of how things are and not by our expectations of how they should be. There are things in life we can never change, and the world will not concern itself with making us happy. We should accept the hand dealt us and take full responsibility to ensure our own happiness.

"A pessimist, they say, sees a glass as being half empty; an optimist sees the same glass as half full. But a giving person sees a glass of water and starts looking for someone who might be thirsty." (G. Donald Gale)Whenever you begin to feel ugly, find someone (and there is always someone) who will appreciate your gesture(s) of friendship. There are many thirsty people all around us. In your own private way, quench their thirst with acts of kindness and consideration, and you may be surprised by the beauty of your existence.

Whining about life's unfairness does nothing to level the playing field. Train yourself to rise above it. Everything that happens to you can be classified under one or more of these three options. Identify yours and try and 'work' at it.

Learning experience, (i.e., to be more compassionate, but not too trusting).

Earning experience, (i.e., make more or less money without losing sight of your roots.)

Turning experience, (i.e., better health, home or career)

One surefire way to acquire beauty is to develop an "educated" heart. An educated heart is like passing the salt before it is asked. When you do someone a favor, do it in such a way that it is perceived as kindness executed in style. If you want to give a beggar a dollar to buy something to eat, ask him if he needs something to drink too. Don't be decorative kind—be substance kind. If a friend or family member is ill and you visit them at the hospital, do you make that your only visit, if their stay is an extended one? Get into the habit of giving that little "extra" in your interactions with others. Many of us are not really kind. When we do an act of kindness, chances are we are repaying a favor or hoping for one. If you make kindness a daily routine of your life, it will happen automatically and without deliberate thought. Kindness *performed with style* is a deep and more lasting form of beauty.

If there is a smile in your heart, your face will show it, but you must start it on its journey. Search the faces you meet and offer them your smile. Some may reject it, but you will never offend another by returning theirs. There is an African proverb that echoes this sentiment. "Judge not your beauty by the number of people who look at you, but rather by the number of people who smile at you."

Beauty advice and words of comfort for those who consider themselves unattractive:

♦ "Put even the plainest woman into a beautiful dress and unconsciously she will try to live up to it." (Lady Duff Gordon, 1863-1935)

♦ Although a rose may smell better than a tomato, that doesn't mean a rose can make a better stew. Your strengths are yours—use them.

♦ "Be who you are and say what you feel, because those who mind don't matter and those who matter don't mind." (Theodor Geisel)

♦ There are beautiful flowers that are scentless, as there are beautiful women who are unlovable.

♦ "There's a difference between beauty and charm. A beautiful woman is one *I* notice, but the charming woman is one who notices me." (John Erskine)

♦ "For attractive lips, speak words of kindness." (Sam Levenson)

♦ "The useful and the beautiful are never separated." (Periander)

♦ Plain women know more about men than beautiful women. (Katherine Hepburn)

- "No one can make you feel inferior without your consent." (Eleanor Roosevelt)

- "A woman whose smile is open and whose expression is glad has a kind of beauty no matter what she wears." (Anne Roiphe)

- "Outer beauty attracts, but inner beauty captivates." (Kate Angell)

- "It is amazing how complete is the delusion that beauty is goodness." (Leo Tolstoy)

- "The Lord prefers common-looking people. That is why he made so many of them." (Abraham Lincoln)

- "Beauty is the first present nature gives to women and the first it takes away." (George Brossin Mere)

- "Although beauty and modesty have been known to occur in the same woman, we'll probably have to settle for one or the other." (Gerald M Weinberg).

- "It is the beautiful bird which gets caged." (Chinese proverb)

- "A beautiful woman uses her lips for Truth, her voice for Kindness, her ears for Compassion, her hands for Charity and her heart for Love. For those who do not like her, she uses Prayer." (Unknown author.)

- "If the words you spoke appeared on your skin, would you still be beautiful?" (Auliq Ice)

"If you look back in history of the women who are most memorable and most stylish, they were never the followers of fashion. They were the ones who were unique in their style, breakers of the rules. They were authentic, genuine, original. They were not following the trends." (Nina Garcia)

"You should look into a mirror: if you look fine, do fine things; if you look ugly, correct by nobility, the defect of your nature." (Bias of Priene)

Speechmaking

W riter & Humorist, Mark Twain (1835–1910) said, "The brain is a superbly designed mechanism which functions even when you're asleep. The only time it fails to function, is when you stand up in front of a group to make a speech."

ILLUSTRATION:

In ancient Rome, a man was thrown into an arena full of lions. The lions were indeed hungry, since they had been deprived of food for some time. Sensing the imminent kill, the crowd in the arena cheered as the big cats circled their prey. The poor man bravely walked up to a lion who appeared to be the leader of the pack and whispered into his ear. The lion immediately backed away with its tail between its legs. It ran toward a corner, where it curled itself into a fetal position and remained crouched there with its face frozen with fright. The amazed emperor had no choice but to declare the man be freed. Being the ruler of the land, he was very curious how an ordinary man was able to conquer such a ferocious beast. Later that evening, the emperor requested the man be brought to his private chambers. After he was questioned, he confessed his secret to the emperor. He said, "Sire, I told the hungry lion, 'You can devour me if you want, but right after you are finished eating me, they are going to ask you to stand up and say a few words.'"

When preparing a speech, begin at the end. Write down what you will want the audience to do or think about after they've heard your speech. Keep these ideas in perspective as you prepare the rest of the speech.

If you've agreed to speak to an audience with which you are not familiar, ask for the names of a half dozen people who will be in the audience. Contact them and determine their backgrounds and expectations for the presentation. Thank them when you start your speech. Doing this type of homework will surely impress your audience.

In his 1988 book, The Complete Speaker's Handbook, author Bob Monkhouse offered the following tip. He wrote: "John Wade a master magician and persuasive speaker advises inexperienced speakers not to look at anyone directly during a speech. He warns that by doing this you seem to be speaking to this person alone and [may]embarrass them. He counsels speakers to move their gaze around the room, both near and far without fixing upon any one person. Occasionally, you can focus on someone's eyes briefly, but otherwise you should keep your look wide, taking in the whole room, and avoiding actual eye contact."(Page #44)

You shouldn't spend five minutes talking about something that can be expressed in one minute nor waste words describing and idea or concept with which everyone is already familiar. You must have something interesting to say.

ILLUSTRATION:

A pretentious bore was putting his audience to sleep with endless stories of his trip to Switzerland. At last, he concluded, "I stood high up on the mountain with a great chasm yawning before me." To which one irritated listener asked, "Was that chasm yawning before you got there?"

Our dogs and our kids recognize our tonal inflections and what we mean by them, so don't think your audience is any different. Make your closing sentences as loud and vibrant as the rest of your speech. Many speakers have a tendency to lower their intonation when they utter their last few words. From his many speaking experiences, author Bob Monkhouse concluded, "I have found a shrewdly chosen tale which combines truth with fun a far more popular finale than an exhortation to work harder or a declaration of some philosophical principle."

A few speechmaking tips and observations

1. The first lesson of speechmaking: stop speaking when you see your audience tapping their watches to make sure they are still working.

2. "A sure-fire formula for making a good speech; have a good beginning and a good ending... and keep them close together.(Author Unknown)

3. When making a speech, think how the word "banana" is spelled – you have got to know when to stop.

4. Your goal should always be to make people "feel" what you say is coming from your heart.

5. "A speech is like a woman's skirt: it needs to be long enough to cover the subject matter but short enough to hold the audience's attention." (Author Unknown)

6. "Speeches are a lot like steer horns—a point here, a point there, and a lot of bull in between." (Alfred E. Neuman)

7. "The mind can absorb no more than the seat can endure." (Morton Blackwell)

Franklin D. Roosevelt on how to give a speech: "Be sincere, be brief, be seated."

Spousal Cheat Sheet

*T*hirty-five percent of all people who use personal ads for dating are already married. A study has revealed that one in every three people in the United States has had at least one affair. Guilty people almost always make slipups, either physical or mental. Here are six clues described in Perry Buffington's book *Cheap Psychological Tricks* that may suggest probable infidelity. (Page # 169)

- **An uncharacteristic obsession with laundry chores.** The spouse having an affair may begin to wash his or her own clothes since washing destroys evidence like lipstick on the collar and any hints of unfamiliar perfume or aftershave.

- **A sudden switch in underwear style.** Men having a fling typically go from cotton to silk, or from boxers to bikinis, flaunting their newfound prowess. Women however, often shift from silky and lacy to cotton and flannel, going out of their way to avoid appearing sexy to their husbands.

- **An unexpected change in social circles.** Spouses having an affair seem to drop their old friends and begin to hang out with people you've never heard of.

- **A sharp drop in domestic sex drive.** After their daily dalliance, women lose interest in lovemaking at home. Men [experience virility issues] and just don't have the ability, after they have strutted their stuff.

- **New hobbies that exclude you.** All of a sudden, a spouse of fifteen years develops an interest in [fine]wines—or takes up fishing, hooks and lures. The new hobby constantly provides an excuse to stay away from home and from you!

- **A sense that your children suspect trouble between mom and dad.** It may be true that the innocent spouse is always the last to know: if you watch your children, you may pick up clues that they know something is wrong, long before the truth comes out."

The following is inspirational author and columnist Shannon L Adler's excellent observation of how we go about lying to ourselves and others. "A deceitful man will go as far as to trample all over a woman's reputation and spirit in order to prove to his ex-love that he was faithful. The irony is, he is still in love with his ex, and the new woman in his life doesn't even realize it."

The man who brings home a young and attractive female with appealing physical attributes is always fearful of other men. Thoughts like, "What if he were" or "Would she consider" are always under contemplation. Before committing to such a relationship, a man must carefully decide whether he is able to balance the worries of jealousy with the pleasures of possession.

"What men desire is a virgin who is a whore."(Edward Dahlberg). Some may construe this statement as true, sexist, or somewhere in between but playwright and novelist William Somerset Maugham offered this sober thought, "My own belief is that there is hardly anyone whose sexual life, if it were broadcast, would not fill the world at large with surprise and horror."

Do you agree with these four observations?

1. "When a husband brings his wife flowers for no reason, there's a reason."(Molly McGee)

2. "The woman who deceives her husband makes her lover swear never to be unfaithful to her." (Chinese proverb)

3. "A jealous man always finds more than he is looking for." (Madeline de Scudery)

4. "He who flatters you more than you desire either has already deceived you or wishes to deceive you." (Italian proverb)

~ *"Do not, that which you have to keep secret."(Periander)*

Success

The following is a poem by nineteenth-century lecturer and theologian Ralph Waldo Emerson (1803-1882), titled "To Laugh Often and Much"

> To laugh often and much;
>
> To win the respect of intelligent people and the affection of children;
>
> To earn the appreciation of honest critics and endure the betrayal of false friends;
>
> To appreciate beauty;
>
> To find the best in others;
>
> To leave the world a bit better, whether by a healthy child, a garden patch or a redeemed social condition;
>
> To know even one life has breathed easier because you have lived.
>
> This is to have succeeded.

Too often, success and winning have caused some of us to become more thoughtless, arrogant, and even cruel. This is because our desire to conquer and dominate invariably invites and promotes those attitudes.

Ask any successful person, and most will tell you they had a person who believed in them i.e., a teacher, a friend, a parent, a guardian, a sister, or grandmother. It only takes one person, and it really doesn't matter who it is.

Successful people shun ambiguity. Those who do not keep promises or avoid duty rely on ambiguity to keep them afloat one more day. Ambiguity's purpose is to neutralize a statement and avoid a commitment: "We didn't fail, we anticipate success." Successful people already know their reputation and honor is what brings them to the table and have no need for fluff or double-talk.

Success can be viewed as a victory for having made a difference in the lives of those with whom we share a common bond. But beware, it matters not if you are a big success at work, if your family considers you a failure at home.

The recipe for success and the recipe for a nervous breakdown is the same. So how do you tell in which direction you're headed? It's quite simple actually. When you are steadfastly following the advice you've given to others, you are on the road to success.

Some other reflections on the subject of success:

- "The worst part of success is trying to find someone who is happy for you." (Bette Midler)

- "Formula for success: Under-promise and over-deliver." (Tom Peters)

- "Success seems to be largely a matter of hanging on after others have let go." (William Feather)

- "Success is how high you bounce after you hit bottom." (General George S. Patton, 1885-1945)

- "Perseverance is a great element of success. If you only knock long enough and loud enough at the gate, you are sure to wake up somebody." (H. W. Longfellow)

- "Regardless of how you feel inside, always try to look like a winner on the outside." (Arthur Ashe)

- A $300 suit does not go well with a facial expression that is worth 10¢.

- A successful man is usually an average man who had an opportunity ... and took it.

- "Work hard in silence. Let success make the noise." (Author Unknown)

Many of us are already familiar with the **Golden Rule,** *Treat others as you would like others to treat you.* But many are not too familiar with the Silver and Iron rules. They are described below:

The Silver Rule of Success: *Do for yourself, but not less than you would do for others.*

The Iron Rule of Success: *Do not do for others what they can do for themselves.*

Be honorable on the inside and the outside because as we already know, when we change the label outside the bottle, we do not alter the contents inside.Former Prime Minister of India, Indira Gandhi (1917-1984) said her grandfather told her, "There are two kinds of people, those who do the work and those who take the credit. Try to be in the first group; there is less competition there." And American President Harry S. Truman offered a similar observation. He said, "It is amazing what you can accomplish if you do not care who gets the credit."

One of the worst uses that can be made of success is to boast about it.

ILLUSTRATION:

> *"After eating an entire bull, a mountain lion felt so good that he started roaring. He kept it up until a hunter came along and shot him. The moral: when you're full of bull, keep your mouth shut." (Texas Bix Bender: Don't Squat With Yer Spurs On!)*

> *"Aim for service, and success will follow." (Albert Schweitzer)*

Tact when Dealing with Sellers

- When asking for a better price, it is best to say, "Can you do a little better?" (Talk to the person in charge, but not within earshot of other customers).

- When negotiating, never make the first offer. Doing so allows the seller to take control of the bargaining process. Start by asking about current bargains or sale offerings, then negotiate upward from there. Do not make the mistake of immediately counteroffering. You do not want the seller to feel that you didn't take his original proposal seriously. Pause and wait a moment, repeat the seller's price to show you are listening, then say, "So you want one hundred dollars for this item? Let me think about it for a minute."

- If possible, invoke a higher authority. For instance say, "I do like the color and texture of that rug, but my wife doesn't want me to spend so much money" (or my financial planner says I can't afford a new car right now or my mechanic thinks I should consider vehicle model XXX instead).

- If you notice a defect in an item, keep it to yourself until you negotiate the best price possible. As the deal nears completion, point out the flaw (or mention a trade-in) and bargain down the sale price a bit more.

- Don't challenge the seller by saying, "I will only give you twenty dollars for this. Do we have a deal or not?" Say instead," I do like this phone case for my grandson, but he is a little picky. Would you consider taking twenty dollars for it?"

- Assume you are looking for a provider in your neighborhood to perform a service, but you are unsure of the going rate for that service. Depending on who you approach, there could be big differences in the quotes you receive. So, how do you tell which quote is fair and who is probably taking you for a ride? Here is a suggestion. Let's say you are in the market for a new pair of prescription eyeglasses. First, you go to a discount provider and obtain a quote for your prescription including the type of lens and features you want. Take that price and add 20% on top of it (i.e., if you received a quote of $99, then multiply $99 x 1.2). In this example, the result of $118. 80.That should be an approximate estimate of the 'ball-park' amount you should consider paying for the desired product or service.

- When confronted with a salesperson who pressures you into making an immediate buying decision, say something like, "I like to do business with sellers who are transparent and fair. If you are transparent, your price should be within an acceptable market range. And if you are fair, I will want to stick around and talk with you some more. So, what will it be? Can we explore whether there's a chance we could do business, or should I head in the opposite direction?"

- Answering harsh criticism with a defiant response may seem justified when it happens unexpectedly, but seldom does it produce the kind of end-result you desire. It would be better if you could pause a moment and then come up with a more graceful response. By doing that, you can still make your point without making an enemy.

ILLUSTRATION:

Once, a man in a department store bought a cigar and attempted to light it when he was informed that smoking was not permitted in the store. "What nonsense! You sell cigars but you prohibit smoking?" he barked. The sales-

clerk politely replied, "Well, sir, we also sell bath towels, but we don't expect you to shower here too."

From a surface level, it's not easy to tell differences in quality. Most sellers tend to gravitate around a set price range, but if another sells far below the market value without justification, you should be wary. Why? Well, as art critic John Ruskin (1819-1900) put it, "The bitterness of poor quality remains long after the sweetness of a discounted price is forgotten."

A word of caution about those no-cost, 10-30 day free-trial offers that guarantee your 'good faith' deposit is fully refundable, if you decline the offer within the stipulated grace period. Yes, they are almost always refundable however there is a disconnect between the flow of funds out of your account and back into it. Withdrawals from your account are often immediate (by the time you hang up, payment is already debited from your account). However, it is seldom so when you request a refund. It isn't unusual to wait 3-10 days after your refund request is fully processed and before your money is returned to you. The larger the company, the greater the probability this is likely to happen.

There is a Chinese proverb that goes: " He who hasn't a penny sees bargains everywhere." A bargain represents an item priced so incredibly low that after you've purchased it and you later find a defect with it, you decide not to return it. Either you 'hold-on' to it or re-gift it, because it is such an awesome one in a lifetime deal. "It is *not* cheaper things that we want to possess, but expensive things that are on sale for a whole lot less."(Rolf White). And Kin Hubbard captured the true essence of that observation this way, "A bargain... anything a customer thinks a store is losing money on."

"Tact is the ability to give a person an injection without him or her feeling the needle. It is all about knowing how far to go without going too far."

Technology's Drawbacks

istorian and social critic, Bertrand Russell (1872-1970, declared: "There will still be things that machines cannot do. They will not produce great art or great literature or great philosophy; they will not be able to discover the secret springs of happiness in the human heart; they will know nothing of love and friendship." And Canadian author and artist, Douglas Coupland offered this corresponding remark, "Before machines the only form of entertainment people really had was relationships."

Electronic mail, YouTube videos, and cell technology have long diluted the travel experience by pre-revealing all the secrets and possible adventures associated with faraway lands. There is little left to the imagination. Rustic hideouts are described in such finite detail, that it robs us of the thrill of discovery. We cease to wonder and now only expect.

Breakaway technological advancements continue to feed our curiosity. Movie producer and director Steven Spielberg advanced the following thought: "Technology can be our best friend, and technology can also be the biggest party pooper of our lives. It interrupts our own story, it interrupts our ability to have a thought or a daydream, to imagine something wonderful, because we're too busy bridging the walk from the cafeteria back to the office on the cell phone." The sad truth about social media is that it has evolved so rapidly in such a short time, that it enables the majority of the *population with little to contribute* to interface with those who are trying to impress them that behind their words, photos, and videos, very important things are taking place. Because of social media, we are now able to experience the joys of life through other people; we take our cues from them; we borrow their happy moments; we dress like them and eat what they eat. At any given time of the day, our ears are tuned to the plinging sound coming from a small glass screen with the latest update. Before we know it, we re-forward the sender's thoughts and opinions to others or hijack the ideas received and promote them as our own. Writer Rita Mae Browne observed,"… Our technologies are driving us apart, only connecting us in terms of information, not in terms of emotions."

Already, our vision of the future is influenced by the promise that technological advancements will transform our lives in unimaginable ways. Gears, circuits, and buttons control and direct almost all of our home and work life. We live in an age where chips and robotics think and do the work for us. Writer Stewart Brand commented, "Once a new technology rolls over you, if you're not part of the steamroller, you're part of the road." Some may feel threatened by that and wonder when the day may come when we'll regret giving up so much authority. But not to worry. That day will not come soon because as playwright and critic, Karel Capek put it, "Man will never be enslaved by machinery, if the man tending the machine be paid enough."

The more choices we have, the less satisfied we are with each. This is because there is always a newer and more advanced updates coming out soon that will "tickle" us in a way like we've never been tickled before. The high-tech gadgetry in today's modern cars are truly astounding, but never forget they are also plagued by the same traffic jams, speed limits, scrapes, and scratches as a twenty-year-old model. Because of voice recognition technology, we're heading in the direction where fingers and arms may no longer be called into service to complete mundane tasks. Data mined and collected about our online shopping behavior is already being used to gauge our sensitivity to price. If that data suggest we 're not likely to seek the services of another provider, then it's likely we may be a prime candidate for an up-charge or higher premium.

"What used to work were effort, education, and saving money. The 'Heartland' was where Americans made things … and prospered. Now, the money is made by people who never break a sweat. In the seventies, stead-fastness and diligence were the motivating factors behind industry. What pays off now? Speculation, knowing somebody in power, or getting a special break from the Feds. The route to success has detoured from the Heartland and moved now toward Washington and Wall Street." (Bill Bonner).

As the days go by, we anxiously await the newest gadget or upgrade to simplify our life further. Decades ago, we marveled at the expertise of surgeon Christian Barnard who successfully completed the first ever heart transplant. Today, we are no longer intrigued by such things. Instead, We're becoming more and more willing to sacrifice privacy for convenience. Our world today is a sea of information with a seemingly endless array of choices, when all we need is a little bit of intelligent direction.

Light Trivia

"Had there been a computer in 1879, it would have predicted that by now there would be so many horse-drawn vehicles that it would have been impossible to clear up all the manure everywhere." (William Kapp)

"The three "R's" -Reading, 'Riting' and 'Rithmetic' are no longer enough. We must add the three "C" – Computing, Critical thinking, Capacity for change" (Fred Gluck)

"I think God's going to come down and pull civilization over for speeding." (Steven Wright)

"It is only when they go wrong, that machines remind you how powerful they are." (Clive James)

Terrorism

Terrorism is demanding the undoable, using hooded garments to execute untenable plans by slaughtering innocents.

ILLUSTRATION by Glenn Van Ekeren from his book "Words for all Occasions."

> *"An elderly woman was standing on a street corner, too scared to cross because there was no traffic signal to control the flow of vehicles. A man joined her on the street corner and asked if he could walk across with her. "Oh, yes!" she replied, grabbing his strong arm for direction and support. They proceeded across the street in a haphazard fashion. Cars were honking, people screaming and the screech of tires filled their ears. Finally [upon] reaching the other side, the elderly lady exclaimed in anger, "You almost got us killed. You walk as if you can't see the nose on your face.""I can't, the man replied, "I'm blind. That's why I asked if I could walk with you." Page # 185)*

So it is too with those who recruit others to fight their battles for them. The recruiters are as "un-seeing" as those whom they enlist. Each side is looking to the other for support and sometimes guidance. It is not too difficult to convince others to enlist in rebellion when there is full and complete trust in the leader's cause. Sixteenth-century historian and philosopher Voltaire observed, "Those who can make you believe absurdities can make you commit atrocities." And incidentally, those very same leaders are always conspicuously absent during live combat.

Jewish diary keeper and Holocaust victim, Anne Frank (1929-1945) made this lucid statement : "I don't believe that the big men, the politicians and capitalists alone, are guilty of war. Oh no, the little man is just as guilty, otherwise the peoples of the world would have risen in revolt a long time ago!"

No other factor in history has produced as many wars as the rallying cry in the name of patriotism. World War II Nazi leader Hermann Goering (1893-1946) declared:

> "Why of course, the people don't want war. Why should some poor slob on a farm want to risk his life in a war when the best he can get out of it is to come back to his farm in one piece? Naturally, the common people don't want war: neither in Russia, nor in England, [and] for that matter in Germany. That is understood. But after all, it is the leaders of a country who determine the policy and it is always a simple matter to drag the people along, whether it is a democracy or fascist or parliament. Voice or no voice, the people can always be brought to the bidding of the leaders. That is easy. All you have to do is tell them they are being attacked and denounce the peace makers for lack of patriotism and exposing the country to danger. It works the same in any country."

Difference of opinions about what is right and acceptable have always fanned the flames leading up to chaos and eventually war. Former US President Abraham Lincoln (1809-1865), concisely captured the rites of passage that precipitate a conflict in the following observation. "The shepherd drives the wolf from the sheep's throat, for which the sheep thanks the shepherd as his liberator, while the wolf denounces him for the same act as the destroyer of liberty. Plainly, the sheep and the wolf are not agreed upon a definition of liberty."

Who better to know about the weapon called propaganda than Nazi leader Adolph Hitler. He proclaimed that for propaganda to be popular, "it has to accommodate itself to the comprehension of the least intelligent of those whom it seeks to reach." Conversely, a guarded secret of those who use propaganda to push their initiatives was expressed by diplomat Abba Eban (1915–2002), who said, "Propaganda is the art of persuading others of what you don't believe yourself."

The tyrant will always find a pretext for his tyranny, and it is useless for the innocent to seek justice through reasoning, especially when the oppressor is bent on being unjust. There will always be tyrants and the degree of their atrocity on the innocent depends on how well they are deterred before they engage in their monstrosities. If their brutality is left unchecked, sooner or later there will be a war. According to an old German proverb, "A great war leaves a country with three armies—an army of cripples, an army of mourners, and an army of thieves." Terrorism of today is no different than the terrorism of old—the only difference is the choice of weapons. War does not and cannot prove which side is right, only which side is stronger. Former US General George S. Patton astutely pointed out, "The object of war is not to die for your country but to make the other bastard die for his."

The traditional dictionary meaning of the word 'martyr' is someone willing to die for what he believes in. Osama bin Laden was quoted as saying, "I'm fighting so I can die a martyr and go to heaven to meet God, as our fight now is against the Americans." And Indian nationalist leader, Mahatma Gandhi defiantly said, "They may torture my body, break my bones, even kill me ... and then, they will have my dead body but not my obedience." So, how do we reconcile the clear disparity in motives between these two men? Perhaps, we should consider the words by psychoanalyst Wilhelm Stekel (1868-1940). He hypothesized, "The mark of the immature man is that he wants to die nobly for a cause, while the mark of the mature man is that he wants to live humbly for one."

Our sense of who we are as a community is often defined by the hardships we've endured together. Many of us feel intimidated when the subject of reconciliation comes up because it brings with it additional responsibility. However, we should resist those fears and take a chance and embrace that which we know to be right and fair. Physicist, Albert Einstein once remarked, "The world is a dangerous place to live, not because of the people who are evil, but because of the people who don't do anything about it."

> *"Throughout history, it has been the inaction of those who could have acted; the indifference of those who should have known better; the silence of the voice of justice when it mattered most; that has made it possible for evil to triumph." (Haile Selassie, 1892-1975).*

This & That

Home sweet home:

We may hesitate inviting friends or family over because our house is a mess or perhaps our furniture is old and shabby, but we should not forget the reason friends come to our house. It is not because we live in a fabulous home but because they like us and enjoy our company. Every house is cozy and attractive when it's filled with friends delighting in each other. The following was taken from the Hindu book of good counsel, the Hitopadesa: "Flee from the house that has false friends, impertinent servants and a bawling wife."

Life is painful:

If we don't accept life as it is, we'll keep wishing for something else and never get it for we'll keep complaining and whining about the way things are or how they should be. Renowned critic George Bernard Shaw said, "The world will not devote itself to making you happy." You should recognize the depth of that statement and take charge of your life. Consider also what philosopher and writer Aldous Huxley observed: "Experience is not defined by what happens to a man during his life, but more so what a man does with what happens to him."

Persuading parents on controversial issues:

First, just as your life is your own to live, so too your parents' lives are their own. Your parents naturally love you and want you to be happy. If you really need to change their minds, don't do it through words—do it by showing them how happy your way of thinking makes you feel. Chances are they'll eventually come around. After all, isn't your happiness what matters to them most?

Rejection:

Rejection prepares us for change. It forces us to do or approach things differently. Rejection makes us stronger (physically and intellectually), and we emerge "fuller" because of it. Rejection never leaves us; it simply moves from the conscious to the unconscious, where it settles and assists us in visualizing things from a different and clearer perspective. So, the next time you are rejected, don't become too disappointed because processes are already at work and preparing you for a new adventure.

The real troublemakers:

"How much of the world's trouble is caused by guys with hammers or wrenches in their hands? How many bakers cause depression? How many masons are mass-murderers? And how many steelworkers, cabinet makers, or delivery men cause mass starvation? The guy who causes real trouble is the guy in the suit." (Bill Bonner)

We are brothers:

"It's silly to go on pretending that under the skin we are all brothers. The truth is more likely that under the skin we are all cannibals, assassins, traitors, liars, hypocrites ..." (Henry Miller,1891-1980). Read the following verse from John 3:17: "But whoever has the world's goods, and sees his brother in need and closes his heart against him, how does the love of God abide in him?" Now ask yourself, are you one of those people?

Making an impression at work:

The following recipe for success was expressed by former Avis CEO, Robert C. Townsend (1920-1998). He said:

> "If asked when you can deliver something, ask for time to think. Build in a margin of safety. Name a date. Then deliver it earlier than you promised. You'll be very valuable wherever you are. The world is divided into two classes of people: the few people who make good on

their promises (even if they don't promise as much), and the many who don't. Get in column A and stay there. You'll be very valuable wherever you are."

Being too cautious:

We often extol the virtues of planning, preparation, vision, and foresight. These things are important, but we're likely to miss out on other joys and opportunities when we lean too heavily on the side of caution. We end up denying ourselves the thrill and freedom of choice. As it sometimes happen, by the time we find greener pastures, we're too old to climb over the fence. Don't deny yourself because you're afraid of punishment or hoping for more or better pleasures. Take chances now and then— but when at it— do heed the truth contained in this observation by 1960's movie actor, Robert Mitchum who said, "The people who can do **you** the most damage, are the ones who are closest to you."

Mercy:

Generally, toddlers are selfish beings, but eventually they learn compassion by observing the pain and discomfort of those around them. They may wonder why a baby is crying but understand only when they themselves have fallen or bruised a knee. Learning to be compassionate should not be restricted to childhood years. Too often, adults are indifferent to the suffering of others and at times blame them for their predicament or treat them as invisible beings. The uneasy sensations we occasionally feel when we see a fellow creature in distress are instinctual and a human quality. And it is this disquiet that causes some of us to react in ways that defy common sense and reason.

Government:

This is the Confucian philosophy toward government: "The requisites of government are that there be sufficiency of food, sufficiency of military equipment, and the confidence of the people in their ruler. If forced to give up one of these—give up arms; if forced to give up two, then give up arms and food. For without the trust of the people, nothing can endure."

Better/best:

Things we perceive to be the best may not necessarily be in our better interest. The most luxurious homes are no more comfortable in a snowstorm than a warm, dry cabin in the woods. The niceties of life do not mean much when our needs are simple ones: warmth when we are cold, food when we're hungry, and sleep when we're tired. Author Linda Picone wrote in her *Book of Positive Quotations,* "We wish for so many things that we think will bring us happiness, yet we often find ourselves looking back fondly on simpler times."

Why be good:

Since we don't want anyone who cheats us or does corrupt things to get away, so too we must guard against becoming like them. We should refuse to allow the negative consequences that flow from others to enter our consciousness and disturb our inner peace. Inner peace doesn't mean an absence of noise and conflict; it means remaining calm in the midst of noise, rowdiness, and loss. Generally, folks who are loud and offensive are so for three reasons: They see you as a threat, they hate themselves, or they want to be like you. Likewise, cheaters and thieves have only one job, and that is to earn your scorn. English Philosopher and critic William Hazlitt (1778–1830) concluded, "Those who are at war with others are not at peace with themselves." While you should not take ownership of their contemptible traits, be consoled in knowing such people are always fearful of being exposed.

Judging:

Don't judge others by their dramatic moments or disturbing reactions during a crisis. Generally, how they are during tranquil moments is more aligned to how they are normally and is a better barometer. Ever notice during sporting events or recaps of those events how sportscasters and journalists focus on a particular disruptive or telling event and seem to miss many other fine moments during the game? "Animals are such agreeable friends - they ask no questions; they pass no criticisms."(George Eliot)

Getting acquainted:

"Would you like to get to know someone better? Ask a new acquaintance to take a ten-minute walk with you. It is amazing how walking with someone can bring you closer" When you are walking toward something, you tend to forget what you are walking away from. (Perry Buffington, *Cheap Psychological Tricks*, page # 54)

The "others" in our lives:

No matter how strong, competent, or talented we are, our attractiveness can only be realized through others. Our most meaningful achievements are actualized through combined efforts of other "helpers." Even when we do something that feels like our sole achievement (painting a picture, winning an award, hitting a home run), there is always a constellation of friends, teachers, and even enemies who've been part of our success. The mighty sun with all its power and glory cannot make a rainbow by itself, for it needs the rain to make that happen. Like the rain that helps create the rainbow, the contributions of others do not detract from our achievements but rather facilitate them. Newspaper columnist George W. Adams (1878–1962) made the following assertion: "There is no such thing as a 'self-made' man. We are made up of thousands of others. Everyone who has ever done a kind deed for us or spoken one word of encouragement to us has entered into the makeup of our character and of our thoughts as well as our success."

Excuses Excuses:

Wilbur to his farmer neighbor: "Can I borrow your rope?"

Farmer: "I am sorry, I am using it right now to tie up my milk."

Wilbur: "That's ridiculous. You can't use a rope to tie up milk."

Farmer: "I know that, but when you don't want to do something, any excuse is as good as the other."

Scandal fears:

Nobody really wants a scandal cleared up, especially a romantic one, because scandal delights our imagination with juicy possibilities. However, a confession causes the scandal follower to become more conscious of their secret sins. When the confessor confesses, the scandal follower may feel uneasy because the light of scrutiny may now shine upon them. So, what does the scandal follower do? He or she advocates for the swift punishment or removal of the guilty for the sake of our children and community.

Recipe for a happy life:

Here are ingredients for a happy life:

Be courageous in spite of the odds;

Go to bed each night with a clear conscience;

Have simple tastes; refrain from being stingy.

Consider these words too by Hungarian academic and psychoanalyst, Thomas Szasz who said, "The proverb warns, 'You should not bite the hand that feeds you' ...but maybe you should, if it prevents you from feeding yourself.'"

What goes into a mind, comes out in a life.

Thoughts at the Time of Death

Physician Bernadine Healey who was privileged to share her patients' last moments, described it this way: "People facing death do not think about what academic degrees they earned, what positions they held, or how much wealth they were able to accumulate. At the end, their last thoughts were mostly about those people who they loved and who loved them. The circle of love is everything and is a good measure of a past life."

Thoughts that may cross our minds when death beckons:

- We make them cry who care for us,
- We cry for those who never care for us,
- And we care for those who will never cry for us.

ILLUSTRATION:

A sick man was visiting his doctor. As he was preparing to leave the examination room, he turned around and said, "Doctor, I am afraid to die. Tell me what lies on the other side."

The doctor replied quietly, "I do not know."

"How could you not know? You are a doctor, and over the years I've come to know you as a man of deep faith."

The patient's hand was about a foot away from the doorknob when he and the doctor heard a scratching and moaning sound coming from the other side of the door. The doctor went ahead and opened the door, and in rushed a dog, wagging its tail, eager to show its gladness at seeing its master.

Turning to the patient, the doctor said. "Did you notice my dog? He has never been in this room before and had no idea what was inside, but he knew his master was here, and when the door was opened, he sprang in without fear. I know little of what is on the other side of death, but I do know one thing. I know my Master and Lord is there, and that is enough for me."

New Zealand writer and poet, Katherine Mansfield (1888-1923) wrote a short narrative titled, "Why I Would Like to Attend My Own Funeral?"This is what she had to say:

" I think you come to conceptualize the value of your life by what others say about you at your funeral. Some people may care or not care what others have to say about them, but for me, if I heard nice things spoken about me and I knew my life would continue, in a different realm, I would like to maintain and keep those traits that defined me. If however, I heard unflattering things about my life and possibly went on to exist in another capacity, I would want to do things to change that former and loathsome perception about me."

Things you can do for your loved one, when death is imminent.

- Sit and talk with them, and if possible, allow them to listen to their favorite music, spiritual verse(s) or proudest accomplishment.

- Let them know that their personal affairs will be handled promptly and that their loved one(s) will continue to obtain the care and attention they deserve.

- When the terminally ill are no longer able to eat or swallow, their mouths become dry. Help them keep their mouths moist and allow them to make their final transition in peace.

The following visionary remark was made by Civil rights leader, Martin Luther King. He said, " In the End, we will remember not the words of our enemies, but the silence of our friends."

"As a well-spent day brings happy sleep, so a life well-used brings happy death." (Leonardo Da Vinci 1452-1519)

Trials of Being Rich

*D*escribed below, are some of the most common reasons cited why wealth and recognition continue to remain in the hands of a select few. While each of these statements may ring true on the surface, there is much more we may want to consider. Know that there are many invisible passions and initiatives that partner with each other to create the image of success. It is unfair to allude, as we often do, that the appearance of prosperity or good-fortune may be the result of descent or unearned windfalls. Dr. Julie White in her 1986 Career Track Publications seminar, "Image and Self-Projection," describes three of these incorrect conclusions or suppositions.

"He was born with a silver spoon in his mouth, or as a West Texan may say, 'Them that has, gets.'"

Dr. White responds by saying, "Ask yourself, can you present and project the image of yourself that will make you be seen as a winner?

"Employers want proven winners. They want people who've demonstrated they are already successful before giving them a chance. Those who carry with them the image of a winner find it easy to project that persona and tend to be viewed as more capable. Don't compare yourself to a 'better' you. (That is a standard of excellence that is very difficult to surpass.) Instead, compare yourself with other people like you or other products and services similar to yours. Then, use the advantage you have over those people or things, and demonstrate why you are already a champion."

In summary: More people earn their success than have it handed to them on a plate.

He must have just been in the right place at the right time.

Dr. White responds by saying, "What big risk have you undertaken recently or what steps have you taken to prepare for the change(s) you hope for tomorrow?"

"Do not focus on the process, but on the outcome of a risk. For instance, instead of asking, 'How many years will it take before I finish medical school?' ask yourself, 'What will I get or gain after I graduate?' If you have not failed at something recently, then your life is too safe. Achievers know, lucky breaks don't come pre-labeled. They take chances and create those breaks." Rear Admiral Grace Hopper once said, "A ship in port is safe, but that is not what ships are made for." Expressed differently: We should sail out with a hopeful vision, and see where the current takes us. "Don't worry about failures, worry about the chances you miss when you don't even try."(Jack Canfield)

It is certainly not what you know; it's who you know that counts around here," or, "Isn't it just like them? You hire one, and they bring in their own kind?"

Dr. White responds by saying, "Ask yourself, how good are you at building alliances with people you already know?

"Alliances are not a one shot deal like a connection. It is built on *you and I* having a history of helping each other out. It works best when we do favors **first** and then call those favors in later, when needed. Over eighty percent of job vacancies are never advertised. Many positions are filled by networking with people with whom we have already developed a working relationship and *who we trust.* Ironically, most careers are advanced because people are *pushed up* by those who work underneath them [through delegation] rather than *pulled up* by those at the top."

In summary: "Networking is marketing yourself and exchanging information with people who can help you professionally." (Michele Jennae)

Common traits of the rich and wealthy:

Wealthy people are not "Jack of all trades," but are proficient in a specific area. Their expertise is obtained through self-education, personal knowledge, or hands-on experience. They generally view mistakes as teaching them what 'not to do' in the future. They aren't preoccupied with blame, but on protecting the image they've carefully nursed throughout the years. Publisher and politician Steve Forbes noted this about the wealthy: "You won't find them watching much TV or spending long hours on social media websites."

Rich people are not in the habit of broadcasting failures or opinions not grounded on facts. Chances are, you wouldn't hear them saying things like, "My parents were drunks; parks are no longer safe for our kids; there is no decency in the world anymore." On the contrary, they serve as beacons who guide the way for a better tomorrow. For them, tomorrow is where all their hard work, hopes, and aspirations will come to fruition. They recognize that the future depends on what they do and say today

Over 90% of rich people tend to save 20% or more of their income, and they begin saving long before they become wealthy. Most do not live beyond their means, and few are lugging around thousands of dollars in credit card debt. Unlike their less-fortunate brothers, they don't expect things to be given to them before they reciprocate. They share first and then reap whatever they've sowed. Like everybody else, they appreciate a good bargain, but unlike most, the thrill of a deal is not contained at the moment of obtainment—but beyond that. They'll look for ways to create a relationship or bond with the gatekeepers of a bargain with the hope of extending the same benefit to those outside themselves, but this time for a profit.

The positives of being rich:

- "Every man thinks God is on his side. The rich and powerful know he is."(Jean Anouilh)

- "The richest man is not he who has the most, but he who needs the least." (Anonymous).
- "A man with money has a claim on the time and possessions of other men." (Bill Bonner)
- "No one would remember the Good Samaritan if he'd only had good intentions; he had to have money too." (Margaret Thatcher)
- "People are fascinated by the rich. Shakespeare wrote plays about kings, not beggars." (Dominic Dunne)
- "The poor is hated even by his own neighbour: but the rich hath many friends." (Proverbs 14:20)
- "When a dog has money, he buys cheese." (Jamaican Proverb)

The negatives of being rich:

- "Fear of death increases in exact proportion to increases in one's wealth." (Ernest Hemingway)
- "Of all classes, the rich are the most noticed and the least studied." (John Kenneth Galbraith)
- Somehow, everybody feels obligated to charge the wealthy more than necessary for the things they buy.
- When the poor choose not to give, their indiscretion is overlooked, but when the wealthy choose not to give, they are immediately branded as stingy or uncaring.
- The rich want to be known for the people they are, not for their money. However, more often than not, they imagine that others like them only because of their money or what they can get from them.
- "The richer your friends, the more they will cost you." (Elizabeth Marbury)
- "It's more pitiable once to have been rich, and not be rich now." (Jean Antoine Petit-Senn)

Words for both rich and poor :

- "The rule is, not to talk about money with people who have much more or much less than you." (Katherine Whitehorn)

- "There are two things needed in these days: First, for rich men to find out how poor men live, and second for poor men to know how rich men work." (Edward Atkinson)

- "Rich people stay rich by living like they are broke. Broke people stay broke by living like they are rich." (Unknown)

- Employees always knock the wealthy for their riches and lifestyles. Canadian educator, Peter J Laurence observed, "Don't knock the rich. When did a poor person[ever] give you a job?"

- "Rich people choose to get paid based on results. Poor people choose to get paid based on time." (T. Harv Eker)

- "About the only difference between the poor and the rich is this: the poor suffer misery, while the rich have to enjoy it."(Henry Wheeler Shaw)

- Wouldn't it be a pleasant life if people with money used it the way people who didn't have any say they would spend it if they had a little extra?

- "Never promise a poor person, and never owe a rich one."(Brazilian Proverb)

- "The poor man is honored for his skill and the rich man is honored for his riches." (Ecclesiasticus)

> *"Wealthy people are no happier than those of modest means." (David Mamet)*

US Politics, the Media & the Government

*J*ournalist Ambrose Bierce (1842-1914) contended that politics is all about interests masquerading as principles for the private advantage of a select group. Let's say that there is an ordinance to permit big trucks to pass through local community roads in an effort to ease congestion on main traffic routes. The bill does not enjoy widespread support and is met with resistance from the local community. That community is supported by political party "A," which brings it up for debate at a local forum. However, political party "B" wants the ordinance adopted immediately and to avoid the spectacle of all that scrutiny. That party may assert the refusal to pass the bill now is a restriction on business activity and stifles competition. They may further assert that all must be done now to protect our "free enterprise" system from those who want to remain in the Dark Ages. Political party "A" makes an official protest and may probably assert that the rush to pass the bill is an erosion of democracy and not in keeping with the principles adopted by the nation's founding fathers. This is a common manifestation of American politics, i.e., one -half of all politicians trying to get something started and the other half trying to get it stopped. At the other end of the spectrum, of course, is the general public and who journalist, Elmer Davis (1890-1958) characterized as follows, "Applause, mingled with boos and hisses, is about all that the average voter is able or willing to contribute to public life."

The tragedy, however, is not that we're so naïve or deceived by this sort of double-talk, the absurdity lies with our deep reliance on partisan news networks and social media sites. Many talk-show hosts along with their associates psychoanalyze every word and statement of day's headlines and intro-duce loaded "trigger" words that they splice among selectively chosen video and audio segments. Seldom is a reader or listener provided with an opportunity to review or analyze the words spoken before and after a pur-ported "incendiary' remark... after all, the audio or video speaks for itself and what other evidence do you need? Each show caters to its loyal audi-ence by giving them more of the 'candy' they've grown to expect. But better than that, is the audience's opportunity to take ownership of those telling "catchphrase" statements and replay them before others, as if it were their own.

The news media has long relinquished its right to open and honest discus-sion, as many of those outlets have forsaken the news function in favor of ratings and advertising revenue. Former politician and diplomat Adlai Stevenson (1900-1965) observed, "Newspaper editors are men who separate the wheat from the chaff, and then print the chaff." To illustrate this point, Lyndon B Johnson, the 36th President of the United States commented, "If one morning I walked on top of the water across the Potomac River, the headline that afternoon would read: 'President Can't Swim.' Journalist, Abbot Liebling (1904-1963) provided a more cheeky response. He added, "Freedom of the press is limited to those who own one." And distinguished British TV host and personality, David Frost (1939-2013) dropped this into the kitty: "TV reality and talk shows permit you be entertained in your living rooms by people whom you will not want to have in your home."

Unflattering labels exchanged between politicians are repeated so often in the media that they tend to stick in the public's mind. And those who dili-gently follow those events are only too eager to latch onto those awkward labels because they are catchy and rouse attention. The US presidential elec-tions have become a cross between a popularity contest and a recital of stale, weary clichés. Political language is now contoured to make lies sound truthful. One sad consequence of that —the growing demand for men and women who can make wrong appear right.

So, how does the everyday citizen navigate all the good and bad rhetoric that assaults his eyes and ears every day? Perhaps the words of former UK Prime Minister William E. Gladstone (1809–1898) might provide a clue. He said, "Nothing that is morally wrong can be politically right. Also, Edward R Murrow, whose name is synonymous with journalistic excellence chipped in by saying, "To be persuasive we must be believable; to be believable we must be credible; to be credible we must be truthful."

Regardless of how you feel about the news media, you shouldn't overlook the role played by the 'top brass' at these organizations. Here's why. Let's say the owner or president of a news agency is firm and strongly against abortion (and that is his or her right), it's unlikely that the 'air-time' assigned surrogates will be used to defend abortion rights—more or less, it'll be the other way around. TV Networks and news services always try to impress their audiences, that they are centrist and their primary function is "to tell it as it is". What they fail to tell you is that, the underlining theme of their messages is almost always a reflection of the agenda(s) of the entity paying them their salaries.

How to differentiate between a Democrat and a Republican

ILLUSTRATION:

One warm summer night, a Republican sees a man who looks like he is drowning about fifty feet from the pier. He throws the man a twenty-five-foot rope and tells him to swim the other twenty-five feet. The man drowns before he can reach the rope. The Republican claims the man did not try hard enough.The next night, a Democrat sees another man drowning fifty feet from the same pier. He throws him a 100--foot rope. As the Democrat is midway through pulling the man to safety, he hears another cry for help. He releases his end of the rope and rushes off to save the other hapless soul. Unable to swim to safety, the drowning man also dies. In his defense, the Democrat claims afterward that there is only so much he can do by himself.

As is usually the case, party affiliation means everything and if you disagree with any aspect of a party's platform or direction, sooner or later you are branded a traitor and a stooge of the opposition. "Democrats never agree on anything, that's why they're Democrats. If they agreed with each other, they would be Republicans."(Will Rogers). An Unknown writer made this observation: "There needs to be fewer Republican Senators and fewer Democratic Senators and many more United States Senators." Thankfully though, there are politicians like Fiorello La Guardia (1882-1947), one of the greatest mayors in American history. He considered himself a 'Pro-new deal, liberal, progressive Republican.' He appealed to his constituents across party lines and had a dualistic approach to governing. One of the many non-partisan remarks he made was: "There is no Democratic or Republican way of cleaning the streets."

French Emperor Napoleon Bonaparte, professed this over two hundred years ago, "In politics... never retreat, never retract, never admit a mistake." It appears that many US politicians have a great appreciation for those principles as many still staunchly adhere to them.

Voters and the electoral college decide who'll be the next President of the United States but Mathematician, Dan Bennett, offered a more revealing glimpse of what actually happens. He calculated, "An elected official is one who gets at least 51 percent of the votes cast by 40 percent of the 60 percent of voters registered [to vote]." In layman terms, he is suggesting that it may only take 12 percent of the *entire US population* to decide who'll be the next President of the United States.

Things that never seem to change in government and politics.

- "Politicians are the same all over; they promise to build bridges even when there are no rivers." (Nikita Krushchev)

- "Laws are like cobwebs which may catch small flies and mosquitoes but allow wasps and hornets to break through." (Jonathan Swift)

- "The mistake a lot of politicians make, is forgetting they've been appointed [and believe] they've been anointed."(Unknown)

- "Politics is the gentle art of getting votes from the poor and campaign funds from the rich, by promising to protect each from the other."(Oscar Ameringer)

- "When it was passed, Republicans voted for it and Democrats voted against it." (Dennis Cohoon)

- "He that goeth about to persuade a multitude that they are not so well governed as they ought to be shall never want attentive and favorable hearers." (Bishop Richard Hooker)

- "Our children await Christmas presents like politicians getting in election returns: there's the Uncle Fred precinct and the Aunt Ruth district still to come in." (Marcelene Cox)

- "An honest politician is one who, when he is bought— will stay bought." (Simon Cameron)

- The middle class: People who are not poor enough to accept charity, but not rich enough to donate anything.

- "A government which robs Peter to pay Paul, can always depend on the support of Paul." (George Bernard Shaw, 1856-1950)

"When you give politicians money, you are actually buying 'access.' There is however the mistaken impression that political big-wigs are in charge. They are not, their aides are. Aides are like super-efficient secretaries who control and feed essential information relevant to their bosses' interests. By appealing to aides, you are more likely to get a hearing because of their access and control of agendas, schedules and talking points." (Art Buchwald, 1925-2007)

Observations by Will Rogers, the American humorist and social commentator: (Wit & Wisdom of Will Rogers, Metro Books)

- "I belong to neither party's political party; each is good when they are out and bad when they are in."

- "Just a few women could stop every war. Wives of Presidents, diplomats, and legislators just have to say, "If you allow war to come, I'll leave you.""

- "Let Wall Street have a nightmare and the whole country has to help get them back in bed again."

- "If you ever injected truth into politics, you would have no politics."

- "So why don't they use a national sales tax? That is the only fair tax. Have no tax on necessary food and moderately prices clothes, but put a tax on every other thing you buy or use. Then the rich fellow who buys more and uses more has no way of getting out of paying his share."

- "I believe a candidate would go over Niagara Falls if he was sure the political wind was with him."

- "Republicans favor tax cut and Democrats favor tax hikes. The crime of taxation is not how it is obtained ... but the way it is spent."

"I propose forthwith that the method of choosing legislators in the United States be abandoned and that the method used in choosing juries be substituted. That is to say, I propose that the men who make our laws be chosen by chance and against their will, instead of by fraud and against the will of all the rest of us, as is now." (H.L Mencken)

"The loudest voices we hear are those who advocate conflict, divisiveness. (John C Danforth)

When!!!

- "When there are two conflicting versions of a story, the wise course is to believe the one in which people appear at their worst." (H. Allen Smith)

- "When a true genius appears in the world, you may know him by this sign: that the dunces are all in confederacy against him." (Jonathan Swift)

- "When a woman behaves like a man, why doesn't she behave like a nice man?" (Edith Evans)

- When packing for a vacation, take half as much clothing and twice as much money.

- When people are laughing, they have a tendency to turn their heads toward the person they like the most.

- When you return mean words with even meaner words, you're closing down the possibility of any fruitful discussion.

- When someone speaks of "one of these days," they mean none of these days.

- "When someone hugs you, let them be the first to let go." (H. Jackson Brown, Jr.)

- When two men in business always agree, one of them is unnecessary. (William Wrigley)

- When you are dealing with a child, sit on the floor.

- "When a man is ill, nothing is so important to him as his own illness." (Anthony Trollope)

- "When your friend or family member dies, mention not his vices." (Hadith)

- When your income reaches the point where the price of food is no longer an issue, calories becomes the new issue!

- "When it comes to getting things done, we need fewer architects and more bricklayers." (Colleen Barrett)

- "When you envy others, they will in turn envy you. The evil of envy is that it knows no limit." (Shinto Nihongi)

- "When someone you love becomes a memory, the memory becomes a treasure." (Author Unknown)

- "When you deny someone an apology, you will remember it at a future time, when you beg them for forgiveness."(Erin Gruwell)

- "When men speak ill of thee, live so as nobody may believe them."(Plato)

- When making an important decision or have ambivalent feelings, consult your mate or your parents. They know more about you than most others and could remind you of things that are important to you.

- When someone promises you something and it is impossible to keep- there is a good chance it'll end up being a lie. (Sweet home movie)

- When you feel disappointed, don't be. Although you think you know the reason for your disappointment- you really don't. You aren't truly aware of all the players and machinery that came together to produce the unhappy result. (Karsh)

"Every action of our lives touches on some chord that will vibrate in eternity." (Edwin Hubbel Chapin)

Wisdom from the World's Living Religions

These are the people who know God: **(Bhagavad-Gita—Hinduism)**

- He who weeps.
- He who yearns to know.
- He who toils to help.
- He who is certain of God's existence.

There are three ways of committing sin: **(SutraKitanga—Jainism)**

- By our own actions.
- By authorizing others.
- By approval.

These are the greatest crimes: **(Hadith—Islam)**

- To seek another God than the one God.
- To vex one's father and mother.
- To commit murder.
- To commit suicide.
- To swear to a lie.

Things that are an abomination to God: (**Old Testament- Judaism**)

- A lying tongue and haughty eyes.
- A heart that devises wicked thoughts.
- Hands that shed innocent blood.
- He who sows discord among his brothers.
- The one who makes a hungry soul more sorrowful.

These are the four evils of government: (**Analects—Confucianism**)

- To inflict punishment without laying down the law—this is tyranny.
- Without hint or clue to always expect total obedience—this is oppression.
- To tax but spend stingily—this is a misuse of the government function.
- To take or demand first and then notify later—this is robbery.

Things we recognize as we grow older: (**Dhammapada—Buddhism**)

- Life is easy for a man who is without shame.
- Hunger is the worst of diseases.
- Victory breeds hatred.
- An evil deed, like freshly drawn milk, does not turn sour at once.
- A man is not learned because he talks much.

Things we should teach our children: (**The Logia—Christianity**)

- As you judge, so shall you be judged.
- When you pray, pray for those who are about to perish.
- Man must give an account of every good word he fails to speak.
- Kind words are better than ointment.
- A man who is not tempted, is not proven.

*These are the qualities of a good ruler: (**Shinto**)*

- Fail not to correct that which is wrong when you see it.

- Be not resentful when others differ with you.

- Either merit or demerit, deal out to each that which is its reward or punishment.

- Turn away from that which is private and set your face on that which is public, for that is the duty of a governing official.

*The results and consequences of more: (**Taoism**)*

- The more prohibitions, the more poverty.

- The more laws, the more crimes.

- The more skills, the more luxuries.

- The more weapons, the more chaos.

Despite newer translations or explanations of sacred texts, people still continue to sin" the same old-fashioned way.

World Proverbs

- A clear conscience never fears midnight knocking. . . . . **Chinese**
- A forced kindness deserves "No thanks!". . . . .**Italian**
- You cannot wake a person who is pretending to be asleep. . . . . **Navajo**
- When the kettle boils over, it overflows its own sides. . . . .**Yiddish**
- When the tide of misfortune moves over you, even jelly will break your teeth. . . . .**Persian**
- When there is no enemy within, the enemies outside cannot hurt you. . . . .**African**
- If all were equal, if all were rich, and if all were at the table, then who will lay the cloth and serve the meal?. . . . .**German**
- Do not choose your wife at a dance, but in the field among the harvesters. . . . . **Czech**
- In the midst of great joy, do not promise anyone anything.. . . . . . . **Chinese**
- Confiding a secret to the unworthy is like carrying grain in a bag with a hole at its bottom. . . . .**African**
- With money in your pocket, you are wise, handsome and people think you sing well, too! . . . .**Yiddish**
- The man who cannot dance will blame the drum. . . . .**African**
- When the mouse laughs at the cat, there is a hole nearby. . . . . . . **Nigerian**
- Don't call a man "honest" just because he's never had a chance to steal. . . . . **Jewish**
- It is the same life, whether you spend it crying or laughing. . . . . . **Japanese**
- Let what is past flow away downstream.. . . . .**Japanese**

◆ To know the road ahead, ask those coming back. . . . . **Chinese**

◆ No matter how far you've gone on the wrong road, turn
back. . . . . **Turkish**

◆ Don't open a shop unless you know how to smile. . . . . **Jewish**

◆ What a man says when drunk has been thought when
sober. . . . .**Belgian**

◆ If God lived on earth, people would break his windows. . . . . **Jewish**

◆ When the sun goes down at sunset, it will take a part of
your life with it. . . . .**Indian**

◆ Three things best to avoid: A strange dog; a flood; a man
who thinks he is wise.. . . . .**Welch**

◆ He who marries a widow will have a dead man's head
thrown on his dish. . . . . **Spanish**

◆ Parents who are afraid to put their foot down usually
have children who step on their toes. . . . . **Chinese**

◆ Free cheese is found only in mousetraps. . . . . **Russian**

◆ If the rich could hire people to die for them, the poor
could make a wonderful living. . . . . **Jewish**

◆ To hide one lie, a thousand lies are needed. . . . .**Indian**

◆ If there is character, ugliness becomes beauty; if there is
none, beauty becomes ugliness. . . . . **Nigerian**

◆ Do not use a hatchet to remove a fly off your friend's
forehead. . . . . **Chinese**

◆ You are permitted in times of great danger to walk with
the devil, until you have crossed the bridge. . . . . **Bulgarian**

◆ Do not stand in a place of danger trusting in miracles. . . . . **Arabian**

◆ The slimming of an elephant or the losses of a rich man
are not noticeable. . . . . **Ethiopian**

◆ Don't ask questions of fairy tales. . . . . **Jewish**

- It's a sad house where the hen crows louder than the cock. . . . . **Scottish**

- Until lions have their own historians, tales of hunting will always glorify the hunter. . . . . **African**

- The reverse side also has a reverse side. . . . . **Japanese**

- Who that is hungry needs no seasoning. . . . . **Italian**

- In every woman there is a queen. Speak to the queen and the queen will answer. . . . . **Norwegian**.

> *"Nothing ever becomes real till experienced—even a proverb is no proverb until your life has illustrated it." (John Keats,1795-1821)*

Worry

A breakdown of all types of worry:

- 40% of all our worries will not happen.
- 30% concern old decisions that cannot be altered.
- 12% is criticism that is mostly untrue and made up by people who feel inferior to you.
- 10% are related to your health, which worsens with worry.
- 8% may be truly legitimate and deserve some attention.

A man once asked famed psychiatrist, Dr. Karl Menninger what action he would recommend if a person were to feel a nervous breakdown coming on. His response: "Lock up your house, go across the railroad tracks, and find someone in need and do something for him." The following story supports that conclusion, but in a more familiar environment.

ILLUSTRATION : (Anonymous Author)

The park seemed deserted that Sunday morning when I sat down on a bench beneath an old willow tree. I was a sad and disillusioned soul, and it seemed the whole world was intent on dragging me down. Suddenly, out of nowhere, a young boy came running up in my direction. As he rushed up, he appeared seemingly out of breath. He managed to stop right before me, and with a slightly bent head blurted out, "Look what I found!" In his hand was an old and shriveled-up flower. I wanted him to take his pitiful dead shrub and just run off somewhere else and play. To force his retreat, I faked a little smile and deliberately shifted my eyes away from him. But instead of moving away, he remained standing next to me. Then, all of a sudden, he shoved the flower closer to his nostrils and blurted out, "I picked it because it smells lovely and I think it is beautiful too—here, I want to give it to you."

The wilted weed was probably already dead, but I knew I had to take it or he would never leave. I reached for the flower and exclaimed, "Just what I needed." However, instead of placing it in my hand, he held it up midair and waited patiently for me to take it from him. It was then I realized the boy was blind. Here I was, sitting feeling sorry for myself, and this little boy with a more significant disability than mine was willing to share with me "a joy" and happiness he found in a shriveled-up flower.

With tears in my eyes, I thanked him for selecting the best flower ever and for wanting to give it to me. "You are welcome," he said, and with that he smiled and sped off in a different direction. How did that little boy know my pitiful soul was in need of cheering up? Perhaps his heart was blessed with true sight, and I was the one who was blind. From that moment, I vowed to see the beauty of life around me, and as I held the wilted flower close to my nose, I watched the little boy with another shriveled weed in hand about to change the life of another unsuspecting soul.

When we worry, what we are doing is focusing too much on something that we do not want to happen. Sometimes, our friends and family help us along by nursing our feelings of helplessness. But once the bothersome thing is over and passed, we experience a sense of enormous relief. We all know we can't change the past, but we sometimes forget that we ruin the present by worrying about the future.

ILLUSTRATION:

A lady went to the market with a shopping list and, upon arriving, realized she had somehow misplaced it. She was very distraught and couldn't stop blaming herself for being so careless. Her anxiety soon manifested itself in the form of a throbbing pain at the back of her neck. But she managed to finish her shopping, and when it was time to pay as she opened her wallet she spotted the list neatly tucked in among her dollar bills. She removed it, glanced at it quickly, folded and placed it into her left coat pocket. Once back at home and was finished with her unpacking, she retrieved the list from her coat pocket and threw it into the wastepaper basket. It was now a useless piece of paper.

ILLUSTRATION:

A vibrant old lady puzzled everyone with her constant cheerfulness despite having an unusual share of troubles. When asked about her secret for staying calm, she replied, "You see, it's like this: the Bible often says, 'and it came to pass,' never does it say, 'it came to stay.' So what I do is wait and hope."

"Worry is like a rocking chair: it gives you something to do but never gets you anywhere." (Erma Bombeck)

You and a Better You

"*Y*es, I know, you are certain that ... your grocer, garbageman, sister-in -law and your dog are all of the opinion that you have put on weight... furthermore, you are convinced that everyone spends two-thirds of everyday commenting ...on your work. I promise you, nobody is thinking about you. They are thinking about themselves —just like you." (Roger Rosenblatt, pg. # 3, in his book, Rules for Aging.). And no, they aren't laughing at how awful you looked in that gown or that swim-wear you wore, and neither are they plotting ways to embarrass or deceive you further. The truth is they are 100% involved with their own concerns and worries, and you, and others like you may be the furthest thing away from their minds. In the words of author David Foster Wallace, "You will become way less concerned with what other people think of you when you realize how seldom they do."

You may sometimes doubt your own goodness because you may have mean thoughts or fail to seize opportunities to be kind to others or perhaps worry if others knew the kind of person you are deep down, they wouldn't like you as much or even think your goodness is all pretense. But stop! No one has the ability to peer into another's soul, nor can they see the goodness that resides there. Let your conscience not be conflicted by what "they" think about you. Just focus on living the best life you know how, and do it without causing harm to anyone. Cleric and writer,Charles Caleb Colton added : "He that is good,will infallibly become better and he that is bad,will certainly become worse— for vice, virtue and time are the three things that never stand still."

If your life is hard because you need a bigger home or your employer does not compensate you enough to pay the bills or your life is loveless because you do not have a partner, then you must change what needs changing: your attitude. Once adjusted, you'll see opportunities open up. "It's easier to put on slippers than to carpet the whole world." (Al Franken)

The following is an excerpt from novelist and playwright J. P. Donleavy's, 1955 novel *The Ginger Man*.

- When you don't have any money, the problem is food.
- When you have money, it's sex.
- When you have both, its health i.e. you worry about getting a rupture or something.
- If everything is simply jake, then you're frightened of death.

A checklist of things you can do to become a better person:

- "Be wiser than other people, if you can, but do not tell them so." (Earl of Chesterfield)

- Say what you mean, mean what you say, and do what you say you'll do!

- "I've learned that people will forget what you said, people will forget what you did, but people will never forget how you made them feel." (Maya Angelou)

- "The more you talk about yourself, the more likely you are to lie." (Johann Zimmermann)

- "Take control of your debt and extravagance and your path ahead will be made easier."(Karsh)

- When someone shows you kindness, be thankful, but be not quick to reciprocate. Instead, pass that kindness along and let it multiply.

- "If you want something new, you have to stop doing something old." (Peter Drucker)

- Do not accept television or a movie's representation of the world to be your picture of the world because you will see greed, waste, and shallowness in everything.

- "We must respect the other fellow's religion, but only in the sense and to the extent that we respect his theory that his wife is beautiful and his children are smart." (H. L. Mencken)

- You never get rewarded for the things you intend to do.

- "You are not judged on the height you have risen but on the depth from which you have climbed." (Frederick Douglas)

- "When making your choice in life, do not neglect to live."(Samuel Johnson) i.e., you should treat yourself, once in a while!

When people extend small courtesies to those around them, they usually feel better about themselves. For example, picking up and returning an object that has fallen from the grasp of the frail or overburdened; sharing an umbrella in a way that the other party obtains the bigger benefit; smiling broadly with a baby or toddler who stares curiously at them. These small solicitations of ours require little effort on our part, but they provide comfort to others and render meaning to our lives.

You may suffer more or suffer less. But your journey will always be unique and different from every other. Rather than obsessing over yourself or where you fit in, you should be on the lookout for ways to be a more endearing guest in the eyes of your maker. "Don't try to be different- just be good, because being good is different enough." (Arthur Freed)

> *"Let right deeds be thy motive, not the fruit that comes from them."*
> *(Bhagavad Gita)*

"LOVE ALL,
TRUST A FEW,
DO WRONG TO NONE."

William Shakespeare

(*All's well that ends well.*)

WORKS CITED

Abby, D. (1918-2013). *Columnist.*

Amiel, H. (1821-1881). *Swiss Poet & Critic.*

Anonymous. (n.d.). *The Flower.*

Anthony, S. B. (1820-1906). *Reformer & Activist.*

Aquinas, T. (1225-1274). *Philosopher/Theologian.*

Ashe, A. (1943-1993). *Tennis Player.*

Assisi, S. F. (1181-1226). *Catholic Friar.*

Bach, R. (n.d.). *American Author.*

Baldwin, J. A. (1924-1987). *Novelist and Critic.*

Baudelaire, C. (1821-1867). *French Poet & Translator.*

Beecher, H. W. (1813-1887). *Minister & Activist.*

Beecher, W. &. (n.d.). Beyond Success & Failure. *SMI Audiocassette.*

Bennett, A. (1867-1931). *British Novelist and Critic.*

Bierce, A. (1842-1914). *Writer/Journalist.*

Bits and Pieces Magazine. (1994, June). p. 17.

Bits and Pieces Magazine. (1995, September). p. 2.

Blaine, P. P. (n.d.). *Hearttouchers.com.*

Bloch, A. (n.d.). Murphy's law 2000. *Price Stern Sloan Publishing.*

Bloch, R. (1917-1994). *Writer.*

Bonner, B. (n.d.). In Hormegeddon (p. 170 & 177). *Lioncrest Publishing.*

Brothers, D. J. (1927-2013). *Psychologist/Columnist.*

Brown, H. J. (1991). Life's Little Instruction Book. *Rutledge Press.*

Bruce Patton, D. S. (n.d.). Difficult Conversations. *Penguins Books.*

Brzezinski, Z. (1928-2017). *Political Scientist.*

Buchwald, A. (1925-2007). *American Columnist.*

Buffington, P. (1996). In P. Buffington, Cheap Psychological Tricks (pp. 2,3,32,33,39,54,169). MJF.

Cameron, C. (1946). *Getting the most out of life.* The Reader's Digest.

Canfield, J. (n.d.). *Author & Motivational Speaker.*

Carter, B. (1979). In H. Faber, *The Book of Laws* (p. 108). Times Books.

Cecil, L. E. (1867-1918). *English Soldier & Administrator.*

Coco, S. (n.d.). Author - *Assertiveness Training.*

Colton, C. C. (1780-1832). *Cleric & Writer.*

Coolidge, C. (1872-1933). *30th President of the United States.*

Corneille, P. (1606-1684). *French Dramatist.*

Coupland, D. (n.d.). *Canadian Novelist.*

Cousins, N. (n.d.). *Anatomy of an Illness.* Bantam Books.

Covey, S. R. (2004). *7 Habits of Highly Effective Families.* Audiobook.

Cox, M. (n.d.). *American Writer.*

Davis, E. (1890-1958). *Author & News Reporter.*

Delaney, S. (1938-2011). *English Dramatist.*

Dickinson, E. (1830-1886). *American Writer/Poet.*

Dryden, J. (1631-1700). *Poet & Critic.*

Dulles, J. F. (1888-1959). *Secretary of State.*

Easwaran, E. (1910-1998). *Author & Spiritual Leader.*

Einstein, A. (1879-1955). *Mathematician & Physicist.*

Eisenhower, D. (1890-1969). *34th US President.*

Ekeren, G. V. (n.d.). *Words for All Occassons.* Prentiss Hall.

Emerson, R. W. (1803-1882). *Essayist, Lecturer & Philosopher.*

Erhard, L. (1897-1977). *West German Chancellor.*

Forbes, S. (n.d.). *Publisher/Entrepreneur.*

Forest, H. (2005). *Wisdom Tales from Around the World.* August House Publishers.

Frank, A. (1929-1945). *German diarist & Holocaust victim.*

Fulghum, R. (n.d.). In R. Fulghum, *It Was On Fire When I Lay Down On It.* Ivy Books.

Fulghum, R. (2004). In R. Fulghum, *All I really need to know I learned in Kindergarten.* Ballantine Books.

Gandhi, I. (1917-1984). *Indian Prime Minister.*

Garcia, N. (n.d.). *Author & Fashion Editor.*

Gates, B. (n.d.). *Microsoft Founder.*

Gita, B. (n.d.). *Chapter11, the Book of Doctrines.*

God's Little Devotional Book. (n.d.). Honor Books.

Goering, H. (1893-1946). *Nazi Military leader.*

Goodman, A. (1899-1982). *Radio & Magazine columnist.*

Gordon, L. D. (1863-1935). *Fashion Designer.*

Gray, J. (n.d.). *Men are from Mars & Women from Venus.* Harper Collins.

Grellet, S. (1773-1855). *Missionary.*

Harris, S. J. (1917-1986). *Author.*

Hartmann, T. (n.d.). *Radio Host & Author.*

Hayakawa, S. (1906-1992). *Academic.*

Hayakawa, S. (1972). *In Language in Thought and Action* (p. 185). Harcourt Brace Jovanovich Inc.

Healey, B. (1994). *Commencement Address.* Vassar College.

Hecht, B. (1894-1964). *Director/Producer.*

Heilbroner, R. (n.d.). *Psychology Today*.

Hobbes, J. O. (1867-1906). *Novelist*.

Hollingsworth, M. (2008). *In And God said..Let there be laughter. (p. 264)*. Guideposts.

Hubbard, E. (1856-1915). *Philosopher & Writer*.

Hubbard, K. (1868-1930). *Humorist & Journalist*.

Ibsen, H. (n.d.). *Norwegian Dramatist*.

Iroh, U. (2005). *Avatar : The Last Airbender*. Nickelodeon.

Jefferson, T. (1743-1826). *President of the United States*.

Johnson, D. S. (1709-1784). *Writer & Poet*.

Keats, J. (1795-1821). *English Poet*.

Keller, J. (1900-1977). *Priest & TV Producer*.

Klein, T. C. (n.d.). *Aristotle and an Aaardvark Go to Washington*. In T. C. Klein. Abrams Image.

Kreider, T. (n.d.). *Essayist*.

Kriedman, D. (n.d.). Relationship Expert. *The Secrets of making Love Great*.

Kushner, H. (n.d.). *Rabbi & Author*.

Kushner, R. H. (2002). In R. H. Kushner, *When All You've Ever Wanted Isn't Enough*. Simon & Schuster.

Landers, A. (1918-2002). *Syndicated Columnist*.

Lawrence, D. P. (1919-1990). *Canadian Educator*.

Leary, T. F. (1920-1996). *Psychologist & Writer*.

Levenson, S. (1911-1980). *Humorist & Teacher*.

Levitt, T. (1925-2006).

Lewis, C. (1898-1963). *Irish Novelist*.

Lieberman, D. J. (1999). *Never be lied to again*. Audio Book.

Liebling, A. J. (1904-1963). *Journalist.*

Lincoln, A. (1809-1865). *16th President of the United States.*

Longfellow, H. W. (1807-1882). *Poet & Educator.*

Lowell, J. R. (1819-1891). *Poet & Diplomat.*

Maltz, M. (1899-1975). Writer & Surgeon. *In Psycho-Cybernetics.* Prentiss Hall.

Marden, O. S. (1997, February 27). Inspirational Author. *Bits & Pieces,* p. 23.

Martin, J. (1938). *Miss Manners.*

McGuire, A. (1928-2001). *Basketball coach.*

Mead, M. (1901-1978). *Anthropologist.*

Meyer, J. (n.d.). *Christian Author/Speaker.*

Midler, B. (n.d.). *Movie actress.*

Miller, A. (1923-2010). *Psychologist & Philosopher.*

Miller, H. (1891-1980). *Writer.*

Monkhouse, B. (1988). In B. Monkhouse, *The Complete Speaker's handbook* (p. 44). Barnes & Noble Inc.

Moore, M. (n.d.). *Author & Motivational Speaker.*

Morley, C. (n.d.). *Writer.*

Myerson, A. (1881-1948). *Researcher & Psychiatrist.*

Niven, D. (n.d.). *100 Secrets of Happy People.* Harper Collins.

Null, C. (n.d.). In B. S. Edward K Rowell, *Humor for Preaching & Teaching* (p. 33). Baker Books.

Osteen, J. (n.d.). *Author, Speaker & Televangelist.*

Parker, P. J. (n.d.). *How to use tact and Skill in handling people.* SMI Audio Cassettes.

Parker, T. (1810-1860). *Abolitionist & Minister.*

Patton, G. S. (1885-1945). *U.S General.*

Picasso, F. (n.d.). *Coach & Motivational Speaker.*

Picone, L. (n.d.). In *The daily Book of Positive quotations* (p. 26). Fairview Press.

Pierre, A. (1912-2007). *French Catholic priest.*

Price, A. (n.d.). *Author.*

Quintilian. (35-96 AD). *Latin teacher & Writer.*

Rama, E. (n.d.). *Albanian Politician & Writer.*

Raskas, B. (n.d.). *Heart of Wisdom.*

Rogers, W. (1879-1935). *Political Humorist.*

Rosenblatt, R. (n.d.). In R. Rosenblatt, *Rules for Aging* (pp. 3,71,127,95,96). Harcourt Inc.

Ruskin, J. (1819-1900). *Art Critic.*

Russell, B. (1872-1970). *Philosopher & Mathematician.*

Sadat, J. (n.d.). *First Lady of Egypt.*

Santayana, G. (1863-1952). *Philosopher & Novelist.*

Schweitzer, A. (1875-1965). *Missionary.*

Seeger, P. (1919-2014). *Folk Singer & Activist.*

Selassie, H. (1892-1975). *Ethiopian Emperor.*

Seneca. (5BC- 65AD). *Philosopher.*

Senn, J. P. (1792-1870). *Genevian Poet.*

Shaw, G. B. (1856-1950). *Critic & Playwright.*

Siegel, D. B. (1998). *Prescription for Living-* Pgs 70,163,180,185 & 199. Harper Collins.

Smith, G. (n.d.). *Businessman and Investment Advisor.*

Smith, L. P. (1865-1946). *Essayist & Critic.*

Sourcebook of Wit & Wisdom. (1996). *Communication Resources, Inc.*

Spielberg, S. (n.d.). *Movie Director & Producer.*

Stephens, J. (1880-1950). *Irish Poet.*

Stevenson, A. (1900-1965). *Statesman/Diplomat.*

Stewart, M. Y. (n.d.). *Little Ways of Caring.* St Martin Press.

Strange History. (n.d.). Portable Press.

Strickland, L. A. (2002). *In L. A. Strickland, The Last Dance* (p. 127). McGraw-Hill Higher Education.

Swindoll, C. (n.d.). *From a sermon by Johnny Creasong.*

Talmud. (n.d.). *Book of Jewish & Ceremonial law.*

Tammeus, W. D. (n.d.). *Columnist.*

The Best of Bits & Pieces. (1994). The economic Press Inc.

The Self-Esteem Companion. (n.d.). In P. F. Matthew Mckay. New Harbinger Publications.

Thompson, E. T. (1928-2018). *Editor at Readers's Digest.*

Thoreau, H. D. (1817-1862). *Philosopher & Historian.*

Tolstoy, L. (1828-1910). *Nobel Peace Prize Author.*

Townsend, R. (1920-1998). *Business Executive.*

Uncle John's, A.-I. B. (2002). In *Uncle John's, Ahh-Inspiring Bathroom Reader.* (p. 305). Bathroom Rader Press.

Vaughan, W. E. (1915-1977). *Columnist & Author.*

Vinci, L. D. (1452-1519). *Painter, Sculptor & Engineer.*

Viscott, D. (n.d.). Author & Psychotherapist. *In How to live with another person.* SMI Audio Cassettes.

Ward, W. A. (n.d.). *Author & Pastor1921-1994.*

White, D. J. (1986). Speaker, Consultant & Author. *Image & Self-Projection.* Career Track Publications.

White, P. (n.d.). *Cardiologist. (1886-1973).*

White, R. (n.d.). *Quick Wits, Worn Shoes & a Fax Machine.* Citadel Press.

Whitehorn, K. (n.d.). *Writer/Journalist.*

Wholy, D. (n.d.). *Author & Producer.*

Wikipedia. (n.d.). Rosalie Ida Straus.
https://en.wikipedia.org/w/index.php?title=Ida_Straus&oldid=936819502.

Wilde, O. (1859-1900). *Irish Novelist.*

Wordsworth, H. (1770-1850). *English Poet.*